AN OPEN THEIST RENEWAL THEOLOGY

GOD'S LOVE, THE SPIRIT'S POWER, AND HUMAN FREEDOM

RORY R. RANDALL

Studies in Open and Relational Theology Series

SacraSage Press (SacraSagePress.com)
© 2021 SacraSage Press and Rory Randall

All rights reserved. No part of this book may be reproduced in any form without written consent of the author or SacraSage Press. SacraSage Press provides resources that promote wisdom aligned with sacred perspectives. All rights reserved.

Interior Design: Nicole Sturk
Cover Photo: Thomas Jay Oord
Print: 978-1-948609-44-9
Electronic: 978-1-948609-45-6

Printed in the United States of America

Library of Congress Cataloguing-in-Publication Data
An Open Theist Renewal Theology / Rory Randall

To my wife Vikki—

for her loving encouragement and sharing of ideas

Table of Contents

Acknowledgments ix
Introduction 1

I. Classical Theism, Open Theism, and Renewal Theology—
Definitions and Literature 7
    A. Classical Theism. 7
    B. Open Theism 12
    C. Renewal Theology 39

II. John Wesley Does Not Entirely Fit Renewal or Open Theist
Paradigms 49
    A. Open Theist Considerations 52
    B. Proto-pentecostal/charismatic Considerations 74

III. John Wesley and John Fletcher Initiate a Trajectory toward
Open Theism 89
    A. Theological Themes Pointing to Open Theism 90
    B. Controversy with Calvinism 104

IV. Open Theism in Another Wesleyan Trajectory—Pentecostalism.... 113

    A. Wesley and Fletcher Initiate a Trajectory toward Pentecostalism 117

    B. Open Theism in Early Pentecostalism 122

V. A Convergence of the Two Trajectories 131

    A. Towards an Open Theist Renewal Theology 132

    B. Towards an Open Theist Renewal Praxis 154

Conclusion... 171
Bibliography 179
Indexes... 203

Acknowledgments

I'd like to thank some people whose thinking, teaching, or mentorship has helped me along the way to the completion of this project. Ward and Laurel Gasque were the first to encourage me to pursue an academic career path and modeled the importance of putting people before ideas. Colin Brown, my ThM mentor, demonstrated how you can do systematic theology that is biblically driven. He gifted his students with the inside information that Reformed and Barthian theological systems don't work. He also liked to quote G. K. Chesterton (in *What's Wrong with the World*), "If a thing is worth doing, it is worth doing badly." I have found that thought liberating and energizing (but not, of course, applicable to this project). David Hubbard in his Hebrew Prophets class started me on a path toward open theism with his appreciation for the Jewish scholar, Abraham Heschel, who described God in dynamic terms as affected by human actions and deeply involved in the world—quite unlike the immovable God of classical theology. Shortly after taking Dr Hubbard's class, another Fuller professor (a hyper-Calvinist) rejected a paper I wrote for my first ThM seminar. The paper argued Augustine's Neoplatonism had overly influenced western theology.

At Regent in Virginia Beach, Professor Stan Burgess demonstrated how the Holy Spirit has been at work throughout the history of the church and broadened my horizons to appreciate the Eastern church. I caught Vinson Synan's enthusiasm for John Wesley and the Pentecostal-holiness tradition. He and Wolfgang Vondey both encouraged me to write papers on Clark Pinnock, whom I knew from Regent College in the 1970s when he taught a remarkable class on the Book of Exodus, and from an Open Theology and Science conference in 2008. The last time I saw Clark Pinnock, he suggested

I talk to John Sanders, who graciously sent me a detailed email with suggestions for dissertation topics. Kevin Spawn skillfully coached me through comprehensive exams. Estrelda Alexander's passion for justice and admiration of William Seymour has influenced this project in ways that will be evident. Amos Yong modeled how much could be accomplished if one gets by on minimal sleep. By assigning a sympathetic historian as my dissertation mentor, he dramatically influenced the structure of the project. I'm particularly grateful to Kimberly Alexander for suggesting the design of the research and her unfailing encouragement. Ken Archer and Néstor Medina have made many helpful suggestions through several iterations of revision. I was gratified by Thomas Jay Oord's interest and reading of an earlier draft.

Thanks go to my daughter, Jessie, and my sons, Joshua and Christopher, who allowed me time to be with the books and for writing and showed genuine interest in what I was working on. Finally, heartfelt thanks to my wife, Vikki, whose support through this multi-year endeavor was instrumental and is deeply appreciated.

Introduction

John Wesley's theology of love began a trajectory towards open theism, just as his emphasis on an experience of holiness and the Holy Spirit began a trajectory towards pentecostalism. Together, these trajectories provide the basis for a constructive theology. This dissertation will lay the groundwork for a coherent renewal theology with the experiential strength of Wesleyan charismatic-pentecostalism and the philosophical advantages of open theism.

The potential for coherence exists because, as will be seen, both charismatic-pentecostalism and open theism owe something to John Wesley and John Fletcher. The compatibility of the two will be demonstrated by first looking at *The Works of John Wesley* and seeing the trajectory toward open theism, especially the open theism that is most concerned with soteriology and the nature of God. Wesley's *Sermons* are relied on as the predominant source for several reasons. (1) The *Sermons* provide an accurate window into Wesley's developing thought. Albert Outler, an outstanding Wesley scholar of the twentieth-century and editor of the critical edition of the *Sermons*, affirms that Wesley's thought "was expounded in unsystematic forms, and yet it was inwardly coherent and relatively consistent in its development."[1] Wesley's regular practice of publishing the sermons shows the weight he gave to them.[2]

---

1. John Wesley, *Sermons I, 1–33*, ed. Albert C. Outler, The Works of John Wesley (Nashville: Abingdon, 1984), 1:57.

2. Randy Maddox observes, "Thus, as Wesley understood and engaged in theological activity (or, as they called it at that time, 'divinity'), the defining task was not to develop an elaborate system of Christian truth-claims; it was to nurture and shape the worldview or disposition that orients believers' lives in the world. Pastor-theologians (divines) may well engage in apologetic dialogues or in debates over doctrinal issues, but ideally because—and to the extent that—these are in service to their more central task.

(2) Although frequently occasioned by the needs of the moment (much like the letters of the New Testament), the *Sermons* are well thought out. Wesley remarked, "Though I am always in haste, I am never in a hurry; because I never undertake any more work than I can go through with perfect calmness of spirit."[3] (3) Because they were written over a period of decades, they provide a convenient way to see how Wesley's thought developed. This development is significant because it is especially the views of the later Wesley which point toward a future charismatic-pentecostalism and open theism. Speaking of the very late sermons, Albert Outler observes, "The *later* Wesley who emerges here is the neglected Wesley…"[4]

John Fletcher's *Five Checks to Antinomianism* are also referenced because they were the decisive statement of the Wesleyan position in the debates with the English Calvinists.[5] Those debates anticipate elements of the open theist conversations with other evangelicals over the last twenty years.

The potential coherence of open theism with charismatic-pentecostalism (at least that segment which holds to a synergistic view of soteriology) will be shown by looking at the publications of the Azusa Street mission as indicative of the broader movement. Why Azusa Street? At the time that the movement became a global phenomenon, for three years the Azusa Street mission was the epicenter of American pentecostalism.[6] The potential coherence will be shown first by noting how the Azusa Street mission was essentially a Wesleyan holiness church, and then by demonstrating that its theological interests were in a direction that is consistent with open theism. The issues of *The Apostolic Faith* produced during the Azusa Street revival and William Seymour's *The*

"This means that Wesley would have considered the first-order literary forms of liturgy, catechism, hymn, sermon, and the like to be central to the work of theologians." *Doctrinal and Controversial Treatises I*, ed. Randy L. Maddox, The Works of John Wesley (Nashville: Abingdon, 2012), 12:3.

3. Letter to Miss March from near London, 10 December 1777 in John Wesley, *The Letters of the Rev. John Wesley, A.M., Sometime Fellow of Lincoln College, Oxford*, ed. John Telford, 8 vols. (London: Epworth, 1931), 6:292.

4. Wesley, *Sermons I*, 1:54.

5. John Fletcher, *Five Checks to Antinomianism* (London: Wesleyan Conference Office, 1872).

6. Mel Robeck writes, "'Azusa Street' rightfully continues to function as the primary icon expressing the power of the worldwide Pentecostal movement." Cecil M. Robeck, Jr., *The Azusa Street Mission and Revival: The Birth of the Global Pentecostal Movement* (Nashville: Thomas Nelson, 2006), 10.

INTRODUCTION

Doctrines and Discipline of the Azusa Street Apostolic Faith Mission of Los Angeles, California will be sampled as representative of the early theological impulses of pentecostalism. I will identify themes important to open theism in these early pentecostal publications.

Another factor brings renewal theology and open theism together.[7] Some hold open theist convictions through studying the Hebrew Prophets and noticing that God is frequently described there as passionate and engaged with his people—in contrast to classical theism's description of God as impassible. It is the reality of that divine presence and activity, both historically and in the present, which is the link with renewal theology. Renewal theology is also, through its interest in the work of the Holy Spirit, attentive to God's engagement with the world.

Why does it matter that open theism is on a trajectory from the theology of John Wesley? The recognition that open theism is not primarily an innovation of the twentieth century, but a reform that has been centuries in the making is significant.[8] It provides impetus going forward because it is encouraging to know that open theism is not trying to get moving from a standing start, but rather it has the momentum of decades of research efforts behind it. It matters because it helps keep alive John Wesley's project with its emphasis on experiential spirituality and personal and social transformation. And it matters because it means that open theism can be resourced by theologians and philosophers who have been working on similar problems for two centuries but have been neglected, suppressed, or forgotten by mainstream evangelicalism.

In Chapter One, I will look at open theism, what it is, its theological concerns, and the major contributors to the movement. I will also define what I mean by the term 'renewal theology' and consider some ways renewal theologians have interacted with open theism, before making an initial assessment of the compatibility of the two. I will propose the theological thinking of John Wesley and John Fletcher as the foundation for a possible open theist renewal theology. In Chapter Two, I will look further into likely points of connection

---

7. See p. 15 for a discussion of the definition of 'open theism' and p. 39 for 'renewal theology'.

8. John Sanders, "Open Theism: A Radical Revision or Miniscule Modification of Arminianism?," *Wesleyan Theological Journal* 38, no. 2 (2003).

between both Wesley and Fletcher and open theism and between Wesley and pentecostalism. I will specifically attend to issues that initially seem problematic in making the connections, such as the early Wesley's view of time and Wesley's understanding of providence. I will note the contribution of the nineteenth-century Methodist scholar, Lorenzo Dow McCabe, who serves as a bridge from Wesley to open theism. I will discuss the early Wesley's attitude toward charismatic gifts and how the Maxfield–Bell crisis provides a remarkable window into Wesley's maturing views. In Chapter Three, I explore ways in which Wesley and Fletcher are moving in a direction toward open theism. I will look at five theological themes: (1) soteriology and God's grace, (2) human freedom and God's omnipotence, (3) God's omniscience and omnipresence, (4) God's capacity for feeling and suffering, and (5) divine love. In the second part of the chapter, I will look at Wesley and Fletcher's controversies with the Calvinistic Methodists. These controversies are at least analogous to the present-day open theism debates, and possibly an incipient stage of those debates. In Chapter Four, I will first look at how Wesley and Fletcher can be seen as at the beginning of a trajectory toward pentecostalism. Then, in the second half of the chapter, I will explore ways that early pentecostalism emphasized themes important to open theism, therefore showing how the two trajectories might come together. In Chapter Five, we will see how the two trajectories might be merged by describing a Wesleyan renewal theology with an open theist identity.

Clark Pinnock drew attention to the compatibility of openness theology with Wesleyan thought.[9] Donald Dayton did the same for pentecostal-

---

9. Those appreciative of the openness model, he writes, "are mostly found in Wesleyan, Arminian and Pentecostal circles of evangelicalism that affirm human freedom and deny absolute divine control. There is a natural affinity there." Clark H. Pinnock, *Most Moved Mover: A Theology of God's Openness* (Carlisle, U.K.: Paternoster, 2001), 12. He adds, "The openness model has intellectual roots in Wesleyan-Arminian thinking prior to the rise of process thought in the work of biblical theologian A. Clarke (d. 1832) and of philosopher L. D. McCabe (d. 1897)." Ibid., 12 n. 36. We will consider the work of Lorenzo Dow McCabe at length in chapter two. Adam Clarke was a British biblical scholar and Methodist theologian. In the General Introduction to his well-known commentary of John Calvin, he writes, "He was a strenuous advocate for the doctrine of salvation by grace through faith, and for what he justly calls the *decretum horribile*, the horrible decree of sovereign, eternal, irrespective reprobation. This opinion, from the manner in which it has been defended by some, and opposed by others, has tended greatly to the disunion of many Christians, and produced every temper but brotherly kindness and charity." Adam Clarke, *The Holy Bible Containing the Old and New Testaments: The Text Printed from the*

ism by tracing its roots back through the holiness movement to Wesley and Fletcher.[10] That both open theism of a particular strand and much of synergistic renewal theology have a common ancestry in the theology of Wesley gives them a genetic relationship and some inherent compatibility. Coherence, however, is not inevitable because they have grown independently. The intent of this dissertation is to indicate how an intentional blend of the two can produce a coherent systematic renewal theology, with the experiential strength of Wesleyan charismatic-pentecostalism and the philosophical advantages of open theism.

Most Correct Copies of the Present Authorized Translation Including the Marginal Readings and Parallel Texts with a Commentary and Critical Notes Designed as a Help to a Better Understanding of the Sacred Writings, Vol. 1 (New York: N. Bangs and J. Emory for the Methodist Episcopal Church, 1825), v.

10. Donald W. Dayton, *Theological Roots of Pentecostalism* (Peabody, Mass.: Hendrickson, 1987).

CHAPTER I

Classical Theism, Open Theism, and Renewal Theology— Definitions and Literature

*I*n this chapter, I will focus on open theism. I will define what is meant by the term and its synonyms and try to get at the theological concerns that drive it. I will enter into the major issues in the current debate between open theists and classical theists by considering the major published contributions of the last twenty years. In the second part of the chapter, I will consider what is meant by the term 'renewal theology' and review some ways renewal theologians have interacted with open theism.

A. CLASSICAL THEISM

Classical theism is the biblical-classical synthesis which arose from the "inevitable encounter between biblical and classical thought" in the first centuries of the Christian church as Christians attempted to "evangelize pagan thought and culture."[1] It is the approach of most evangelicals who are not open theists.[2]

---

[1] John Sanders, "Historical Considerations," in *The Openness of God: A Biblical Challenge to the Traditional Understanding of God*, ed. Clark H. Pinnock (Downers Grove: InterVarsity Press, 1994), 99.

[2] I'm using the term 'evangelical' in the sense defined by David Bebbington. He identified a quadrilateral of characteristics: (1) biblicism, a particular regard for the Bible (e.g., all essential spiritual truth is to be found in its pages), (2) crucicentrism, a focus on the atoning work of

H. P. Owen defines classical theism as "belief in one God, the Creator, who is infinite, self-existent, incorporeal, eternal, immutable, impassible, simple, perfect, omniscient and omnipotent."[3] Owen states, "So far as the Western world is concerned, theism has a double origin: the Bible and Greek philosophy. All the divine properties [those just mentioned] are implied in the Bible; the expression and, still more, the amplification of them were due to the influence of Greek philosophy." Owen explains where classical theism originated:

> The philosophical presentation of theology (by which I mean the basic theory of God's nature) was begun by the Apologists (2) and continued by both the ante- and post-Nicene Fathers. (3) It reached its climax in the writings of the two great theologians St Augustine (354–430) and St Thomas Aquinas (*c.* 1225–74). Above all it was Aquinas who systematised and gave authoritative form to this lengthy and complex process of reflection.[4]

Also important to contemporary classical theism would be the thinking of Martin Luther (1483–1546) and especially John Calvin (1509–1564). The biblical-classical synthesis finds expression in Stephen Charnock's *Discourses on the Existence and Attributes of God* (published in 1853 although Charnock lived 1628–1680) and has been influential in conservative evangelical theology ever since.[5] Charnock emphasizes God's transcendence, with chapters

---

Christ on the cross, (3) conversionism, the belief that human beings need to be converted, and (4) activism, the belief that the gospel needs to be expressed in effort. *Evangelicalism in Modern Britain: A History from the 1730s to the 1980s* (Grand Rapids: Baker, 1989), 2–3. Donald Dayton, on the other hand, takes a contrary view. Donald W. Dayton, "Some Doubts about the Usefulness of the Category 'Evangelical'," in *The Variety of American Evangelicalism*, ed. Donald W. Dayton and Robert K. Johnston (Downers Grove: InterVarsity, 1991), 245–51. Dayton thinks the term 'evangelicalism' is meaningless because it refers to three unrelated things: "Sixteenth-century Reformational theology, eighteenth-century Pietism and twentieth-century fundamentalism all formed subsets of Evangelicalism." Peter Althouse, *Spirit of the Last Days: Pentecostal Eschatology in Conversation with Jürgen Moltmann*, JPT Supplement Series 25 (London: T & T Clark, 2003), 17.

3. Huw Parri Owen, *Concepts of Deity*, ed. John Hick, Philosophy of Religion Series (London and Basingstoke: Macmillan, 1971), 1.

4. Ibid., 1–2.

5. Sanders, "Historical Considerations," 94.

I. CLASSICAL THEISM, OPEN THEISM, AND RENEWAL THEOLOGY

on God's eternity, immutability, omnipresence, knowledge (exhaustive foreknowledge), wisdom, power (omnipotence), holiness, goodness, dominion (sovereignty), and patience (impassibility, non-suffering [II:477]).[6]

Classical theism's view of God is constructed around the assertion that God is perfect and can be described in terms of certain perfections. In his ontological argument for the existence of God, Anselm defined God as "the being than which nothing greater can be conceived." Here he is building on those Greek philosophical ideas that God is perfect, immovable, unchangeable, and incapable of being influenced.

To highlight the main features of classical theology, a brief analysis of a recent text in wide use will be instructive. Wayne Grudem's *Systematic Theology* is an excellent example of classical theology for that purpose in that Grudem, while Calvinist, is noncessationist and has been open to the Vineyard movement and should therefore be sympathetic to at least the renewal aspect of this project.[7] In an introductory chapter, Grudem explains his method. He says he will emphasize biblical theology (rather than historical theology or philosophical theology or apologetics) which is a little narrower than typical for systematic theologies.[8] He then follows a traditional structure of seven parts, beginning with scripture, going on to the doctrine of God, the nature of humanity (what he calls the "doctrine of man"), the doctrines of Christ and the Holy Spirit (four chapters on Christ and one on the Holy Spirit), the doctrine of salvation, the doctrine of the church, and ending with the doctrine of the future. In the section on scripture, he defends an inerrantist position.

Grudem's chapters on the doctrine of God are of particular interest. He mentions twenty communicable attributes of God: spirituality, invisibility, knowledge (omniscience), wisdom, truthfulness (and faithfulness), goodness,

---

6. Stephen Charnock, *Discourses upon the Existence and Attributes of God*, 2 vols. (Grand Rapids: Baker, 1853 [Robert Carter & Brothers], rprt. 1996), I:iii–iv, II:iii.

7. Wayne Grudem, *Systematic Theology: An Introduction to Biblical Doctrine* (Leicester, England: InterVarsity and Grand Rapids: Zondervan, 1994, 2000). The classical theist approach is also exemplified in Millard Erickson's recent systematic theology. He defends the classical attributes of God while suggesting Charnock is guilty of "excessive analysis." Millard J. Erickson, *Christian Theology*, 2nd ed. (Grand Rapids: Baker, 1998), 291. Interestingly in the second edition, Erickson very briefly summarizes and responds to open theism. Ibid., 307–08.

8. Grudem, *Systematic Theology*, 21.

love, mercy (grace, patience), holiness, peace (or order), righteousness (or justice), jealousy, wrath, will, freedom, omnipotence (or power and sovereignty), perfection, blessedness, beauty, and glory.[9] In discussing incommunicable attributes of God, he mentions independence (aseity), unchangeableness (immutability), eternity (timelessness), omnipresence, and unity. What is interesting is how he qualifies the immutability of God: "God is unchanging in his being, perfections, purposes, and promises, yet God does act and feel emotions, and he acts and feels differently in response to different situations."[10] The qualification is a modification of classical theology where God is immovable and impassible because these involve change and God is thought to be incapable of change because God is already perfect. For the question of God's impassibility, Grudem takes a position that essentially follows Wesley rather than the more traditional classical view as exemplified by Louis Berkhof, whose categories for God's immutability he adopts.[11] Anselm expresses the more traditional classical view of impassibility:

> How art thou at the same time compassionate and impassible? For if thou art impassible thou dost not feel pity; if thou dost not feel pity thy heart is not made miserable by sympathy with the miserable, which is what it means to be compassionate. But if thou art not compassionate whence do the miserable receive so great consolation? How then, Lord, art thou both compassionate and not compassionate, unless because thou art compassionate from our point of view but art not compassionate in thyself? Thou art so indeed in our sense and not in thine. For when thou lookest upon us miserable men we experience the effect of compassion, but thou does not experience the feeling. Thou art therefore both compassionate because thou savest the miserable and sparest those that sin against thee, and

---

9. Ibid., 185–86.
10. Ibid., 163.
11. Ibid., 163–65. Berkhof's categories are being, perfections, purposes, and promises. Louis Berkhof, *Systematic Theology* (Grand Rapids: Eerdmans, 1939, 1941), 58.

I. CLASSICAL THEISM, OPEN THEISM, AND RENEWAL THEOLOGY

not compassionate because thou art not affected by sympathy with misery.[12]

Grudem follows a more traditional classical approach in discussing God's eternity. He asserts that "God is timeless in his own being" although the first text he cites in support affirms not timelessness but everlasting duration: "from everlasting to everlasting you are God" (Psalm 90:2).[13] Secondly, Grudem states that "God sees all time equally vividly."[14] He says, "Thus God somehow stands above time and is able to see it all as present in his consciousness."[15]

Grudem's discussion of God's omnipresence is also in line with classical theism. He makes a concession to modify Plato's idea of God's immovability when he affirms God acts. The biblical basis of his theology requires this. Grudem says, "God's omnipresence may be defined as follows: God does not have size or spatial dimensions and is present at every point of space with his whole being, yet God acts differently in different places."[16]

Lastly, on the incommunicable attributes of God, Grudem's discussion of the divine unity affirms that "God is not divided into parts, yet we see different attributes of God emphasized at different times."[17] He states, "When Scripture speaks about God's attributes it never singles out one attribute of God as more important than all the rest."[18] This section on the doctrine of God discusses the Trinity, providence, miracles, prayer, angels, Satan, and demons.

Grudem's section on the "doctrine of man" covers creation, the nature of humans, the nature of sin, and covenants between God and humans. The section on the doctrine of Christ and the Holy Spirit has chapters on the person of Christ, the atonement, the resurrection and ascension, the offices of Christ (prophet, priest, and king), and one chapter on the Holy Spirit.

---

12. Arthur Cushman McGiffert, *A History of Christian Thought: Volume II, The West from Tertullian to Erasmus* (New York and London: Charles Scribner's Sons, 1933, 1954), 194.
13. Grudem, *Systematic Theology*, 169.
14. Ibid., 170.
15. Ibid., 171.
16. Ibid., 173.
17. Ibid., 177.
18. Ibid., 178.

The fifth section covers soteriology with chapters on common grace, election and reprobation, effective calling, regeneration, conversion, justification, adoption, growth in sanctification, baptism in and filling with the Holy Spirit, the perseverance of the saints, death and the intermediate state, glorification, and union with Christ. Some topics that are selected indicate Reformed theological preoccupations.

Grudem's sixth section is on ecclesiology and engages the nature of the church, the purity and unity of the church, the power of the church, church government (women are held not to be eligible to be pastors), the means of grace, baptism, the Lord's Supper, worship, and the gifts of the Holy Spirit.

The last section in Grudem's introductory *Systematic Theology* text is on eschatology. He discusses the return of Christ, the millennium, final judgment and eternal punishment, and the new heavens and new earth.

Even in this highly abbreviated synopsis, it will be clear that classical theism covers a remarkably extensive theological landscape. This summary of Grudem's text has allowed us to view it through a wide-angle lens and sets us up to look at open theism and see how it differs.

B. OPEN THEISM

1. Open Theism and Love

God is good and the most important thing we can say about him is that he is loving.[19] That conviction is at the heart of open theism. Other theologies prioritize God's power, emphasizing divine sovereignty, yet others start with God's righteousness and thus emphasize divine justice. But for open theists,

---

19. I'd like to acknowledge the desirability of using gender-neutral pronouns with respect to God and the Holy Spirit. In the biblical witness, God has both male and female aspects. However, given the limitations of English grammar in its present state, I'll occasionally use gender-specific pronouns in reference to God to avoid constructions which draw attention to themselves. The issue can become especially awkward in working closely with historical and biblical texts. It is also more acute in discussing relational theologies like open theism where God's personal interaction with humans is emphasized so language like 'godself' which is technically more correct can put God at a distance.

I. CLASSICAL THEISM, OPEN THEISM, AND RENEWAL THEOLOGY

the affirmation that God is love sets the theological agenda; for many, love is not just one among God's attributes but the most important one.[20]

Love is relational, non-coercive, and seeks the good of others, sometimes at cost to self. Love is *relational* because it seeks active expression in interacting with another person. Love that is not communicated is incomplete. Jesus told his disciples, "I give you a new commandment, that you love *one another*."[21] Love is *non-coercive* because it does not seek to control the other person with whom it is in relationship.[22] Paul writes, "Love... does not insist on its own way."[23] Love seeks the *good of others*. Thomas Jay Oord defines love in this way: "To love is to act intentionally, in sympathetic/empathetic response to God and others, to *promote overall well-being*."[24] More particularly, divine love has been defined by other Godly love researchers in similar terms as "the dynamic interaction between divine and human love that enlivens and expands benevolence."[25]

These qualities of love find theological expression in open theism. In open theism, God is highly *relational*. He created the universe to make possible loving relationships with humans. Open theism gives expression to the *non-coercive* nature of how love prefers to act by emphasizing the measure of freedom that God has given humans. God gives up some control in order to make real choices possible for humans. Without this freedom, humans could

---

20. The Swiss theologian Hans Urs von Balthasar quotes Pascal: "L'unique objet de l'Ecriture est la charité" then attempts to show from scripture (both Old and New Testaments) that revelation has a center in the theme of divine love. *Love Alone Is Credible*, trans. D. C. Schindler (San Francisco: Ignatius, 1963, 2004), 5, 83-98. He goes on to argue that not only is love alone credible, but that only love ought to be believed (p. 101). By this he means that faith requires belief in absolute love—the love that Jesus showed in dying for us. This faith (here landing on common ground with open theism) is "against every 'rational' concept of God, which thinks of him in terms of impassibility or, at best, totally pure goodness, but not in terms of this inconceivable and senseless act of love" (p. 102).

21. John 13:34.

22. Exceptions can be thought of, as a temporary expedient, as with a parent keeping a child from danger. Parents who seek to control their children after they have become adults are perceived as acting out of insecurity rather than love.

23. 1 Corinthians 13:4–5.

24. Thomas Jay Oord, *The Nature of Love: A Theology* (St. Louis, Mo.: Chalice Press, 2010), 17. Italics mine.

25. Matthew T. Lee and Amos Yong, *Godly Love: Impediments and Possibilities* (Lanham, Md. and Plymouth, UK: Lexington Books, 2012).

not genuinely love. Open theists affirm the partial openness of the future as a consequence of the non-coercive way God prefers to act in history and the non-deterministic nature of reality. Lastly, open theism emphasizes how God *seeks the good* of humanity, even at cost to self. Jesus on the cross dying for the salvation of humanity is the epitome of self-sacrificial love.

2. Concerns of Open Theism

Does God control everything? If so, it is hard to escape the conclusion that he is responsible for all the evil in the world. Open theism rethinks this question. Is God, above all, loving? If so, it is difficult to continue to describe him in the terms of classical theism as incapable of response and being influenced (immutable), as immovable, and incapable of feeling (impassible). Open theism seeks to recover a more biblical description. Does God know the future in complete detail? If so, how can human beings have genuine free will to change what is going to happen? What is the future? Does it even exist yet? These are questions that open theists seek to answer.

Why does it matter what we think about God? We become like whatever or whoever it is we worship. Who we are and how we think influences how we live out our lives. Open theism's vision of a God who loves passionately, and its view of a partially open future, inspires us also to love radically and to be intentional in how we influence what the future will be.

Open theism occupies a position between classical theism and process theology. In classical theism, God stands outside of time and space, and is not changed by events and people in the world.[26] In process theology, God is evolving and depends on humanity.[27] In open theism, God is engaged with humanity in time and space, and seeks to work cooperatively with people to further his purposes.

---

26. Classical theism was discussed above beginning at p. 7.

27. Process theology is indebted to the philosophy of Alfred North Whitehead (1861–1947, British mathematician, logician and philosopher) as developed by Charles Hartshorne (1897–2000). (Hartshorne and Paul Weiss edited the *Collected Papers of Charles Sanders Peirce*.) Hartshorne addressed the problem of evil and God's omnipotence. For Hartshorne, God's perfection lies in his superlative ability to relate to every creature. God changes and grows in his knowledge of the world and in empathy. God's power lies in his ability to persuade free creatures towards the good. Hartshorne's student, John Cobb, Jr. is probably the best-known proponent of process theology today. Process is interested among other diverse things in (1) emphasizing

I. CLASSICAL THEISM, OPEN THEISM, AND RENEWAL THEOLOGY

3. Definitions

'Open theism' describes a theological and philosophical movement which is not homogeneous. Its precise definition can be nuanced in several ways. The terms 'open theism,' 'open theology,' and 'openness theology' are essentially synonymous and do not provide a basis for distinction. 'Relational theology' is a related term referring to a range of views—of which open theism is one—which stress two ideas: (1) God affects his creation and his creatures, and (2) creatures affect God.[28]

What is meant by 'open theism' usually goes in one of two directions. If the interest is primarily philosophical, the tendency is to define open theism in terms of a view of the future. If the interest is primarily theological, frequently the intent is to identify a position on soteriology and the nature of God. John Sanders exemplifies the theological approach.[29]

Alan Rhoda illustrates a philosophical interest in the nature of time with a focus on the openness of the future, rather than the openness of God.[30] He proposes a taxonomy that describes five different ways of viewing the future as open. The future is *casually* open if there are multiple possible futures

---

God's immanence over transcendence, (2) providing an explanation for reality that provides a unified explanation for the universe, and (3) addressing the problem of theodicy. Some of the range of the next generation of Process interests can be seen in Jay B. McDaniel and Donna Bowman, eds., *Handbook of Process Theology* (St. Louis, Mo.: Chalice Press, 2006).

[28]. Thomas Jay Oord, "What Is Relational Theology?," in *Relational Theology: A Contemporary Introduction*, ed. Brint Montgomery, Thomas Jay Oord, and Karen Winslow (Eugene, Ore.: Point Loma Press/Wipf & Stock, 2012), 2. Under the umbrella of 'relational theology' Oord includes missional, Arminian & holiness, feminist/womanist, open, trinitarian, process, Wesleyan, and liberation/postcolonial theologies. He observes that a theologian might hold one or a cluster of these views and be emergent and/or pentecostal as well. Ibid., 3. He says, "Of course, those who embrace relational theology typically embrace other theological ideas too…. Most emphasize the importance of relationships in the Church, outside the Church, and relationships with all creation. Most think relational categories are central to Christian ethics and should be guides to get along with others—both human and nonhuman—on our planet." Ibid., 2.

[29]. Clark Pinnock's interest is also primarily theological. "We chose this term because 'openness' was an attractive and unused metaphor which evoked the notion of God's open heart toward his creatures. It suggests the vision that we have of God's glory which is characterized by voluntarily self-limitation and self-sacrificing and which extols a divine power that delights more in nurturing than in subjugating creatures." Clark H. Pinnock, "Open Theism: 'What Is This? A New Teaching?—and with Authority!'," *Ashland Theological Journal* 34 (2002): 39.

[30]. Alan R. Rhoda, "The Fivefold Openness of the Future," in *God in an Open Universe: Science, Metaphysics, and Open Theism*, ed. William Hasker, Thomas Jay Oord, and Dean Zimmerman (Eugene, Ore.: Wipf & Stock, 2011), 69–93.

which are logically possible extensions of the past and which are consistent with being caused and consistent with the laws of nature and supernature.[31] The future is *ontically* open if the nature of time is dynamic (rather than static) and a unique and complete series of future world states does not exist. One way we can express this is to say that only the present world state exists. "Past world states no longer exist, and future ones do not yet exist." We know this view as presentism. Alternatively, the future could be ontically open if past world states still exist, but not future ones. Thirdly, the future is *alethically* open if there is no unique series of events which describe *the* actual future.[32] If a state of affairs *might* happen, then the future is alethically open. Fourthly, the future is *epistemically* open if a future state of affairs cannot be infallibly known. Fifthly, the future is *providentially* open if some or all future events have not been efficaciously ordained.[33] If this view is true, then meticulous providence is not. Rhoda argues that "if the future is causally open then it is open in all five respects."[34]

In summary, open theism is a movement with both theological and philosophical concerns. Philosophically, it advocates for a partially open, nondeterministic view of the future. Theologically, it is centered on God's love and the freedom he gives humans.

4. Major Contributors to the Debate

While we can find antecedents to the current interest in open theistic themes in the nineteenth century, and even much earlier,[35] a group of recent writers

---

[31]. "I include 'laws of supernature' in order to allow for the existence of non-physical beings (God, angels, Cartesian souls, etc.) capable of influencing the course of events. Such beings, if they exist, presumably have natures or essences that constrain or limit what they can do, much as the laws of nature constrain what physical beings can do." Ibid., 73.

[32]. The term 'alethic' derives from ἀλήθεια, the Greek word for 'truth'. It has been used to describe four different ways a proposition could be true or false: necessity, contingency, possibility, and impossibility (the alethic modalities). Christopher Menzel, "Alethic Modalities," in *The Cambridge Dictionary of Philosophy*, ed. Robert Audi (Cambridge: Cambridge University Press, 1999). If future contingencies exist then the future is alethically open.

[33]. Rhoda, "The Fivefold Openness of the Future," 69–93.

[34]. Ibid., 91.

[35]. John Sanders mentions Calcidius, writing in the late fourth century, who wrote a book challenging Stoic determinism. Sanders mentions as well some of the Remonstrants (Dutch Arminians), Andrew Ramsay (John Wesley's contemporary), Isaak Dorner (nineteenth century

has been responsible for articulating a more in-depth and comprehensive theological vision. These particular scholars are highlighted because they were the ones who happened to be catalytic in creating much of the energetic discussion of open theist themes of recent years. Surveying their work will provide a contextual overview of open theism.

Richard Rice in 1980 wrote *The Openness of God: The Relationship of Divine Foreknowledge and Human Free Will* with a revised version issued as *God's Foreknowledge & Man's Free Will*.[36] We can credit him with inventing the term Openness theology.[37]

David Basinger and Randall Basinger's *Predestination and Free Will: Four Views of Divine Sovereignty and Human Freedom* (Downers Grove:

German theologian), Adam Clarke (Methodist author of a well-known biblical commentary), and many others in the nineteenth and twentieth centuries. John Sanders, *The God Who Risks: A Theology of Providence*, 2nd ed. (Downers Grove: InterVarsity Press, 2007), 165–172.

Of particular interest is Lorenzo Dow McCabe (1817–1897), a Methodist theologian and philosopher who taught at Ohio Wesleyan University and provoked debate for decades. The second of his two books is *Divine Nescience of Future Contingencies a Necessity: Being an Introduction to "The Foreknowledge of God, and Cognate Themes"* (New York: Phillips & Hunt, 1882). The prior book is *The Foreknowledge of God, and Cognate Themes in Theology and Philosophy* (Cincinnati: Walden & Stowe, 1882). McCabe's significance as a precursor to open theism is highlighted in three articles:

George M. Porter, "Things That May Be Only? Lorenzo Dow McCabe and Some Neglected Nineteenth Century Roots of Open Theism in North America," *Forum of The Oxford Society of Scholars Meeting in Rewley House/Kellogg College* (January 12–14, 2004), http://opentheism.info/information/things-may/ [accessed 14 May 2014].

William McGuire King, "God's Nescience of Future Contingents: A Nineteenth-Century Wesleyan Theory," *Process Studies* 9 (Fall 1979).

David Alstad Tiessen, "The Openness Model of God: An Evangelical Paradigm in Light of Its Nineteenth-Century Wesleyan Precedent," *Didaskalia* (Spring 2000).

Tom Lukashow has prepared a timeline and detailed annotated bibliography of writers expressing views compatible with an open view of the future as well as writers critiquing such views, beginning in the seventeenth century. Tom Lukashow, "Historical Research," *The Open View* (2014), http://theopenview.org/historical-research/ [accessed 12 May 2014].

36. Richard Rice, *God's Foreknowledge and Man's Free Will* (Minneapolis, Minn.: Bethany House, 1985); Richard Rice, *The Openness of God: the Relationship of Divine Foreknowledge and Human Free Will* (Nashville, Tenn.: Review and Herald, 1980).

37. Rice studied Whitehead and Hartshorne at the University of Chicago Divinity School, suggesting the probable influence of process thought in the development of open theism. Richard Rice, "Process Theism and the Open View of God: The Crucial Difference," in *Searching for an Adequate God: A Dialogue Between Process and Free Will Theists*, ed. John B. Cobb and Clark H. Pinnock (Grand Rapids: Eerdmans, 2000), 165–66.ed. John B. Cobb and Clark H. Pinnock (Grand Rapids: Eerdmans, 2000

InterVarsity, 1986) also provoked discussion.[38] Clark Pinnock contributed a chapter in which he says, "God is omniscient in the sense that he knows everything which can be known, just as God is omnipotent in the sense that he can do everything that can be done. But free actions are not entities which can be known ahead of time. They literally do not yet exist to be known."[39] Pinnock here is giving voice to an incipient openness theology.

William Hasker's *God, Time, and Knowledge* is an outstanding contribution.[40] Hasker is associated with Huntington University, now Emeritus Professor of Philosophy. He argues God knows all possible future contingencies and the relative likelihood of each taking place.[41] He has a particular interest in showing the weaknesses of Molinism as an alternative to open theism.[42] For Hasker, the future doesn't exist, so future events are unknowable even to God. Hasker wants to say that God knows all that can be known, but can't know a future that doesn't yet exist.

John Sanders teaches at Hendrix College and is a leading contemporary advocate for open theism.[43] Sanders was a contributor to Clark Pinnock's

---

38. David Basinger and Randall Basinger, *Predestination and Free Will: Four Views of Divine Sovereignty and Human Freedom* (Downers Grove: InterVarsity, 1986).

39. Clark H. Pinnock, "God Limits His Knowledge," in *Predestination and Free Will: Four Views of Divine Sovereignty and Human Freedom*, ed. David Basinger and Randall Basinger (Downers Grove: InterVarsity, 1986), 157.

40. William Hasker, *God, Time, and Knowledge*, Cornell Studies in the Philosophy of Religion (Ithaca: Cornell University Press, 1989). Later he wrote *Providence, Evil and the Openness of God* (London: Routledge, 2004). More recently he has done a historical study of the Trinity and ends with developing a social trinitarianism in *Metaphysics and the Tri-Personal God*, Oxford Studies in Analytic Theology (Oxford: Oxford University Press, 2013). Here he is revisiting the subject of his doctoral dissertation, "The Social Analogy in Modern Trinitarian Thought" (Ph.D. thesis, University of Edinburgh, 1961).

41. Hasker, *God, Time, and Knowledge*, 188.

42. Molinism, originated by the Jesuit Luis de Molina in the sixteenth century, sought a "middle knowledge" with a balance of free will and theological determinism. God knows the future because he knows which choices free humans will make. God knows the choices because he knows what every free agent will choose to do in every situation. These options have recently been termed 'counterfactuals'. Molina's book is available in a modern translation: Luis de Molina, *On Divine Foreknowledge*, trans. Alfred J. Freddoso, Part IV of the *Concordia* (Ithaca and London: Cornell University Press, 1588, 1988).

43. He has near martyr status, having been almost voted out of the Evangelical Theological Society for his views: Ted Olsen, "ETS Leadership Issues Recommendations on Kicking Out Open Theists: Evangelical Theological Society's Executive Committee Unanimously Recommends

I. CLASSICAL THEISM, OPEN THEISM, AND RENEWAL THEOLOGY

1989 book advocating Arminianism, *The Grace of God, The Will of Man* (as was Richard Rice).[44] *The God Who Risks: A Theology of Providence* is Sander's fullest treatment of openness theology.[45]

Greg Boyd is a prolific and articulate proponent of open theism. Boyd graduated from Yale Divinity School in 1982 and Princeton Theological Seminary in 1988, taught for sixteen years at Bethel University and continues to adjunct there.[46] He is currently senior pastor of Woodland Hills in St. Paul, Minnesota. His *God of the Possible* is one of the most accessible introductions to open theism.[47] A more scholarly treatment is found in *Satan and the Problem of Evil*.[48]

The late Clark Pinnock, as he was moving from what he called paleo-Calvinism to a more Arminian position, tracked down Rice's book and read it appreciatively.[49] That his pilgrimage was not without both detractors and defenders is evidenced in "Reconstructing Evangelical Theology" a paper that was first presented at the Evangelical Theological Society annual meeting

---

Clark Pinnock Stay; Majority Says John Sanders Should Go," *Christianity Today* 47, no. 10 (October 2003), http://www.christianitytoday.com/ct/2003/octoberweb-only/10-27-41.0.html.

See also David Neff, "Dispatch from Atlanta: What Fireworks? Anxieties and Attack Turn to Grace as the Evangelical Theological Society Votes on Open Theism Proponents' Membership," *Christianity Today* 47, no. 11 (Nov 2003), http://www.christianitytoday.com/ct/2003/novemberweb-only/11-17-41.0.html.

Sanders lost a post at Huntington College (now Huntington University) in Indiana for being an out-spoken advocate: John Dart, "College to Close Out 'Open Theism' Scholar," *Christian Century* 121, no. 26 (Dec 28, 2004).

44. John Sanders, "God as Personal," in *The Grace of God, The Will of Man*, ed. Clark H. Pinnock (Grand Rapids: Zondervan, 1989), 165–80.

45. Downers Grove: InterVarsity Press, 1998.

46. Bethel Seminary website: http://cas.bethel.edu/catalog/personnel/faculty.html.

47. Gregory A. Boyd, *God of the Possible: A Biblical Introduction to the Open View of God* (Grand Rapids: Baker, 2000).

48. Gregory A. Boyd, *Satan and the Problem of Evil: Constructing a Trinitarian Warfare Theodicy* (Downers Grove: InterVarsity, 2001).

49. At The Word Made Fresh and Society of Evangelical Scholars meeting with the theme "Exploring the Life and Theology of Clark Pinnock," (November 18, 2011 in San Francisco as part of the annual meeting of the American Academy of Religion), Richard Rice recalled receiving a letter in the mail from Pinnock asking how he could obtain a copy of the book (which seems to have been suppressed by the publisher after creating some controversy in Rice's Adventist denomination).

in Colorado Springs, November 14–16, 2001.[50] Pinnock's departure from Calvinism began around 1970 when he was teaching the Book of Hebrews at Trinity Evangelical Divinity School. It was the tension introduced by biblical texts, particularly Hebrews 3:12 (on persevering) and 10:26 (on the possibility of falling away), that led him to question the doctrine of absolute security. Calvinism is a logically tight system and needs all of its components to hold together. "The thread was pulled, and the garment must begin to unravel, as indeed it did."[51] This insight led him toward Arminianism, and ultimately to openness theology: "What had dawned on me was what I had known experientially all along in my walk with the Lord, that there is a profound mutuality in our dealings with God."[52]

Pinnock generated remarkable interest in open theism in the 1990s with the publication of *The Openness of God* in collaboration with Richard Rice, John Sanders, William Hasker, and David Basinger.[53] This watershed book built on the prior work by the authors and others to make the case for open theology.[54] The publication of *The Openness of God* twenty years ago made open theism an identifiable movement. For that reason, I will consider the book in some detail.

Richard Rice, in his chapter in *The Openness of God*, describes classical theism and in what way it sees God as immutable, omnipotent, and

---

50. Clark H. Pinnock, "Reconstructing Evangelical Theology: Is the Open View of God a Good Idea?," *Andrews University Seminary Studies* 41, no. 2 (2003): 215–27.

51. Clark H. Pinnock, ed. *The Grace of God, The Will of Man: A Case for Arminianism* (Grand Rapids: Zondervan, 1989), 17.

52. Ibid., 17–18.

53. Clark H. Pinnock et al., *The Openness of God: A Biblical Challenge to the Traditional Understanding of God* (Downers Grove: InterVarsity Press, 1994), 69.

54. Significantly:

William Hasker, "Foreknowledge and Necessity," *Faith and Philosophy* 2 (April 1985).

David Basinger and Randall Basinger, *Predestination and Free Will: Four Views of Divine Sovereignty and Human Freedom* (Downers Grove: InterVarsity, 1986).

William Hasker, *God, Time, and Knowledge*, Cornell Studies in the Philosophy of Religion (Ithaca, N.Y.: Cornell University Press, 1989).

Clark H. Pinnock, ed. *The Grace of God, The Will of Man: A Case for Arminianism* (Grand Rapids: Zondervan, 1989).

omniscient.[55] He discusses the key biblical texts for this position and how they lead to an elevated view of God. Then he lays out the alternative that openness theology is proposing and reviews the most significant biblical texts which support that position.

Two hermeneutical keys significant for open theism are that love is God's most significant attribute and that God is best understood dynamically—by what he does—rather than statically. This dynamic understanding of God is exemplified in Scripture, where we see many interactions between God and humans. What has been lost in classical theism is how responsive God is to his creatures. This responsiveness comes out in Old Testament texts where God is described as having several different feelings ranging from joy to sorrow and anger to satisfaction. God's responsiveness goes beyond inner experience to how the future is being shaped.

The claim of open theism is that in some situations God reacts to human decisions and acts accordingly. There are also situations where God acts by fiat, for example, in the world's creation. In turning from the Old Testament to the New Testament, Rice finds that here we also find a portrayal of God that is primarily dynamic rather than static and supports the open view. Jesus uniquely reveals who God is—passionate and self-giving to the point of dying on the cross. He is the antithesis of the aloof, unmoved God of classical theism. Rice grapples with the texts that seem to support the classical position and shows how they can be understood as consistent with the open view. For example, Malachi 3:6, James 1:17, Numbers 23:19, and 1 Samuel 15:29 seem to support the view that God does not change.[56] Rice points out that most of these and similar biblical texts are saying that God's character does not change. It is not speaking of God's experience.[57] He mentions how the South African scholar Adriö König observes that the issue in these passages is

---

55. Richard Rice, "Biblical Support for a New Perspective," in *The Openness of God: A Biblical Challenge to the Traditional Understanding of God*, ed. Clark H. Pinnock (Downers Grove: InterVarsity Press, 1994), 11–58.
56. Ibid., 47.
57. Ibid.

divine faithfulness—for example, can God be trusted to keep his word?—not immutability.[58]

Rice discusses the nature of prophecy, observing that a prophecy "may express God's intention to do something in the future irrespective of creaturely decision."[59] A prophecy "may also express God's knowledge that something will happen because the necessary conditions for it have been fulfilled and nothing could conceivably prevent it."[60] Thirdly, a prophecy "may also express what God intends to do *if* certain conditions obtain."[61] This understanding of how prophecy is functioning makes good sense of the biblical data and does not require absolute divine foreknowledge.

In the second chapter, John Sanders looks at the historical background.[62] He notes how Greek philosophical concerns shaped early Christian theology. Early Christian thinkers were trying to make sense of Christianity for the intellectual world in which they lived. This thinking came through Plato's thought. Their primary concern was to move away from the anthropomorphisms of the Greek religions toward perfections which describe ultimate reality. For Philo, God is immutable and impassible, but can intervene in history. The church fathers took a similar approach, producing a synthesis of Greek philosophy and biblical theology, beginning as early as A.D. 100. For Ignatius, God is timeless and impassible. Justin Martyr describes God as unchangeable, eternal, impassible, anonymous, and incomprehensible. Tertullian swam against the current and resisted the synthesis. He noted God could respond to human actions and change his mind. Origen declares God to

---

58. Adriö König, *Here Am I!: A Christian Reflection on God* (Grand Rapids: Eerdmans, 1982). This volume is out-of-print but is available as a Wipf & Stock reprint. Adriö König was John Sanders' doctoral advisor.

59. Rice, "Biblical Support," 51.

60. Ibid.

61. Ibid. Surprisingly, John Calvin concedes the implied conditional nature of some Old Testament prophecy: "Who now does not see that it pleased the Lord by such threats to arouse to repentance those whom he was terrifying, that they might escape the judgment they deserved for their sins? If that is true, the nature of the circumstances leads us to recognize a tacit condition in the simple intimation." John Calvin, *Institutes of the Christian Religion*, ed. John T. McNeill, trans. Ford Lewis Battles, The Library of Christian Classics, Vol. XX (Philadelphia: Westminster, 1960), 1:228, Book 1 ch. 17 §14.

62. Sanders, "Historical Considerations," 59–100.

be impassible, immutable, omnipotent, and omniscient (with foreknowledge of human choices). Augustine was very influenced by the Neoplatonism of Plotinus. With Augustine, the conception of God as impassible, unchangeable, all-powerful, all-knowing, and timeless became embedded in Western theology. In the Reformation, Luther, because of his emphasis on salvation and the cross, distinguished God as known rationally through philosophy and God as known through the Bible. And yet Luther can speak of God's will as immutable and eternal.[63] Calvin also tried to move toward a more biblical theology and away from philosophical speculation, but was influenced by Augustine. For Calvin, God is not affected by his creation. God preordains all that takes place and certainly doesn't change his mind.

Sanders describes how, in recent times, the idea of God has been reexamined by progressives, conservatives, and moderates alike. Paul Tillich developed a panentheism.[64] Wolfhart Pannenberg is helpful in distinguishing panentheism from pantheism. In discussing God's unity, he says, "It is not all in one (pantheism) but transcends the difference of one and all."[65] In pantheism, God and the creation are ontologically one. In panentheism, they are ontologically distinct, but God is in all. "Precisely as the one who incommensurably transcends his creation, God is still present to even the least of his creatures.... The biblical sayings about God's dwelling in heaven are especially significant because they imply the distinction of heaven from earth and therefore God's giving his earthly creatures room to live their own lives in their own present but alongside him."[66] Process theology describes a relationship between God and the creation which is mutually dependent.[67] Scholars

---

63. Pinnock et al., *The Openness of God*, 88.

64. Tillich writes, "The being of God is being-itself. The being of God cannot be understood as the existence of a being alongside others or above others. If God is *a* being, he is subject to the categories of finitude, especially to space and substance." Paul Tillich, "God as Being and as Living (1951)," in *Paul Tillich: Theologian of the Boundaries*, ed. Mark Kline Taylor, The Making of Modern Theology (London: Collins, 1987), 163.

65. *Systematic Theology: Volume I*, trans. Geoffrey W. Bromiley (Grand Rapids: Eerdmans, 1991), 443–44.

66. Ibid., 412.

67. Charles Hartshorne's dipolar theism also describes God's relationship to the world as 'panentheism'. The "dipolar view of God enables us to affirm the theistic insight that God is distinct from the world *and* the pantheistic insight that God is inclusive of the world. In his contingent

like Stephen Charnock, William G. T. Shedd, Louis Berkhof, Lewis Sperry Chafer, A. W. Tozer, Charles Ryrie, J. I. Packer, Carl Henry, and J. Rodman Williams represent a continuation of the classical philosophical-biblical synthesis.[68] Theologians such as Charles Hodge and Millard Erickson hold a modified position: God must have feelings such as love because the Bible says so.[69] Theologians such as James Oliver Buswell Jr., Richard Foster, Greg Boyd, and others represent a moderate position between the classical theists and the progressives (for example, Paul Tillich or Charles Hartshorne). Under the banner of the "openness of God," these scholars are seeking to reformulate our idea of God to consider how God can be intimately involved in human history and how his love requires that he not impose his will on humanity.

---

pole, God includes the world, so his reality incorporates all the value of the creaturely existence. But in his necessary pole, God is distinct from the world, so God would be God no matter what world actually existed. For panentheism, there must be some creaturely world or other, not necessarily *this* world. Any world will do. There is nothing greater than God, because God includes the entire value of the creaturely world. God can enjoy genuine relations with his creatures, because his concrete experience is contingent, just as theirs is." Rice, "Process Theism and the Open View of God," 175–77.

68. There is some diversity in the views of these theologians but one of the common elements would be an allegiance to the synthesis achieved by Augustine. Augustine distinguishes God's internal and external relations. "The internal relations between the Father, Son and Spirit are eternal and immutable but do not convey the being (or substance) of God.... Augustine says that God's external relations with the temporal creation are accidental, and so do not affect the being of God. Since neither internal nor external relations involved the essence of God, God has no 'real relationship' with any other, including creation." Sanders, "Historical Considerations," 83–84. Augustine's distinction was further clarified by Gregory Palamas (1296–1359), Archbishop of Thessalonica. Ralph Del Colle explained: "In God there is an ineffable distinction between what is communicable and what is incommunicable, between the divine essence or nature properly so-called, and the 'energies of divine operations', which, going forth from God, manifest, communicate, and impart the divine being to created reality." *Christ and the Spirit: Spirit-Christology in Trinitarian Perspective* (New York: Oxford University Press, 1994), 14–15. This distinction is sometimes expressed as the immanent trinity (what the Godhead is in itself) versus the economic trinity. The metaphysical principle of economy means "that God's transcendent causality intervenes in the world sparingly and with the utmost discretion.... Where God's activity manifests itself *within* the succession of events we have saving history, culminating in the Incarnation." Karl Rahner and Herbert Vorgrimler, *Theological Dictionary* (New York: Herder and Herder, 1965), 114. Rahner famously said, "The Trinity is a mystery of *salvation*, otherwise it would never have been revealed.... The 'economic' Trinity is the 'immanent' Trinity and the 'immanent' Trinity is the 'economic' Trinity" because God the Father could not have done on the cross what the Son did." *The Trinity*, trans. Joseph Donceel (New York: Herder and Herder, 1970), 22.

69. Pinnock et al., *The Openness of God*, 96.

I. CLASSICAL THEISM, OPEN THEISM, AND RENEWAL THEOLOGY

Clark Pinnock, in the third chapter, argues that we experience God to be responsive and involved.[70] The trouble comes when we do our theological formulations. A tradition which has stressed the transcendence of God at the expense of ways in which he is immanent has overly influenced us. Pinnock argues God has all power but freely surrenders some of that control so that human beings can be free agents—free to love the Creator. In another departure from classical theism, Pinnock argues God is changeable, at least in his response to human actions, while immutable in his Trinitarian being and in his nature. God is always faithful, but he is not immovable and inert. A third way Pinnock distances himself from classical theism is regarding the doctrine of God's impassibility. He asks, "How can God be loving and not pained by evil? How can God be impassible when the incarnate Son experienced suffering and death?"[71] A fourth refinement Pinnock would make is in the definition of God's eternity. He affirms God has always existed and always will. However, God is not timeless. If he were timeless, he could not engage in history and form relationships with humans. God does not stand outside of time and predetermine all future events. The future is partly open and partly already determined by what has already occurred and by God's intentions. How, then, does God know the future? Pinnock asserts God knows everything that can be known.[72] Omniscience does not require that God have detailed foreknowledge of every event. If that is the case, the future is predetermined. But Pinnock argues that for actual choice to be possible the future cannot be foreknown in complete detail because it does not yet exist. Rather, God and humanity are working together to create that future because an open God has made us free creatures.

In the fourth chapter, William Hasker offers a philosophical perspective on what is at stake in choosing between classical theism's self-sufficient God and the open view.[73] One issue is the relation of God and time. In the view of

---

70. Clark H. Pinnock, "Systematic Theology," in *The Openness of God: A Biblical Challenge to the Traditional Understanding of God* (Downers Grove: InterVarsity Press, 1994), 101–25.
71. Pinnock et al., *The Openness of God*, 118.
72. Ibid., 121.
73. William Hasker, "A Philosophical Perspective," in *The Openness of God: A Biblical Challenge to the Traditional Understanding of God*, ed. Clark H. Pinnock (Downers Grove: InterVarsity

classical theism, God is timeless. The open view is that God is temporal, "that he lives and interacts with us through the changes of time."[74] Hasker argues, "If God is truly timeless, so that temporal determinations of 'before' and 'after' do not apply to him, then how can God *act* in time, as the Scriptures say that he does? ... And above all, if God is timeless and incapable of change, how can God be born, grow up, live with and among people, suffer and die, as we believe he did as incarnated in Jesus."[75]

A second issue is how God is changeless—immutable and impassible. For classical theism, God is perfect in the sense that God is "the being than which nothing greater can be conceived" (Anselm). God is without change because a perfect being cannot change, because any change would either be for better or worse, and thus denying perfection.[76]

Open theists would affirm the changelessness of God's character but affirm that God can experience change. Hasker argues that Plato's argument for God's immutability is fallacious because it is based on the false assumption that all change must be either for better or for worse. Hasker's example is a watch which one moment reads 6:05 but seven minutes later reads 6:12. The watch has changed but neither for the better or the worse. "It is, in fact, an example of a *change that is consistent with and/or required by a constant state of excellence.*"[77]

In the fifth and final chapter, David Basinger discusses five practical implications of the openness theology being proposed.[78] He considers petitionary prayer, divine guidance, human suffering, social responsibility, and evangelistic responsibility.

In summary, *The Openness of God* lays out a clear alternative between classical theism and the open approach. We may highlight several concerns of open theism. One is the nature of God. Is God the immovable, immutable,

---

Press, 1994), 126–54.

74. Ibid., 128.

75. Ibid., 128–29.

76. Ibid., 131.

77. Ibid., 132–33.

78. David Basinger, "Practical Implications," ibid., 155–76.

impassible deity of classical theism who exists outside of the space-time continuum? Openness, on the contrary, describes the nature of God as most essentially love, and God as intimately involved in history and creation. Has God, in his omnipotence, foreordained the future as in classical theism? Openness theology, rather, argues that God has granted genuine freedom to human and spiritual beings and has in his grace given up some of his power and control in order to make room for that freedom to be real. The actions of human beings partially determine what the future will be. The future is not exhaustively predetermined and is not yet even an ontological reality. Is the eternal destiny of individuals predestined and entirely decided by God, as in the monergism of classical theism? Openness theology understands initial justification as entirely an act of God's grace and initiative—freely available to all—but the process of salvation as requiring human response and synergistic cooperation. Openness theology seeks for an understanding of God that is consistent with our experience of God as engaged with people through his Spirit and involved in the world he has created. Openness theology seeks to describe reality, not in neoplatonic terms, but in ways consistent with how it is experienced as present (and possibly past) existence and future possibility.

5. Responses

The Openness of God, in launching the open theist movement, has generated two decades of debate. An initial response came from Timothy George, Douglas Kelly, Alister McGrath, and Roger Olson in *Christianity Today*.[79] A more formal response came from Gerald Bray in his short monograph *The Personal God*.[80] Bray discusses what he sees as positive in the open approach (not a lot), reviews the biblical story of salvation history, defends classical theism by stressing God's sovereignty and how language of God must be analogous, discusses the personhood of God, and argues that it is us rather than

---

79. Roger Olson et al., "Has God Been Held Hostage by Philosophy? A Forum on Free-will Theism, a New Paradigm for Understanding God," *Christianity Today* 39, no. 1 (January 1995): 30–34. In one of the responses, Alister McGrath says he is "outraged" by Sanders' lack of discussion of Martin Luther then curiously spends a quarter of his space to ask why Charles Wesley is not mentioned.

80. Gerald Lewis Bray, *The Personal God* (Carlisle, U.K.: Paternoster Press, 1998).

God who changes when we pray.[81] He concludes God does not change, and what looks like change is God's infinite flexibility. Bray is simply concerned to restate classical theism and is not significantly engaging in the debate. *The Openness of God* is his topic, but it is rarely mentioned except at the beginning and end of the book.

A second major book proposing open theism was published in 2000, Gregory Boyd's *God of the Possible: A Biblical Introduction to the Open View of God*, mentioned earlier. The book is provoked by the story in 2 Kings 20 where God, through Isaiah, tells Hezekiah he is going to die. Hezekiah, however, prays and God says he will heal him and give him another fifteen years. How could the traditional view of God's complete foreknowledge be consistent with this and other similar biblical texts?[82] Boyd argues that the future is partly open because of future time.[83] The future does not exist yet. God's foreknowledge is based on his intentions. God knows what he will do and what the outcome will be.

The challengers to the open model responded energetically. Bruce Ware produced a substantial critique in 2000, *God's Lesser Glory*.[84] To Ware, the idea that God does not comprehensively know the future is very frightening, and therefore must be untrue.[85] As he develops his argument, he is not really fair as he describes the openness position. For example, he assumes God is outside of time and imposes that on the open theist position without arguing his case.[86] He plays off Arminianism and open theology but fails to be convincing because he is obviously unsympathetic to both. Unsurprisingly, he concludes Calvinism is the only viable option.[87] He is really interested in de-

---

81. Bray, *The Personal God*, 64 and 71.
82. Here 'traditional' view and 'classical' view are synonymous.
83. Boyd, *God of the Possible*, 16.
84. Bruce A. Ware, *God's Lesser Glory: The Diminished God of Open Theism* (Wheaton, Ill.: Crossway Books, 2000).
85. Ibid., 13. One is tempted to say to Ware that while it is initially unsettling to consider that the future may not be known comprehensively to God, whether we are bothered by it doesn't change whether it is true or not. It is more important that our thinking be faithful to the Bible than it is for us to be comfortable.
86. Ibid., 35.
87. Ibid., 42.

fending an inherited system, the philosophical-biblical synthesis, rather than attempting to engage in fresh theological construction. He insists that the same hermeneutic be used for an Old Testament text and a New Testament text.[88] He makes much of particular passages in Isaiah, but these texts do not require foreknowledge because God is declaring what he is going to do.[89] Ware raises some good points. For example, he asks how Jesus could have known that Peter would deny him precisely three times if divine foreknowledge is not exhaustive.[90]

Michael Saia, in *Does God Know the Future?* responds to Ware with a detailed discussion of the exegetical issues and a chapter-by-chapter response.[91] The tone of the book is helpful because it is respectful and limits its focus to the issues. Saia addresses philosophical, biblical, and practical issues. In the philosophical chapters he is asking questions like, "Does God live outside of time? Does God know what people will choose to do in the future?"[92] In the biblical chapters, he takes time to lay out exegetical and hermeneutical methodologies, then looks at the nature of prophecy and whether God is timeless from a biblical point-of-view. Then he deals with texts that support or oppose divine foreknowledge. In the practical chapters Saia discusses holiness, prayer, evangelism, and the believer's sense of security.

Beyond the Bounds is another response to Boyd by eleven contributors including Wayne Grudem, John Piper, and Bruce Ware.[93] It discusses a range of topics: historical influences, philosophical presuppositions, anthropomorphisms, cultural context, revelation, hermeneutics, inerrancy, God's trustworthiness, the gospel, and drawing of boundaries. As with Ware's *God's Lesser*

---

88. Ibid., 127.

89. Ibid., 105.

90. Ibid., 42. Perhaps the passage demonstrates that God sometimes intervenes in history—as the exception rather than the rule—to make things happen in a particular way. In that case, Jesus' words were performative, i.e., he made it happen by speaking it. He did it not to override Peter's free will and make Peter do something he wouldn't have otherwise done, but as a sign to Peter of the grace that awaited him on the other side of the betrayal.

91. Hasker, "The Openness of God," 132–33.

92. Michael R. Saia, *Does God Know the Future?: A Biblical Investigation of Foreknowledge and Free Will* (Fairfax, Va.: Xulon, 2002).

93. John Piper, Justin Taylor, and Paul Kjoss Helseth, *Beyond the Bounds: Open Theism and the Undermining of Biblical Christianity* (Wheaton, Ill.: Crossway, 2003).

Glory, what most alarms these scholars is open theism's denial of exhaustive, definite divine foreknowledge.[94] Referring to open theism, the first page has adjectives such as *stunning* (in a negative sense) and *damaging,* and nouns like *fantasy, dishonor,* and *heresy.* The book is not an irenic, engaging conversation, but an attack. It is an extended defense of classical theism which might have been more conducive to dialogue if the tone had been less apologetic and alarmist.[95]

Meanwhile, Clark Pinnock and the foremost contemporary proponent of Process Theology, John Cobb, Jr. edited a book that simultaneously seeks common ground and highlights differences.[96] The quality of the debate is much more respectful than the one Pinnock faced on his other flank. John Cobb identifies the core of the differences by saying, "On the one hand, openness theists are closer to the Bible and affirm its tendencies to anthropomorphism in its representation of God.... Process theists, on the other hand, are keenly aware that supposing that God must be thought of anthropomorphically has led many moderns (and postmoderns) to reject all belief in God."[97] In common, process and openness critique a concept of God who is unaffected by the world and preoccupied with his own glory. Richard Rice writes, "The idea that God's relation to the world is interactive, or dynamic, makes it possible for us to develop coherent concepts of divine love and creaturely freedom."[98] God in his love has given creatures a measure of real freedom. "Love and power are the prominent elements in this shared vision of God."[99] Both process and openness affirm that divine power is not usually exercised through coercion but through persuasion.[100]

---

94. Ibid., 9.

95. For example Piper says, "As a pastor I see open theism as theologically ruinous, dishonoring to God, belittling to Christ, and pastorally hurtful." Ibid., 371.

96. John B. Cobb and Clark H. Pinnock, *Searching for an Adequate God: A Dialogue Between Process and Free Will Theists* (Grand Rapids: Eerdmans, 2000).2000

97. Ibid., xiii.T%

98. Rice, "Process Theism and the Open View of God," 166.

99. Ibid., 183–84.+

100. Ibid., 184.

Another book which takes the form of friendly debate is Christopher Hall and John Sanders' *Does God Have a Future?*[101] Here, two friends talk through issues raised by open theism in an engaging manner.

The debate ignited by *The Openness of God* still has energy left in it. We can expect to see further contributions on both sides because the open approach has a lot to commend it, and those who defend classical theism show no sign of backing down. Many of these proponents of classical theism see open theism as heretical.[102]

From their opponents' point-of-view, the denial by open theists of exhaustive definite foreknowledge is the central issue in the debate.[103] For the authors of *The Openness of God* and many open theists, the central issue is what God is like. They see the biblical God as supremely revealed in Jesus Christ and therefore highly relational and completely loving. Their interest in the nature of the future and the decisions of creatures with free will flows from that starting point. The impassible, wholly immutable, omnicontrolling God of classical theism seems to open theists as inconsistent with the biblical portrayal of God, and thus in need of substantial revision. It is the project of open theism to provide a coherent and biblically defensible vision of God and the nature of the future.

6. The Philosophical Advantages of Open Theism

With its emphases on human freedom, the centrality of love, and the partial openness of the future, open theism shows promise for providing assistance with one or two pressing theological questions.

By highlighting the measure of genuine freedom that God has chosen to give to humanity, open theism avoids a deterministic description of the nature of reality. If humans believe themselves to be genuinely free to act within the constraints of their historical and social contexts and the resources available to

---

101. Christopher A. Hall and John Sanders, *Does God Have a Future?: A Debate on Divine Providence* (Grand Rapids: Baker Academic, 2003).

102. For example, "The fantasy that God is ignorant of the future is a heresy that must be rejected on scriptural grounds." Thomas Oden in a *Christianity Today* article (Feb. 9, 1998) cited by John Piper in *Beyond the Bounds*, 9.

103. John Piper writes, "Open theism's most obvious departure from historic Christianity is its denial of the exhaustive, definite foreknowledge of God." Ibid.

them, hope is engendered, and altruistic action can be galvanized. Despair and immobility result from believing that nothing can change in your situation. People who believe they have the power to change the world around them are more likely to make investments for the future in infrastructure and human capital (education, for example).[104]

An emphasis on human freedom also goes a long way to helping with questions of theodicy, trying to account for pain and suffering in the world while affirming that God is good. The bad choices that humans have made out of ignorance, fear, greed, or lust for power account for much of the suffering we see.

Some open theists, notably Greg Boyd, also emphasize the freedom of non-human spiritual beings.[105] For those who take their cue from the sort of worldview found in the New Testament, there is considerable explanatory power in acknowledging the reality of Satan and his demons to account for evil in the world. Human choices do not account for natural evil but the malevolent actions of fallen spiritual beings can.

Greg Boyd and William Hasker have addressed the problem of evil at length (Boyd emphasizes spiritual warfare but Hasker does not).[106] John Polkinghorne offers an alternative explanation for natural evil. He hypothesizes by analogy to the free will which God has given to humans that God has allowed to the natural world its own freedom.[107] Which of these approaches

---

104. Bryant L. Myers, *Walking with the Poor: Principles and Practices of Transformational Development* (Maryknoll, N.Y.: Orbis, 1999), 93.

105. See especially Gregory A. Boyd, *God at War: The Bible and Spiritual Conflict* (Downers Grove: InterVarsity, 1997); Gregory A. Boyd, *Satan and the Problem of Evil: Constructing a Trinitarian Warfare Theodicy* (Downers Grove: InterVarsity, 2001).

106. In addition to the two volumes just mentioned: Gregory A. Boyd, *Is God to Blame?: Moving Beyond Pat Answers to the Problem of Evil* (Downers Grove: InterVarsity, 2003). Also, Hasker, *Providence, Evil and the Openness of God*.

107. "There remains the problem of natural evil.... I think the only possible solution lies in a variation of the free-will defense, applied to the whole created world. One might call it 'the free-process defense.' In his great act of creation, I believe that God allows the physical world to be itself, not in Manichaean opposition to him, but in that independence which is Love's gift of freedom to one beloved. That world is endowed in its fundamental constitution with an anthropic potentiality which makes it capable of fruitful evolution. The exploration and realization of that potentiality is achieved by the universe through the continual interplay of chance and necessity within its unfolding process. The cosmos is given the opportunity to be itself." John C. Polkinghorne, *Science and Providence: God's Interaction with the World* (Philadelphia: Templeton

seems more helpful comes down to a question of worldview. Experiences in Africa make plausible to me a world where malevolent spirits are active, so I find Boyd's explanation convincing.

Having something to say on the question of theodicy is an important philosophical advantage of open theism. Not only does it go some distance in explaining evil and suffering (at least on a macro level), its dynamic relational theology describes God as active in history and engaged in interpersonal relationships. One of open theism's greatest strengths is its vision of God as caring passionately for the world he has made. He does not stand aloof. He does not control everything that happens. God suffers with us.

The centrality of love in open theism is also an important philosophical advantage. Ethics, philosophical considerations, and theological thought are most satisfying when they function together in mutual dialogue. Putting love at the core provides one possible interpretive framework and consistent rationale. It could easily be argued that love is the most important aspect of human existence, so there is something to be said for making the main thing the main thing.

A fourth philosophical advantage of open theism is its understanding of the nature of time and the partial openness of the future. Most of us don't live as if we believe we are in a universe where everything is predetermined. We feel that we freely make choices within our power and to exert our human agency. The open view of the partially open future is happily consistent with our experience of reality. In the open view, the future is not completely open for at least three reasons. First, everything that has happened in history until this point constrains us. It is determined and cannot be changed. Second, we are limited by whatever resources of physical ability, money, power, social location, and geography we may or may not have at our disposal—although some of these can be conditioned by concerted effort, prayer, or the help of others. Third, open theists assert that the future is not entirely open because

---

Press, 2005), 77. This view is perhaps a more sophisticated version of Wesley's. Wesley overlooks the influence of evil spirits on animals and the natural world: "In the natural world all things roll on in an even, uninterrupted course. But it is far otherwise in the moral world. Here evil men and evil spirits continually oppose the divine will, and create numberless irregularities." Sermon 68: "The Wisdom of God's Counsels" [1784] in John Wesley, *Sermons II, 34–70*, ed. Albert C. Outler, The Works of John Wesley (Nashville: Abingdon, 1985), 553.

God acts in history and has determined ahead of time some things he is going to do.

Open theism's view of time also has philosophical advantages in relation to the physics of time and space. For a period in the twentieth century, it seemed that science said that time is reversible—which would be incompatible with the open view.[108] The open view is wedded to the idea that time is an arrow, moving forward. The nature of time is again a significant debate in the physics community, somewhat parallel to the open theist debate in the theological community. Is time reversible, or is it an arrow progressing from past to future? Coveney and Highfield argue for the latter:

> The fundamental reality in our world is not to be found in its smallest parts but in the capacity of vast assemblies of atoms and molecules for change, as expressed in the Second Law of Thermodynamics.... The onset of chaos, and thus the arrow of time, is overwhelmingly evident when we deal with the world, where objects contain countless atoms.... These new ideas about complexity would seem to turn conventional science upside down. The Second Law of Thermodynamics, which describes the behaviour of vast numbers of molecules, is one element of the fundamental truth. Reductionism, with its attempts to explain the world in terms of the behavior of its microscopic components alone, is invalid. Rather than maintaining that the arrow of time is an illusion, we must ask whether it is the

---

108. The assumption that people at different places in the universe have the same 'now' was challenged by Einstein. "Einstein's theories of relativity, an extension of Newtonian physics, deal with the concepts of space, time and matter. Special relativity starts from the premise that the laws of physics are the same for observers moving at constant speeds relative to one another. General relativity is based on the idea that the laws of physics should be the same for all observers, regardless of how they are moving relative to one another." Peter Coveney and Roger Highfield, *The Arrow of Time: A Voyage Through Science to Solve Time's Greatest Mystery* (New York: Fawcett Columbine, 1990), 364.

Quantum mechanics is the physics that "rules the microscopic world, where energy changes occur in abrupt quantum jumps." Ibid.

"The great edifices of modern science—Newton's mechanics, Einstein's relativity and the quantum mechanics of Heisenberg and Schrödinger—would all appear to work equally well with time running in reverse.... Uni-directional time, in fact, comes to appear as simply an illusion created in our minds." Ibid., 23.

time-symmetric 'fundamental' laws that are approximations or illusions. After all, they only apply to extraordinarily simple systems.[109]

Coveney and Highfield from the point-of-view of physicists conclude: "We are at last beginning to grasp how the notion of an open future fits within the most basic of the sciences as surely as it does in the more complex."[110]

While there are no clear winners or losers regarding the physics as yet, open theism can at least claim to be consistent with one of the more credible scientific theories in play.[111]

In this section, we've considered human freedom, theodicy, dynamic relationality, the centrality of love, and the partial openness of the future. The philosophical advantages of open theism will be noted as well in the next section where aspects of open and classical theism are looked at side-by-side.

7. Open and Classical Theism Compared and Contrasted

Because open and classical theists both largely identify as evangelicals, they have in common theologically far more than what distinguishes them.[112] Let me revisit the categories of Grudem's systematic textbook.[113] Prominent open theists all take the Bible as authoritative. God is affirmed as triune, creator, savior, sanctifier, and coming king. Humans were created male and female, and have fallen away from God, but can reenter relationship with God through covenant. Jesus is fully human and fully divine, atoned for our sins, was resurrected and ascended, functions as prophet, priest, and king; and sent the Holy Spirit, who is active in the church and the world. Salvation entails regeneration,

---

109. Ibid., 295–96.

110. Ibid., 38.

111. Recent developments in physics in the area of quantum entanglement are providing additional support for the idea of the arrow of time. "The astronomer-philosopher Sir Arthur Eddington in 1927 cited the gradual dispersal of energy as evidence of an irreversible 'arrow of time.'... Physicists are unmasking a more fundamental source for the arrow of time: Energy disperses and objects equilibrate, they say, because of the way elementary particles become intertwined when they interact—a strange effect called 'quantum entanglement.'" Natalie Wolchover, "Time's Arrow Traced to Quantum Source," *Quanta Magazine* (April 16, 2014), https://www.quantamagazine.org/20140416-times-arrow-traced-to-quantum-source/.

112. I've discussed Bebbington's definition of evangelicalism above in the note on p. 7.

113. Wayne Grudem's *Systematic Theology* was considered above at p. 9.

conversion, justification, adoption, sanctification, glorification, and union with Christ. The church is the context for the sacraments of Eucharist and baptism, the worship of God, expressing the gifts of the Holy Spirit, and service to the world. Jesus will return, the nations will be judged, and there will be new heavens and a new earth.

Even with so much in common, there are significant differences with implications for how we relate to God and engage in the world. Some of the differences are accounted for by the Reformed interpretive grid through which contemporary classical theologians typically process these themes and Wesleyan theology's Arminian grid.[114] For example, classical theology will emphasize God's sovereign will while Wesleyan theology will pay particular attention to human freedom. Open theism resists the classical description of God because a perfect unchanging being existing outside of time is incapable of relationship since relationships occur in time and entail change.

The open view of God's immutability can be contrasted with the classical view.[115] Classical theists in the last century have modified aspects of their understanding of divine immutability so differences with open theists are not as sharp as they would have been. For example, classical theologians will acknowledge that God is not immovable, and therefore can act. On divine impassibility, some classical theologians, especially under the influence of Jürgen Moltmann's *The Crucified God*, acknowledge God's capacity for suffering. Moltmann wrote:

> It was Abraham Heschel who, in controversy with Hellenism and the Jewish philosophy of religion of Jehuda Halevi, Maimonides and Spinoza which was influenced by it, first described the prophets' proclamation of God as *pathetic theology*. The prophets had no 'idea' of God, but understood themselves and the people in the *situation of God*. Heschel called this situation of God the *pathos of God*. It has nothing to do with the irrational human emotions like desire,

---

[114]. Greg Boyd comments, "The question of the openness of the future... is an in-house Arminian discussion on how to render the freewill defense most coherent, biblical and credible." Boyd, *Satan and the Problem of Evil*, 87.

[115]. More will be said on this subject below starting at p. 98.

anger, anxiety, envy or sympathy, but describes how God is affected by events and human actions and suffering in history.... God takes man so seriously that he suffers under the actions of man and can be injured by them. At the heart of the prophetic proclamation there stands the certainty that God is interested in the world to the point of suffering.[116]

Reformed theologians seem increasingly willing to acknowledge the possibility that God suffers and so are modifying the idea of divine immutability in that respect. However, the idea that God could be capable of change in his thought processes meets greater resistance. This is a point of contrast with many open theists. Theologians who see the future as partly open and who believe humans have some genuine freedom to act as they choose are usually not particularly committed to the idea that God's thoughts are frozen in time.

A second point of contrast between open theism and classical theism is in their respective understandings of time. Open theism's view of the nature of time is consistent with how most philosophers view it.[117] Open theism is consistent with the view that time is a progression from the past to the future. The present has a privileged reality (although some see the past as continuing to exist as well). The alternate eternalist view sees all events in time as equally real. The eternalist position is consistent with a view of God who stands outside of time. But the eternalist view has almost no support among philosophers, so it is an advantage of open theism that it can have a constructive dialogue with philosophers of science on this issue.[118]

---

116. Jürgen Moltmann, *The Crucified God: The Cross of Christ as the Foundation and Criticism of Christian Theology (Der gekreuzigte Gott)*, trans. R. A. Wilson and John Bowden, 2nd ed. (New York: HarperCollins, 1974, 1991), 270–71.

117. Further discussion of the nature of time from the point of view of the philosophy of science will be found below starting at p. 52.

118. In November 2014, the Randomness and Foreknowledge Conference in Dallas explored issues of common interest to philosophers and open theists. I've uploaded several of the talks with hopefully more to come:

Thomas Jay Oord, "Randomness and Foreknowledge Conference Overview" (http://vimeo.com/user34346634/review/112032708/48a5a958dc)

William Hasker, "How to Make a World"

Closely related to God's relationship to time is the nature of God's knowledge of the future. This is a third point of contrast between open theism and classical theism. In typical classical theism, God stands *outside* of time and sees all of history at once. Therefore, the future is completely known to God. Open theists usually view God as existing *in* time in order to be in relationship with his creation. What is knowable about the future is known to God. We can characterize this view as 'dynamic omniscience'.[119] God can accurately predict near field events based on his comprehensive knowledge of the present. He knows events in the distant future that are determined by his action because he knows what he is going to do. Open theists usually take the view that God does not have exhaustive knowledge of future events because he does not know with certainty in advance the free actions of his creatures. If true, the open theist universe must be much more interesting to God as he passionately engages with an unfolding reality than what would be his static role in the classical view.

These points of contrast between classical and open theism have implications for how we relate to God and how we engage the world. If God responds to our prayer because he is fully engaged in time and open to influence as the open view claims, then that should make a difference in how we pray.[120] In addition, if the future is partly open to us, it was partially open to previous

(The Randomness and Foreknowledge Conference, Session 19) (http://vimeo.com/user34346634/review/112287680/4766e9a6c5)

Richard Swinburne, "Causation, Time, and God's Omniscience"

(The Randomness and Foreknowledge Conference, Session 20) (http://vimeo.com/user34346634/review/112420375/da64c2be42)

Robert Russell, "Does 'The God Who Acts' Really ACT? Randomness, Divine Foreknowledge, Flowing Time, and Non-Interventionist Divine Action in Light of Relativity and Quantum Mechanics"

(The Randomness and Foreknowledge Conference, Session 10) (http://vimeo.com/user34346634/review/112512953/69b730a5de)

119. On November 23, 2014, in San Diego as part of the annual meeting of the American Academy of Religion at the session celebrating the twentieth anniversary of the publication of *The Openness of God*, John Sanders mentioned that he prefers the term 'dynamic omniscience' for describing God's knowledge.

120. Kenneth J. Archer writes, "Our way of praying indicates that we, because of God's grace, can enter into a dynamic reciprocating relationship of rich fellowship with the Social Trinity. God encourages us to participate with him in creating the future." *The Gospel Revisited: Towards a Pentecostal Theology of Worship and Witness* (Eugene, Ore.: Pickwick/Wipf & Stock, 2011), 86.

generations as well. We inherit the consequences of their choices so we don't have to accept things as they indicate God's perfect will. We can influence events toward his revealed will. We should feel empowered to pour out our lives in the cause of the emerging kingdom of God.

C. RENEWAL THEOLOGY

1. Definitions

The term 'renewal theology', as I use it here, includes at least pentecostal,[121] charismatic,[122] and neocharismatic theologies.[123] A more precise definition has proved elusive, but it probably should be broad enough to encompass the thinking of Oneness Pentecostals on the one hand and Orthodox and Catholic charismatics on the other. Using 'renewal' as an inclusive term for Spirit-empowered movements is gaining acceptance: a recent study of the Pew Forum on Religion and Public Life used 'renewalists' as "an umbrella term used to refer to pentecostals and charismatics" in ten different countries.[124]

---

121. 'Pentecostal' when capitalized here refers to the classical Pentecostals with origins in Charles Parham's Bethel Bible School in Topeka, Kansas and William Seymour's Apostolic Faith Mission at Azusa Street. See Stanley M. Burgess and Eduard M. van der Maas, eds., *The New International Dictionary of Pentecostal and Charismatic Movements* (Grand Rapids: Zondervan, 2003), xviii–xix. Following the practice of the *NIDPCM* when lower-cased, 'pentecostal' will usually be intended more generally to include charismatic and neocharismatic movements; a synonym for 'renewal'.

122. With roots in Pentecostalism, the charismatic renewal emerged "in 1960 with the publicity surrounding remarkable happenings in the ministry of Dennis Bennett, an Episcopal rector in Van Nuys, CA. As the movement grew, it spread to other Protestant churches, the Roman Catholic Church, and finally also to the Orthodox churches." Charismatics tended to stay within their mainline churches rather than join Pentecostal denominations. "The charismatic renewal represents a transdenominational movement of Christians who emphasize a 'life in the Spirit' and the importance of exercising extraordinary gifts of the Spirit, including but not limited to glossolalia, both in private prayer and in public worship." Ibid., xix.

123. Stan Burgess defines 'neocharismatic' as "a catch-all that comprises 18,810 independent, indigenous, postdenominational denominations and groups that cannot be classified as either pentecostal or charismatic but share a common emphasis on the Holy Spirit, spiritual gifts, pentecostal-like experiences (*not* pentecostal terminology), signs and wonders, and power encounters. In virtually every other way, however, they are as diverse as the world's cultures they represent." Ibid., xx.

124. Luis Lugo, "Spirit and Power: A Ten-Country Survey of Pentecostals," in *The Pew Forum on Religion and Public Life* (Washington, D.C.: The Pew Research Center, October 2006), 12.

In the recent past, the term 'renewal theology' has had an association with Regent University and its late Emeritus Professor of Renewal Theology, J. Rodman Williams. His three-volume *Renewal Theology* is a (moderately Calvinistic) systematic theology written from a charismatic point-of-view.[125] However, Williams used the term 'renewal' to refer primarily to the charismatic spiritual renewal of which he was a part from 1965, and so used it more narrowly than is intended here. I want to keep from Williams the connection to twentieth and twenty-first century contemporary movements of the Spirit, only including classical pentecostals and neocharismatics.

If Williams's definition is too narrow, another Regent professor's is for our purposes too wide. Wolfgang Vondey writes: "Renewal is not easy to define. It is neither the 'old' nor the 'new' but the process of change that takes us from one to the other.... It is the Spirit of God who drives the old to the new.... To speak of renewal as a dynamic of the Holy Spirit is to acknowledge the presence and activity of God in all things...."[126] Vondey's is a valid expansive vision of the work of the Spirit in the world, but here we must be content to consider predominantly theology and history.

Another defining limit on what is meant here by 'renewal theology' is to exclude Spirit movements which might have similar expressions of extra-biblical revelation such as prophecy, tongues speech, dreams, and visions, but which do not have a focus on Jesus. These groups may correctly be considered within pentecostalism as defined phenomenologically, but are a little too far theologically from the central core to be included in this discussion.[127]

Kenneth J. Archer makes the case for maintaining a distinction between 'pentecostal' and 'charismatic'. Speaking of 'renewal' theology gives us a way

---

125. J. Rodman Williams, *Renewal Theology: Systematic Theology from a Charismatic Perspective* (Grand Rapids: Zondervan, 1996).

126. Wolfgang Vondey, "Renew Your Mind ... And the Rest Will Follow," *Renewal Dynamics* (February 24, 2010), http://renewaldynamics.com/2010/02/24/renew-your-mind-and-the-rest-will-follow/ [accessed 11/1/2012].

127. As used here, the term 'renewal theology' is not intended to be all-encompassing but that current of pentecostal/charismatic/neocharismatic theology that can be traced, directly or indirectly, to the Spirit movements originating at the beginning of the twentieth century, e.g., the Azusa Street revival.

of referring to them together (and 'neocharismatic' as well) while preserving the uniquenesses.[128]

What then are the defining characteristics of renewal theology? Vinson Synan in defining "pentecostal/charismatics," follows the Catholic scholar Kilian McDonnell in saying they are "those Christians who stress the baptism in the Holy Spirit and the gifts of the Spirit toward the proclamation that Jesus Christ is Lord, to the glory of God the Father."[129] Those elements—an emphasis on the activity of the Holy Spirit, particularly the baptism in the Spirit, the gifts of the Spirit, and the focus on Jesus—work well as defining characteristics for renewal theology.

Kimberly Alexander argues convincingly that pentecostalism should be defined not entirely in terms of its distinctive teaching (which can be diverse) but by the spirituality of the movement.[130] Here she is thinking of Walter Hollenweger's description of the heart of pentecostalism as lying in its African or black root.[131] Characteristic of this root would be orality, narrativity, community participation, inclusion of dreams and visions, healing, and dance. Renewal theology would be cognizant of a pentecostal spirituality, and hopefully avoid the present situation where "the *living faith* has given way to a *rule of faith*, anxious and guarding its boundaries."[132]

What does renewal theology look like in practice? Amos Yong sets an inspiring agenda: "This renewal theology is not just descriptive about what happened at Pentecost. It invites a living out of this claim. I'm inviting us to go, to be obedient, but also to engage and discern about these realities.

---

128. Archer, *The Gospel Revisited*, xvi–xvii.

129. Vinson Synan, "A Healer In the House? A Historical Perspective on Healing in the Pentecostal/Charismatic Tradition," *Asian Journal of Pentecostal Studies* 3, no. 2 (2000): 189. Although 'pentecostal/charismatic' is only a subset of 'renewal' there is little in Synan's definition that would be objectionable to neocharismatics and renewalists who are not pentecostal or charismatic. For example, The Vineyard USA's statement of faith reads, "WE BELIEVE that the Holy Spirit was poured out on the Church at Pentecost in power, baptizing believers into the Body of Christ and releasing the gifts of the Spirit to them." John McClure and Don Williams, *Theological and Philosophical Statements* (Stafford, Tex.: Vineyard USA, 2004), 14.

130. Kimberly Ervin Alexander, "Standing at the Crossroads: The Battle for the Heart and Soul of Pentecostalism," *Pneuma* 33, no. 3 (2011): 331–349.

131. Walter J. Hollenweger, *Pentecostalism: Origins and Developments Worldwide* (Peabody, Mass.: Hendrickson, 1997), 18–19.

132. Alexander, "Standing at the Crossroads," 339.

Ideas inform practices and in return our practices inform our pneumatological ideas."[133] "For these, and other, reasons, pentecostal theology can be said to be 'renewal theology'. It is not static, but is renewed and always being renewed (hopefully, by the Holy Spirit). Further, it is open to future encounters, to unseen horizons, to unexpected visitations of God's breath."[134] So, to the historically-oriented definition of 'renewal theology', we can add the dimension of an openness to God's Spirit in the endeavor. If open theism provides a theological rationale for prayer and action to further the kingdom of God, renewal theology with its emphasis on the Holy Spirit points to the motivator and source of power to make it happen.

2. Connections between Renewal Theology, Open Theism, and Wesleyan Theology

Where does the nexus of open theism and renewal theology lie? Keith Warrington observes, "Because of its Wesleyan and Holiness background, there has been a tradition, in Pentecostalism, of Arminian theology."[135] Arminian theology and open theism are both, in part, reactions to Calvinism. While going as far as he could to preserve Christian unity, John Wesley's issues with Calvinism led to a split with Whitefield.[136] Wesley preached with some passion against Reformed doctrines like predestination and had an ally

---

133. Amos Yong, remarks on June 25, 2008 at Regent University on the occasion of presenting the paper mentioned in the next note. The paper is a synopsis of *The Spirit Poured Out on All Flesh: Pentecostalism and the Possibility of Global Theology* (Grand Rapids: Baker Academic, 2005).

134. Amos Yong, "Poured Out on All Flesh: The Spirit, World Pentecostalism, and the Renewal of Theology and Praxis in the 21st Century," *PentecoStudies* 6, no. 1 (2007): 36.

135. Keith Warrington, *Pentecostal Theology: A Theology of Encounter* (New York and London: T&T Clark, 2008), 38.

136. John Wesley, *Journal and Diaries*, ed. W. Reginald Ward and Richard P. Heitzenrater, 7 vols., The Works of John Wesley (Nashville: Abingdon, 1990), 19:188–89. In the journal entry for Saturday, March 28, 1741, Whitefield tells Wesley they preach two different gospels and refuses him the right hand of fellowship. Over the years they are reconciled to some extent in spite of their theological differences. Wesley's entry for Friday, January 31, 1766: "Mr. Whitefield called upon me. He breathes nothing but peace and love. Bigotry cannot stand before him, but hides its head wherever he comes." Ibid., 22:29. Wesley also preached one of Whitefield's funeral sermons. He said, "There are many doctrines of a less essential nature, with regard to which even the sincere children of God (such is the present weakness of human understanding!) are and have been divided for many ages. In these we may think and let think; we may 'agree to disagree.'" Sermon 53: "On the Death of George Whitefield" [1770] in *Sermons II*, 324–347.

here in his Swiss-born assistant and friend John Fletcher. Open theism inherits both the theological impetus to correct Calvinism and the irenic spirit to argue in such a way as to try to preserve peace. It is arguable that open theism is a natural progression on a trajectory from Wesley based on this affirmation of Arminianism. Instead of a focus on God's power and sovereignty, Wesley's theological anchors are God's love, human participation in God's work of restoration, and the possibility of transformation. Barry Callen has recently observed that the "orienting concern of Wesley," i.e., his focus on divine love, "appears highly compatible with" relational theology—of which open theism is a subset.[137]

A definition of Wesleyan theology is also appropriate at this point. An astonishing breadth of theologies sometimes claim a Wesleyan resonance: pentecostal-holiness, evangelicalism, open theism, relational theology, process theology, feminism, and liberation theology (based on Wesley's opposition to slavery and concern for the poor).[138] Rather than use the phrase "Wesleyan theology" with reference to these diverse expressions, I will use it in a more historical sense, limiting its use primarily to the writing of John Wesley, but also to his like-minded contemporary and designated successor, John Fletcher.

Not all renewal theology has a direct connection with John Wesley or John Fletcher.[139] This study will concentrate on the holiness-pentecostal stream of renewal theology. Without this arbitrary limitation, the research would become an exercise in identifying degrees of separation.[140]

Sometimes the connections exist in unexpected places. As was mentioned above, Richard Rice, a Seventh-day Adventist open theist, coined the term 'openness theology.' Admittedly, the connection between Adventism

---

137. Barry L. Callen, "John Wesley and Relational Theology," in *Relational Theology: A Contemporary Introduction*, ed. Brint Montgomery, Thomas Jay Oord, and Karen Winslow (Eugene, Ore.: Point Loma Press/Wipf & Stock, 2012), 9.

138. A recent session of the AAR tried to bring some definition to Wesleyan biblical interpretation. The discussion highlighted the breadth of contemporary theologies with roots in historical Wesleyanism. The Wesley Studies interest group, "What Makes it Wesleyan?" (November 20, 2011, in San Francisco).

139. Edith L. Waldvogel, "The "Overcoming" Life: A Study in the Reformed Evangelical Contribution to Pentecostalism," *Pneuma* 1, no. 1 (1979).

140. For example, the Assemblies of God does not self-identify as Wesleyan theologically, but it does identify historically with Azusa Street which clearly was Wesleyan.

and Wesleyan theology is not necessarily immediately apparent. For example, Rice's own introduction to Adventist theology, *The Reign of God*, does not mention John Wesley.[141] There is a strong historical connection, however, between Adventism and Wesleyan theology. The passage below refers to Ellen Harmon who is better known by her married name, Ellen White, one of the founding Seventh-day Adventists:

> Seventh-day Adventists may not always recognize the debt of gratitude we owe to our Methodist brethren. Yet we owe it, and not altogether because Ellen Harmon's spiritual nature was first quickened and nourished within the Methodist Church.... John and Charles Wesley, under the impulse of the Holy Spirit, restored to modern Christianity the primitive evangelistic zeal and heartfelt Christian experience that have been outstanding characteristics of the Seventh-day Adventist movement.[142]

Similarly, the pentecostal-holiness branch of renewal theology has deep roots in Wesleyan theology. Donald Dayton describes the progression from Wesley and Fletcher on through key figures of Methodism in America and especially the holiness movement, such as Phoebe Palmer.[143]

Open theism and renewal theology both strongly affirm the loving engagement of God with his world in the present. For open theists, prayer is efficacious because God is responsive and able to act.[144] Renewal theologians celebrate God's presence in the world through the activity of his Spirit.[145] This shared worldview can draw open theism and renewal theology together.

---

141. Richard Rice, *The Reign of God*, 2nd ed. (Berrien Springs, Mich.: Andrews University Press, 1997). I had a chance meeting with Richard Rice on March 22, 2013 in Seattle at the joint meeting of the Wesley Theological Society and the Society for Pentecostal Studies. He confirmed that Wesley is not mentioned in *The Reign of God* but that Adventism owes a debt to John Wesley.

142. Kathleen B. McMurphy, "John Wesley and the End of the World," *Ministry: International Journal for Pastors* 33 (April 1960).

143. Dayton, *Theological Roots of Pentecostalism*, 65.

144. Kenneth J. Archer, "Open Theism View: Prayer Changes Things," *The Pneuma Review* 5, no. 2 (Spring 2002): 32–53.

145. E.g., Yong, *Spirit Poured Out on All Flesh*.

3. Renewal Theologians Who Have Written on Open Theism

Four prominent theologians who could be identified as renewalist have written significant pieces on open theism: Amos Yong, Kenneth Archer, Greg Boyd, and Clark Pinnock. The criterion for choosing these four scholars is really a personal one. These four have been influential in helping me think through the issues at the intersection of renewal theology and open theism. They illustrate the compatibility of open theism and renewal theology.

Amos Yong, the prominent renewal theologian, while not overtly committed to the approach, has described the open position sympathetically.[146] He has also been a contributor to relational theology collaborations.[147]

Interestingly, Yong makes note of the affinity between open theism and Wesley: "Given Wesley's well-known synergism, it is clear that Wesleyan

---

146. Amos Yong, "Divine Omniscience and Future Contingents: Weighing the Presuppositional Issues in the Contemporary Debate," *Evangelical Review of Theology* 26, no. 3 (2002): 240–264. In this fascinating analysis, Yong contrasts the hermeneutical options chosen by open theism and classical theism. He observes that both positions have root metaphors for the God-world relationship which influence how they read scripture. Classical theists see God as primarily a triad of creator, judge, and sovereign. For open theists, the root metaphors for God are saviour, lover, and friend. Ibid., 242. Yong notes that a major issue in the debate is the nature of biblical language and just when it is that texts are describing God anthropomorphically. For open theists, the texts that describe God as changing his mind or making conditional statements tell us "something about the future, namely that the future is open; some things are determined, but other things, specifically that connected to what free creatures have yet to determine, are not. What has formerly been understood anthropomorphically is now, in the open theist scheme of things, literally predicable of God." Ibid., 244. Yong goes on to associate classical theism with the "elitist" hermeneutics of the Alexandrian school and open theism with the more "democratic" hermeneutics of the Antiochians. Moving to theological presuppositions, he hypothesizes that "if God's essence is conceived of in terms of the patristic and medieval doctrines of divine simplicity and aseity, then classical theism's constructs are sustained. However, if God is conceived of in social trinitarian and, especially, relational terms, then the central openness convictions take on further plausibility." Ibid., 249. Yong thinks that "two different conceptions of divine freedom are driving the classical and openness projects. The former is predicated on the freedom of God to create any world. The latter begins with the freedom of God to respond to the created order in general and to free agents more specifically." Ibid., 254. Yong's is a remarkable insight about assumptions, sometimes unacknowledged, at play in the debate. In a third section on philosophical presuppositions, he highlights the problem of theodicy, the meaning of creaturely freedom, and God's relationship to time and eternity as concerns driving the debate. Ibid., 255–62. Yong's piece is remarkable in its perspicuity and potential for helping each side of the debate to appreciate the concerns of the other.

147. Amos Yong, "Relational Theology and the Holy Spirit," in *Relational Theology: A Contemporary Introduction*, ed. Brint Montgomery, Thomas Jay Oord, and Karen Winslow (Eugene, Ore.: Point Loma Press/Wipf & Stock, 2012), 18–20. Here, he emphasizes the Spirit as the bond of love between the Father and the Son. He writes, "Relationality is what reality is all about, because it characterizes the very life of the Triune God who is spirit and whose Holy Spirit is the bond of love between the Father and the Son." Ibid., 20.

sympathies would reside with those who resist the monergism of the Augustinian-Calvinist tradition."[148]

Kenneth Archer identifies himself as Wesleyan-pentecostal and is the current President of the Society for Pentecostal Studies. He engaged early in the debates as one of the first pentecostal theologians to affirm an openness model. He did so by primarily grounding the discussion in pentecostal spirituality and prayer.[149] In a book of essays on hermeneutics and theology, he says, "I believe a warm kinship exists between the pietistic Wesleyan evangelical open theistic Christianity and Wesleyan-Arminian Pentecostal Christianity because we believe that our present prayer really affects God, ontologically, and the future, potentially. A future that is not yet entirely determined."[150] That intuition is precisely what I'm arguing for.

Gregory Boyd is not only a committed open theist but also a functional charismatic who brings a blend of passion and rigor to his writing. He has a pentecostal background so understands renewal theology from the inside.[151] He also has a long association with openness theology and was quoted appreciatively by Clark Pinnock in *Openness of God*.[152]

---

[148]. Amos Yong, "Possibility and Actuality: The Doctrine of Creation and Its Implications for Divine Omniscience," *Wesleyan Philosophical Society Online Journal* 1, no. 1 (2007). Here, 'synergism' refers to human and divine co-working—not in justification (which God alone can do)—but in the redemptive process of renewing creation.

[149]. Archer, "Open Theism View," 32–53. He also followed a more Narrative approach to the interpretation of scripture. *A Pentecostal Hermeneutic for the Twenty-First Century: Spirit, Scripture and Community* (London and New York: T&T Clark, 2004).

[150]. Archer, *The Gospel Revisited*, 84.

[151]. Gregory A. Boyd, *Oneness Pentecostals and the Trinity: A World-wide Movement Assessed by a Former Oneness Pentecostal* (Grand Rapids: Baker, 1992). The website of Woodland Hills Church where Boyd is senior pastor indicates that the church holds charismatic-friendly positions: http://whchurch.org/about/beliefs/controversial-issues.

[152]. Pinnock, "The Openness of God," 109, 124. Pinnock's longest and his last quote are from Boyd's Princeton dissertation, including this sentence: "Only a God who is socially and self-sufficiently triune as lover, beloved, and loving can take the radical and completely unprovoked initiative to take on within this One's self the full nature of a non-divine self in order to effect wholeness in the whole of the non-divine creation." Gregory A. Boyd, *Trinity and Process: A Critical Evaluation and Reconstruction of Hartshorne's Di-Polar Theism Towards a Trinitarian Metaphysics* (New York, San Francisco, and Bern: Peter Lang, 1992), 332–33. Pinnock's last quote from Boyd highlights how the openness vision of God exalts rather than diminishes God: "It takes far more self-confidence, far more wisdom, far more love and sensitivity to govern that which is personal and free than it does to govern that over which one has absolute control." Ibid., 336.

I. CLASSICAL THEISM, OPEN THEISM, AND RENEWAL THEOLOGY

Boyd contributes uniquely at the intersection of open theism and renewal theology with his work on spiritual warfare. Pentecostals and charismatics, who have a particular interest in the work of the Holy Spirit, often report encounters with not-so-holy spirits.[153] Open theism, with its emphasis on the freedom of humans to resist God's will, asserts that God does not always get his way on the path to ultimate reconciliation of the world to himself. In *God at War*, Boyd brings into focus non-human spiritual beings that resist the divine will as well, working through the biblical material and ending with a description of the Christian life as spiritual warfare.[154] Boyd builds on that

---

153. Boyd writes, "I call this basic understanding of the cosmos a *warfare worldview*. Stated most broadly, this worldview is that perspective on reality which centers on the conviction that the good and evil, fortunate or unfortunate, aspects of life are to be interpreted largely as the result of good and evil, friendly or hostile, spirits warring against each other and against us." Boyd, *God at War*, 13. The late missiologist Paul Hiebert observed that since the Enlightenment, the western world has largely ignored the middle everyday spiritual realm between the empirical material world and the questions of "the origin, purpose and destiny of the individual, a society, and the universe." Paul Hiebert, "Flaw of the Excluded Middle," in *Perspectives on the World Christian Movement Reader*, ed. Ralph D. Winter and Steven C. Hawthorne (Pasadena, Calif.: William Carey Library, 1999), 412. "On the middle level, a holistic theology includes a theology of God in human history—in the affairs of nations, of peoples, and of individuals. This must include a theology of divine guidance, provision and healing; a theology of ancestors, spirits and invisible powers of this world; and a theology of suffering, misfortune and death." Ibid., 413.

154. Walter Wink interprets the "principalities and powers" of the New Testament as any kind of created social structure. "The Powers are good. The Powers are fallen. The Powers are redeemed." Walter Wink, *Engaging the Powers: Discernment and Resistance in a World of Domination*, The Powers, Volume Three (Minneapolis, Minn.: Fortress, 1992), 10. Boyd appreciates Wink's insight into oppressive structures while not going along with the "demythologizing" of the principalities and powers and spiritual warfare. Boyd, *God at War*, 59–60. Beth Snoddlerly (president of William Cary International University) writes, "Boyd points out that Water Wink and others have shown that combating evil powers is not just a matter of prayer but also a matter of social activism. Winter would add, 'and of scientific activism.'" Beth Snoddlerly, "The Warfare Missiology of Ralph D. Winter," (Pasadena, Calif.: William Carey International University, no date), 336, www.wciu.edu/docs/resources/34_warfare_missiology.pdf. Snoddlerly illustrates how Greg Boyd's and Ralph Winter's work reinforce each other to help explain natural evil. Ralph Winter advanced the bold thesis that Satan interfered with evolution: "The Evil One stirs up hate, authors suffering and destruction of God's good creation, perhaps even distorting DNA sequences. Satan's devices may very well include devising virulent germs in order to tear down confidence in God's loving character." Ralph D. Winter, "The Kingdom Strikes Back," in *Perspectives on the World Christian Movement Reader*, ed. Ralph D. Winter and Steven C. Hawthorne (Pasadena, Calif.: William Carey Library, 1999), 210. Ralph Winter's most detailed working out of this thesis is in "The Most Precarious Mission Frontier," *International Journal of Frontier Missions* 21, no. 4 (Winter 2004): 167–72. Boyd and Winter were in conversation (see reknew.org/2007/07/ralph-winters-modified-gap-theory/).

book to contribute significantly to the problem of theodicy in his *Satan and the Problem of Evil* by elaborating a spiritual warfare worldview.[155]

Clark Pinnock was probably the most intentional in developing the themes of open theology for a work on grace and pneumatic theology.[156] Pinnock's sympathies with pentecostal ethos probably stem from his own charismatic experience in 1967.[157] Although he remained a baptist rather than joining a pentecostal denomination, he continued to have charismatic connections. In *Flame of Love*, his pneumatological systematic theology, Pinnock mentions his thankfulness to God for the Toronto Blessing and how it has nourished him.[158]

These four writers—Amos Yong, Kenneth Archer, Greg Boyd, and Clark Pinnock—illustrate the feasibility of blending renewal theology and open theism. Open theism is a movement which offers an alternative to the Calvinistic wing of evangelicalism by reconsidering the traditional understanding of who God is and how he interacts with us in time. In this chapter, we saw how open theism emerged and heard its theological concerns. Secondarily, we saw how 'renewal theology' may be defined and noted that significant renewal scholars have addressed open theism. This chapter described the context for the theme of the dissertation—that open theism and renewal theology have an inherent compatibility through their common genetic relationship to John Wesley and John Fletcher.

---

155. Boyd writes, "I thus suggest that we have no compelling philosophical or biblical reason to locate the primary cause of tornadoes that kill children, genetic mutations that reduce them to vegetables or mudslides that bury them alive to any other source than the enemy of God." Boyd, *Satan and the Problem of Evil*, 292.

156. Clark H. Pinnock, *Flame of Love: A Theology of the Holy Spirit* (Downers Grove: InterVarsity Press, 1996).

157. Clark H. Pinnock, *Three Keys to Spiritual Renewal* (Minneapolis, Minn.: Bethany House, 1985), 50–51.

158. Pinnock, *Flame of Love*, 250 fn 10.

CHAPTER II

John Wesley Does Not Entirely Fit Renewal or Open Theist Paradigms

In the previous chapter, we saw how a theological commitment to the primacy of divine love drives open theism. I surveyed the debate of the past twenty years between open theists and evangelicals of a more Calvinist leaning and noticed how this debate has affinities to the controversies of eighteenth-century Calvinists with John Wesley and John Fletcher. Finally, I mentioned some renewal theologians who illustrate the compatibility of open theism and renewal theology. In this chapter, I explore more deeply the potential points of connection between both Wesley and Fletcher and open theism and between Wesley and pentecostalism. In particular, I will examine areas that initially seem problematic in making the connections.

John Wesley and John Fletcher draw our attention, not because they were famous and influential in the eighteenth century. But they were that, and a brief biographical summary will establish a context for our consideration of their theological thinking.

John Wesley (1703–1791) was an Oxford-educated Anglican priest who was central in the founding of the Methodist movement. After two unsuccessful years as a missionary in Georgia, he returned to London and was influenced in a Pietist direction by the Moravian Peter Böhler. During a reading of Martin Luther's *Preface of the Letter of St. Paul to the Romans* at a meeting in Aldersgate Street in London on May 24, 1738, he felt his heart "strangely warmed," and felt an assurance of salvation. He found it necessary to break with the Moravians in 1740 over several issues, including a perception that they taught all Christians were entirely sanctified and that they downplayed the importance of both the sacraments and good works. Then, in 1741, there was a breach with George Whitefield and the Calvinist Methodists over election. Wesley had a lifelong loyalty to the Church of England and only ordained Methodist preachers when the there was a shortage of ministers qualified to perform the sacraments in America after the Revolutionary War. Beginning in 1744, Wesley held conferences for his lay preachers which became annual events. He evangelized throughout the British Isles, travelling some 200,000 miles on horseback (and later in carriages), preaching over 40,000 sermons. At the time of his death, there were 71,668 members and 294 preachers in Great Britain, 19 missionaries and 5,300 members at mission stations, and 43,265 members with 198 preachers in America.[1]

John Fletcher (1729–1785) was born and educated in Switzerland. He trained as a pastor, but his views on predestination prevented him from taking a pastorate so he served instead as a soldier in Lisbon. He migrated to England in 1750, served as a tutor to a wealthy family in Shropshire (in the middle of England between Bristol and Liverpool), joined a Methodist society in 1753, had an experience of assurance of salvation in 1755, and in 1757 was ordained a Church of England priest then immediately began assisting John Wesley. He enjoyed a warm friendship with both John and Charles Wesley and George Whitefield. In 1760, he became vicar of Madeley in Shropshire, turning down a less demanding and more lucrative pulpit, and resisting the wish of John Wesley to continue as his assistant and to itinerate with him.[2] From 1768 to 1771 he simultaneously helped the Countess of Hungtindon start Trevecca

---

1. *The Encyclopedia of World Methodism* (Nashville, Tenn.: United Methodist Publishing House, 1974), s.v. "Wesley, John."

2. The 1755 experience is described in Benson's biography of Fletcher: Joseph Benson, John Wesley, and Joshua Gilpin (Vicar of Wrockwardine), *The Life of the Rev. John W. de la Fléchère: Compiled from the Narrative of Rev. Mr. Wesley; the Biographical Notes of Rev. Mr. Gilpin; From His Own Letters, And Other Authentic Documents, Many of Which Were Never Before Published* (London: T. Mason and G. Lane, 1840), 23.

College and served as its founding president *in absentia*.[3] He became well-known among his contemporaries, especially through the publication of the *Checks to Antinomianism* (1771–1775) which defended John Wesley's theology convincingly. Fletcher was the first to use the phrase "baptism of the Holy Spirit" to refer to entire sanctification. Wesley's unsympathetic biographer Robert Southey could be remarkably effusive when speaking of Fletcher: "A man of rare talents and rarer virtue. No age or country has ever produced a man of more fervent piety, or more perfect charity; no Church has ever possessed a more apostolic minister."[4] He died six years before Wesley, at age fifty-five, and so could not fulfill Wesley's intention that he succeed him as leader of the Methodist movement.[5]

Wesley and Fletcher attract our interest because their theological thinking, reinforced by their consistent manner of life, was formative for early pentecostals. Coincidentally, Wesley and Fletcher are significant for our exploration of open theism. We can see their debates with Calvinists as an early phase of the same discussion that open theists have been having with Calvinistic evangelicals.

From the outset, I have to acknowledge that John Wesley and John Fletcher do not entirely fit renewal or open theist paradigms. They were not proto-open theists and probably not proto-pentecostals. However, once the considerations that make them not full-blown open theists or proto-pentecostals have been discussed, I will be free to describe the impulses in Wesley and Fletcher toward these movements.

---

3. Laurence W. Wood, *The Meaning of Pentecost in Early Methodism: Rediscovering John Fletcher as John Wesley's Vindicator and Designated Successor*, Pietist and Wesleyan Studies (Lanham, Md.: Scarecrow, 2002), 17.

4. Robert Southey, *The Life of Wesley; And the Rise and Progress of Methodism*, rev. ed. (London and New York: Frederick Warne and Co., 1889), 383.

5. Wood, *The Meaning of Pentecost in Early Methodism*, 6.

A. OPEN THEIST CONSIDERATIONS

1. John Wesley and the Nature of Time

There are occasions in Wesley's writings where the direction of influence runs counter to open theism. For example, as would be expected of a scholar of his time, he viewed God as experiencing time without past, present, or future.[6] This reflects the Christian Platonism which was part of the thought world of his academic environment.[7] Albert Outler says, "He was an avowed empiricist

---

6. Sermon 58: "On Predestination" [1773] in Wesley, *Sermons II*, 417.

7. Christian Platonism in the eighteenth century was known to John Wesley through the Anglican philosopher and rector John Norris of Bemerton (1657–1711), a representative of the Cambridge Platonists. As a group, the Cambridge Platonists were resisting the rationalism of Thomas Hobbs and responding to the scientific discrediting of Aristotelianism by taking advantage of Platonic and Neoplatonic traditions (Antony Flew, *A Dictionary of Philosophy,* 2nd ed.: 54–55). Norris was influenced by Plato and Nicolas Malebranche (1638–1715), who in turn was influenced by Augustine and René Descartes.

Norris opposed the empiricism of John Locke (1632–1702). Outler mentions that the influence of Norris and Malebranche on Wesley was "pervasive" (*Sermons,* note on IV:334 and IV:19). Of the best-known Cambridge Platonists—Ralph Cudworth, Nathaniel Culverwel, Richard Cumberland, Joseph Glanvill, Henry More, John Norris, and Benjamin Whichcote—only John Norris and Henry More are represented in John Wesley's books. Cornelius Bayley's catalogue of books held in the Kingswood library from around 1775, found in Randy Maddox's article in *Methodist History*, 41:1 (October 2002) lists a biography of Henry More: Richard Ward [1657?–1723], *The Life of the Learned and Pious Dr. Henry More* (London: Joseph Downing, 1710) [#228 in Bayley's Catalogue] and Nicolas Malebranche [1638-1715], *Father Malebranche's Treatise concerning the Search After Truth*, translated by Thomas Taylor (Oxford: Lichfield, 1694) [#12 in Bayley's Catalogue]. Of particular interest, Bayley lists John Norris's *A Collection of Miscellanies: Consisting of Poems, Essays, Discourses, and Letters, Occasionally Written* (Oxford: J. Crosley, 1687) and *Reflections upon the Conduct of Human Life*, probably Wesley's 3rd edition (London: Cock, 1755).

Two passages (with spelling and capitalization modernized) give a flavor of Norris's thought and interests. The first, from "A Discourse concerning Perseverance in Holiness" demonstrates why Wesley would include Norris in the Kingswood library: "For if you look upon Christianity as some men are pleased to hold the perspective, it is no way accommodated for the promotion of holiness and virtue, but is rather a perfect discharge from all duty, and a charter of licentiousness. For among other misrepresentations of the gospel, this is one (and I think the most pernicious one that the sophistry of hell could ever suggest) which suggests that it requires nothing to be done by its proselytes. A notion so ridiculous and mischievous as is fit for none but a profane Epicure to embrace, who may be allowed to make his religion as idle and sedentary as he does his God. Nay, 'tis not only ridiculous and mischievous, but in the highest measure anti-Christian. For what greater Antichristianism can there be than that, which strikes not only at some of the main branches, but at the very root of Christianity, and at once evacuates the entire purpose and aim of the gospel." John Norris, *A Collection of Miscellanies: Consisting of Poems, Essays, Discourses,*

in an age of empiricism; yet he was also an unembarrassed intuitionist who openly claimed his heritage of Christian Platonism."[8]

This neoplatonic influence is seen nowhere as clearly as in Wesley's understanding of God's relationship to time. In his view, God inhabits all space and eternity. David Naglee describes Wesley's perspective: "The eternity of God is a constant *NOW*—a never-ending present, without beginning, past, future, or end. As for time, it is a segment of eternity marked with a beginning, a middle, and an end—a past, present, and future—surrounded by the eternal *NOW* of God. As God looks at time, he sees it all at once, Wesley believed.... Hence God knows all time-bound things from an infinite, eternal perspective."[9] This was Augustine's view.[10] Wesley could have learned it in

---

and Letters, Occasionally Written (Oxford: John Crosley Bookseller, 1687; reprint 1978, New York and London: Garland), 213.

A second passage (from "Another Letter to the Same Person, Concerning the True Notion of Plato's Ideas, and of Platonic Love") highlights Norris's philosophical location: "And now, that the grossness of this abuse [the concept that Ideas, thought of as universal natures or abstract essences, subsist eternally apart from the mind of God and separate from particular instances; for example, individual men or women from the universal Man or Woman] may the more fully appear, I will in the next place present you with another sense of Plato's Ideas, and such as by a more than ordinary acquaintance with his works, I know to be the true and genuine one. Know then that Plato considering the world as an effect of an intellectual Agent, ... thought it necessary to suppose ... eternal Forms, models or patterns, of all the species of being in nature existing in the mind of God. And these he calls Ideas. I say existing in the mind of God, for there is not the least intimation in all Plato's works of any such Ideas existing separately from the divine intellect, nor do the great masters of Platonic philosophy, Plotinus, Porphyrius, Procles, or any other that I know of make mention of any such spectres and ghosts of entity. No, this monster was hatched in Aristotle's brain, and believe did never enter Plato's head so much as in a dream." Ibid., 437–38. It is interesting to see Norris defending Platonism while attacking Aristotelianism.

8. Wesley, *Sermons I*, 59. Nevertheless, when Wesley is placed side-by-side with John Norris, the Cambridge Platonist quoted in the previous note, he is seen to be leaning rather more to empiricism than to that Platonic tradition.

9. David Ingersoll Naglee, *From Everlasting to Everlasting: John Wesley on Eternity and Time*, 2 vols., American University Studies, Series 7, Theology and Religion, Vol. 65–66 (New York: Peter Lang, 1991), 1:111. Wesley doesn't say why he thinks all time is present to God at once. He's assuming what is a crucial point. See Sermon 58: "On Predestination" [1773] in Wesley, *Sermons II*, 417.

10. "It is not that God's knowledge varies in any way, that the future, the present, and the past affect that knowledge in three different ways. It is not with God as it is with us. He does not look ahead to the future, look directly at the present, look back to the past. He sees in some other manner, utterly remote from anything we experience or could imagine. He does not see things by turning his attention from one thing to another. He sees all without any kind of change. Things which happen under the condition of time are in the future, not yet in being, or in the present, already existing, or in the past, no longer in being. But God comprehends all these in a stable and eternal present.... Nor is there any difference between his present, past, and future

any number of places, for example, from Malebranche, Norris, or Augustine himself.[11] Naglee asserts, Wesley's "reliance on the thought of Augustine is overwhelmingly obvious."[12]

Wesley writes, "But what is *time*? It is not easy to say, as frequently as we have had the word in our mouth. We know not what it properly is: we cannot

---

knowledge. His knowledge is not like ours, which has three tenses: present, past, and future. God's knowledge has no change or variation. 'With him there is no alteration, or shadow of movement.'" Augustine of Hippo, *Concerning the City of God, against the Pagans*, trans. Henry Bettenson (Harmondsworth, Middlesex, England and Baltimore, Md.: Penguin, 1467, 1972), 452. The neoplatonic commitment to the immutability of God (inherited from Aristotle) is the controlling factor here.

McGiffert argues that Augustine became a neoplatonist when he left Manichaeism behind. "Platonism and Catholic Christianity, he believed, were at bottom really one." McGiffert, *A History of Christian Thought, vol. II*, 77. (Although McGiffert is an old source, it has the serendipity of having been highly recommended by the Reformed professor who rejected an early version of the research that led to this dissertation.) "He was helped out of his skepticism not by Plato himself, but by the writings of Plotinus, which had recently been put into Latin by the North African Victorinus. He found in Neoplatonism much to attract him: the conception of a realm of spiritual being altogether different from the realm of things, the notion that all visible objects are but the types or expressions of invisible ones, the belief in the immateriality and immortality of the soul and in man's possession of a spiritual sense by which he may know God and the realities of the unseen world. Most of all he was influenced by the Neoplatonic solution of the problem of evil, the fundamental problem of the Manichaeans. According to Plotinus, evil is in itself nothing, it is simply the absence of the good." Ibid., 76.

There is much here that open theists would resist but of particular concern is the last point on the nature of evil. One of the motivations behind open theism is providing a more adequate theodicy than that of classical theism. The horrors of the last century and the attempts made to minimize evil appear implausible. Theodicy and the problem of evil was discussed above on p. 32.

The similarity of Karl Barth (the dominant Reformed theologian of the twentieth century) and Augustine on this point is interesting. JoAnn Ford Watson summarizes: "Barth thus ontologically explains evil as nothingness behind God's good creation. The darkside of God's good creation is similar to Augustine's concept of evil as lack in that which is inherently good." "Contemporary Views on the Problem of Evil," *Ashland Theological Journal* 24 (1992): 28.

11. Wesley's personal library had a copy of Augustine's *Confessions*. Randy L. Maddox, "John Wesley's Reading: Evidence in the Book Collection at Wesley's House, London," *Methodist History* 41, no. 3 (April 2003): A copy of the 1648 edition was catalogued as C28.

John Newton in a comprehensive and nuanced way examines Augustine's use of neoplatonic ideas. John Thomas Newton, "Neoplatonism and Augustine's Doctrine of the Person and Work of Christ: A Study of the Philosophical Structure Underlying Augustine's Christology" (Ph.D. dissertation, Emory University, 1969). Interestingly, while Newton demonstrates Augustine's dependence on the neoplatonists at many points, Augustine also finds reason to oppose them: "His criticism of Neoplatonism begins in the *Confessions* [VII, 9 (13–14)] and is sharply stated in the *De civ. Dei* [X, 24, attacking Porphyry's rejection of the incarnation]. He found no foundation in paganism for a concept of humility, rather he found only pride and this was most evident among the best of the pagans, the Neoplatonists." Ibid., 286.

12. Naglee, *From Everlasting to Everlasting*, 1:2.

well tell how to define it. But is it not in some sense a fragment of eternity, broken off at both ends? That portion of it which is at present measured by the revolution of the sun and planets, lying (so to speak) between two eternities, that which is past, and that which is to come?"[13] While Wesley acknowledges the convention of measuring the passage of time by objects in the solar system, he thinks of time in relation to an eternity past and an eternity future. Here he is following Augustine.[14]

The nature of time is closely tied to the issue of the nature of God's foreknowledge. Wesley says, "God *foreknew* those in every nation who would believe, from the beginning of the world to the consummation of all things." Then he follows Augustine: "For if we speak properly there is no such thing as either *foreknowledge* or *after-knowledge* in God. All time, or rather all eternity (for time is only that small fragment of eternity which is allotted to the children of men) being present to him at once, he does not know one thing before another, or one thing after another, but sees all things in one point of view, from everlasting to everlasting."[15]

Wesley denies God *causes* an event just because he *knows* about it.

> But observe: we must not think they *are* because he *knows* them. No; he knows them because they are. Just as I (if one may be allowed to compare the things of men with the deep things of God) now know the sun shines. Yet the sun does not shine because I know it; but I know it because he shines. My knowledge *supposes* the sun to shine, but does not in any wise *cause* it. In like manner God knows that man sins; for he knows all things. Yet we do not sin because he knows it; but he knows it because we sin. And his knowledge *supposes* our sin, but does not in any wise *cause* it.... Men are as *free* in believing, or not believing, as if he did not know it at all.[16]

---

13. Sermon 54: "On Eternity" [1786] in Wesley, *Sermons II*, 360.
14. Outler notes the reference to Augustine, *Confessions,* XI. xiv–xxvi, XII. xxix.
15. Sermon 58: "On Predestination" [1773] in Wesley, *Sermons II*, 417.
16. Sermon 58: "On Predestination" [1773] in ibid.

This only works if God is outside of time, otherwise the knowing of the thing in advance makes it unchangeable and predestined because God's knowledge is perfect. But our experience of God is in time because he relates to us. The biblical story of God relating to people sequentially makes the idea that God is not in time something that cannot be assumed or barely asserted, but must be argued for.

Augustine's (and the early and middle Wesley's) view of time is consistent with what has been labeled the B-theory (or stasis theory or tenseless theory) of time.[17] This way of distinguishing the nature of time was proposed early in the twentieth century by the Cambridge Idealist philosopher John McTaggart.[18] The B-theory considers events in time being defined by their sequential relation to other events—prior, simultaneous with, and subsequent. In the B-theory, all events are equally real. For most A-theorists, only events occurring in the present are real. The present has an existence which the past may not have and the future does not have. In the A-theory (also known as the tensed or process theory), events are defined by being in the past, present, or future, not just in relation to each other. The idea of God being atemporal depends on the B-theory being true. "Many philosophers think that if the A-theory of time is true, then God must be a temporal being."[19] Open theists hold to the A-theory of time.

The B-theory understanding of time has fallen out of favor with philosophers. Gregory Ganssle observes that as recently as 1975 in an article by Nicholas Wolterstorff it could be assumed that the predominant view was that God is atemporal.[20] But in continuing a project of "de-Hellenizing" theology which foreshadows open theism, Wolterstorff argued God is temporal rather than eternal (and neither immutable nor impassible). He writes, "All Christian theologians agree that God is without beginning and without end. The vast majority have held, in addition, that God is *eternal*, existing outside of time.

---

17. Gregory E. Ganssle, ed., *God and Time: Four Views* (Downers Grove: InterVarsity, 2001), 14–15.

18. J. M. E. McTaggart, *The Nature of Existence*, Vol. 2 (Cambridge: Cambridge University Press, 1927), ch. 33.

19. Ganssle, *God and Time*, 15.

20. Ibid., 13.

Only a small minority have contended that God is *everlasting*, existing within time."[21] A quarter century later, in 2001, it is interesting to note that after the debating is over, of the philosophers including Wolterstorff invited to contribute different views to Ganssle's study, only Paul Helm holds out for a B-theory of time. His view of the timeless eternity of God and his use of eternal decrees to appear to interact with the world is clearly wedded to Calvinistic commitments.[22] Alan Padgett flatly asserts, "The stasis theory of time is false."[23] This brings us back to a tensed or process view of time where time is progressing toward the future through the now of the present. This view is consistent with God being active in time and in the world he created. It is consistent with a teleological view of history. That the tensed view of time has essentially won out over the static view does not imply that the nature of time is settled. The philosophy and science of time have undergone several revolutions since the seventeenth century, and there is work yet to be done.

John Wesley lived when the scientific era was emerging. "We can trace the birth of a truly scientific time back to Sir Isaac Newton, who discovered mathematical expressions for the movement of bodies."[24] Newton died in 1727, the year Wesley earned his master's degree. Although Newtonian science had been introduced at Oxford at least twenty years prior to Wesley's studying there, he was given Thomeson Bartholin's *Specimen philosophiae*

---

21. Nicholas Wolterstorff, "God Everlasting," in *God and the Good: Essays in Honor of Henry Stob*, ed. Clifton Orlebeke and Lewis Smedes (Grand Rapids: Eerdmans, 1975), 181. Wolterstorff notes that the "most noteworthy contemporary example" of the minority view is Oscar Cullmann, *Christ and Time: The Primitive Christian Conception of Time and History*, trans. Floyd V. Filson, rev. ed. (London: SCM, 1962).

22. Paul Helm, "Divine Timeless Eternity," in *God and Time: Four Views*, ed. Gregory E. Ganssle (Downers Grove: InterVarsity, 2001), 216–17.

23. Alan Padget, "Eternity as Relative Timelessness," ibid., 95. A broader search only turns up four recent philosophers of time who hold to the B-series view, two associated with Cambridge and two with Harvard. The first is D. H. Mellor who is Professor Emeritus and past president of the Aristotelian Society. Mellor holds that time is real but tense is not. The second is the late John Jamieson Carswell Smart who was born and schooled in Cambridge then Glasgow. He became Emeritus Professor of the Australian National University. Smart believed time is illusory. Willard Van Orman Quine (1908–2000) believed and Hilary Whitehall Putnam (b. 1926) believes that special relativity and quantum mechanics provide support for the B-theory. In an odd twist, Alfred North Whitehead was Quine's academic supervisor (*Stanford Encyclopedia of Philosophy*, q.v. "Alfred North Whitehead").

24. Coveney and Highfield, *The Arrow of Time*, 29.

naturalis Praecipua Physicaes capita exponens (1697) to summarize as an exercise. Bartholin was an eclectic who depended heavily on Aristotle and Descartes.[25] The view of Newtonian physics was that time is absolute: "Time flows at the same rate throughout the universe and people at different locations experience the same 'now'."[26]

Given Wesley's willingness to part company with Augustine on topics like divine foreknowledge and predestination, it is not a stretch to think that if the alternative understanding of the nature of time and God's relation to it had been readily available in the eighteenth century, he might have gladly adopted it. Of God, Wesley says,

> Yet when he speaks to us, knowing whereof we are made, knowing the scantiness of our understanding, he lets himself down to our capacity and speaks of himself after the manner of men. Thus in condescension to our weakness he speaks of his own "purpose," "counsel," "plan," "foreknowledge...." It is merely in compassion to us that he speaks thus of himself as "foreknowing" the things in heaven or earth, and as "predestinating" or "foreordaining" them. But can we possibly imagine that these expressions are to be taken literally?[27]

But what do they mean if they are not to be taken literally? Wesley here realizes that Paul's language and his view of how God relates to time are in conflict. That Wesley is struggling to be consistent can be seen when his language seems to slip toward the A-theory of time. The late Wesley can imply that God is *in* time rather than being timeless: "Does there not seem to be some

---

25. John C. English, "John Wesley's Scientific Education," *Methodist History* 30, no. 1 (October 1991): 43. English comments: "I have the impression that a tilt in the direction of Newtonianism took place about the time that Wesley finished his undergraduate studies. Referring to Oxford in 1721, Nicholas Amhurst wrote 'that Locke, Clarke and Sir Isaac Newton begin to find countenance in the schools, and that Aristotle seems to totter on his antient [sic] throne.' The reference to Aristotle, suitably modified, could be applied to Descartes as well." Ibid., 51. [Amhurst's quote is from William R. Ward, *Georgian Oxford: University Politics in the Eighteenth Century* (Oxford: Clarendon Press, 1932).]

26. Coveney and Highfield, *The Arrow of Time*, 360.

27. Sermon 58: "On Predestination" [1773] in Wesley, *Sermons II*, 421.

sort of analogy between boundless duration and boundless space? The great Creator, the Infinite Spirit, inhabits both the one and the other."[28] A viable alternate view of God and time does not seem to have been available to him.[29]

Wesley's adherence to what we now call the stasis theory of time leads to a weakness in his theodicy.[30] This view of time goes along with God foresee-

---

28. Sermon 54: "On Eternity" [1786] in ibid., 360. Duration implies being in time and here Wesley says God "inhabits" boundless duration. Similarly, three years later, he writes, "Nearly allied to the eternity of God is his omnipresence. As he exists through infinite duration, so he cannot but exist through infinite space;…" Sermon 120: "The Unity of the Divine Being" [1789] in John Wesley, *Sermons IV, 115–151*, ed. Albert C. Outler, The Works of John Wesley (Nashville: Abingdon, 1987), 61. He is no longer speaking of God existing in an "eternal now" but having "infinite duration." He does continue to use the language of 'eternity', but by this he means 'everlasting'. He says from scripture we learn that "God is an eternal being: 'His goings forth are from everlasting,' and will continue to everlasting. As he ever was, so he ever will be; as there was no beginning of his existence, so there will be no end." Sermon 120: "The Unity of the Divine Being" [1789] in ibid. For the late Wesley, God has "goings forth," or movement, which implies he is not timeless because movement requires time.

29. While sources antecedent to open theism proliferated in the nineteenth century, they are much rarer prior to or contemporaneous with Wesley. The Italian-Polish reformer Faustus Socinus (1538–1604) was one possible source having written an essay where he suggests God cannot foreknow what free agents will do, but Wesley would have been put off by Socinus' anti-Trinitarian views. George Porter summarizes the early sources (his footnotes are in square brackets): "Not only did the Socinians hold an understanding of divine omniscience close in wording to the current omniscience of open theism, but the medieval Jewish theologian Gersonides said that in creating beings with genuine free will God limited the divine omniscience, even abdicating some dimensions of divine foreknowledge. [Richard L. Purtill, "Foreknowledge and Fatalism," *Religious Studies* 10 (1974): 319. See also, Douglas P. Lackey, "A New Disproof of the Compatibility of Foreknowledge and Free Choice." *Religious Studies* 10 (1974): 318.] Likewise, Ambrose is reported to have said concerning prayer that 'if God foreknows the future, and if this must needs come to pass,' and 'if all things come to pass by the will of God, and his counsels are fixed, and none of the things he wills can be changed, prayer is vain.' [Quoted by Vincent Brümmer, *What Are We Doing When We Pray? A Philosophical Investigation* (London: SCM, 1984), 35, 41.] Contemporaries of Ambrose—Porphyry, Albinus and Calcidius—held similar ideas. The latter was reputed to have been a Christian, possibly even a Milanese deacon. He wrote that 'it is true that God knows all things, but that he knows everything according to its own nature: that which is subject to necessity as submissive to necessity, the contingent, however, as provided with such a nature that deliberation opens a way for it.' [Calcidius in J. Den Boeft, *Calcidius on Fate: His Doctrine and Sources*, Philosophia Antiqua Vol XVIII, ed. by W. J. Verneius and J. H. Waszink (Leiden: E. J. Brill, 1970), 52.]" Porter, "Things That May Be Only?" Calcidius was a fourth-century philosopher, known as the translator of Plato's *Timaeus* from Greek to Latin. He is the earliest Christian philosopher or theologian found so far espousing views which can be seen as moving in the direction of open theism. Outler observes, "Wesley's direct knowledge of church history from the fifth to the sixteenth centuries turns out to be no better than nominal." Wesley, *Sermons I*, 76. Even though Calcidius predates that range, it wouldn't be surprising if his views on time and divine foreknowledge were unknown to Wesley.

30. Wesley's theodicy does have its strengths. For example, he says, God could "abolish wickedness out of his whole creation, and suffer no trace of it to remain. But in so doing he would counteract himself, he would altogether overturn his own work, and undo all that he has been

ing future actions of free creatures. God's goodness means he is committed to work for the greatest possible good. If God can foresee a great evil, the question arises why he does not work ahead to prevent it (in such a way as to not compromise the free will of creatures). The early Wesley goes in a different direction: "Do not all men know that whatever evil befalls them, it befalls them by God's appointment?" He seems at this early stage to be making God responsible for evil.[31]

The early Wesley's view is that God allows evil in the world only that it may result in a greater good:

> That even no temporal evil shall befall him, unless to clear the way for a greater good! What though he wrestles not only against inanimate enemies, but against flesh and blood, the depravity of his own nature, with the perverseness, malice, and injustice of other men; nay, and not only against flesh and blood, but against principalities, the rulers of the darkness of this world, the wicked spirits in high places?[32]

The flaw in the theodicy that God allows evil in order that greater good may result is demonstrated by William Hasker. He observes that it is difficult to continue to argue that each specific occurrence of evil results in a greater good for the person suffering the harm.[33] The innocent suffering of the holocaust in Germany in the 1940s, the Rwandan genocide of 1994, the earthquake in Haiti in 2010, or the tsunami in Japan in 2012 outweighs any incidental

---

doing since he created man upon the earth. For he created man in his own image: a spirit, like himself; a spirit endued with understanding, with will, or affections, and liberty—without which neither his understanding nor his affections could have been of any use, neither would he have been capable either of vice or virtue. He could not be a moral agent, any more than a tree or a stone." Sermon 67: "On Divine Providence" [1786] in Wesley, *Sermons II*, 540–41. He is saying the creation of free intelligent beings is an endeavor that God has a lot invested in. That freedom is necessarily accompanied by the consequences of poor choices.

31. Sermon 143: "Public Diversions Denounced" [1732] in Wesley, *Sermons IV*, 319. Perhaps Wesley later became dissatisfied with this position which would account for why the sermon was never published in his lifetime.

32. Sermon 135: "On Guardian Angels" [1726] in ibid., 234.

33. Hasker, *Providence, Evil and the Openness of God*, 46.

good and cannot represent the judgment of God because the determination of who is to suffer is too arbitrary.[34] While Hasker advocates giving up the justification of each individual evil event, thus acknowledging gratuitous evil in the world, he argues, "We would still, however, have available the appeal to *general divine policies of governance* as the explanation for why particular evils are permitted."[35] It might have been credible in Wesley's England to say that God allows evil in order to bring about a greater good but it is not convincing from our location where the extent and depth of the world's suffering is so proximate.[36]

2. Lorenzo Dow McCabe as a Bridge to Open Theism

That the early and middle Wesleyan view of time is inconsistent with the process or tensed view of open theists would initially appear to be a major obstacle in seeing a trajectory from one to the other. For most of his long life, Wesley held a B-theory view of time, while open theists hold an A-theory view. This is a problem because the nature of time, and specifically the nature of the future, is a one of the main concerns of open theism.[37] The gap

---

34. Romans 8:28, "Οἴδαμεν δὲ ὅτι τοῖς ἀγαπῶσιν [present active participle masculine plural dative] τὸν θεὸν πάντα συνεργεῖ εἰς ἀγαθόν, τοῖς κατὰ πρόθεσιν κλητοῖς οὖσιν" has frequently been read to support the view that God always brings a greater good out of evil. The most familiar translation is probably, "We know that all things work together for good for those who love God, who are called according to his purpose" (NRSV). But Richard Rice has observed that the passage can be translated in at least three ways. These options are mentioned in David Larson, "The Spectrum Blog," (12 Nov 2007). http://spectrummagazine.org/blog/2007/11/12/richard-rice-discusses-open-theism. "A second legitimate option is 'God makes all things work together for good.' The third is 'in all things God works for good.' Given its overall understanding of God and humanity, 'Open Theism' opts for the third alternative." The NIV comes close to the third option: "And we know that in all things God works for the good of those who love him, who have been called according to his purpose." In the open theist view, even though God did not cause a tragic event, he works in and through it for good.

35. Hasker, *Providence, Evil and the Openness of God*, 55 (italics his).

36. Wesley is sometimes a little too quick to attribute suffering to God: "Here is the ground for resignation to God, enabling us to say from the heart, in every trying hour, 'It is the Lord: let him do what seemeth him good.'" Sermon 59: "God's Love to Fallen Man" [1782] in Wesley, *Sermons II*, 429. He is not here taking account of attacks from opposing spiritual forces, for example. He is not, however, oblivious to these: "For to him [the devil] we may reasonably impute many little inconveniences which we suffer." Sermon 72: "Of Evil Angels" [1783] in John Wesley, *Sermons III, 71–114*, ed. Albert C. Outler, The Works of John Wesley (Nashville: Abingdon, 1986), 26.

37. "If the future is settled in the sense that it is exhaustively and truly describable in terms of what either *will* or *will not* obtain, then divine omniscience (the thesis that God knows all and

is bridged, however, by noticing that it is Wesleyans (among others) in the eighteenth century who are advocating for a change of view.[38] They were interested in modifying the Wesleyan theological tradition to make it more consistent. While Wesley departed from Augustine on issues like free will, predestination, and election, they wanted to add to the list the issues of the nature of time, God's relation to time, and particularly the nature of divine foreknowledge.

The Wesleyan theologian and philosopher Lorenzo Dow McCabe (1817–1897) is the leading nineteenth-century advocate for removing this inconsistency in the tradition.[39] He writes,

> "Explain," said an anxious inquirer to John Wesley, "how it is that God can foreknow with certainty the future choices of a free agent." "I frankly confess I can offer no explanation," was his humiliating reply. Sitting beneath the effulgence of so great a light as that which Mr. Wesley poured upon a darkened theological world, and yet finding that he could not explain the most torturing problem of my existence, has deeply moved me. In my mental distress I have inquired, Is there no way to remove these great difficulties? Can not a theology be constructed that will remove such perplexities?… A thoughtful study of the subject has convinced me that a denial of absolute divine foreknowledge would invalidate many of the objections of the infidel

---

only truths) entails exhaustively definite foreknowledge. Conversely, if the future is open in the sense that a complete, true description of it must include reference to what *might and might not* obtain, then divine omniscience entails open theism and the denial of exhaustively definite foreknowledge. The nature of the future is, therefore, a key issue in the open theism debate." Alan R. Rhoda, Gregory A. Boyd, and Thomas G. Belt, "Open Theism, Omniscience, and the Nature of the Future," *Faith and Philosophy* 23, no. 24 (2006): 432.

38. For example, Daniel Curry (1808–1887). "One of the ablest thinkers American Methodism has yet produced says: 'The denial of absolute divine foreknowledge is the essential complement of the Methodist theology, without which its philosophical incompleteness is defenseless against the logical consistency of Calvinism.' 'Theology,' says Dr. Daniel Curry, 'has very much to unlearn before it will be either reasonable or Scriptural.'" McCabe, *The Foreknowledge of God*, 18.

39. See note on p. 17 and for biographical details see note 33 in Porter, "Things That May Be Only?"

to Christian theology, and shed a clear light upon some of the deepest and most perplexing mysteries of that theology.[40]

In his subsequent book, McCabe also makes explicit his desire to modify the tradition. As he tries to persuade Calvinists to give up double predestination, he offers himself as an example. He himself has renounced a doctrine of a founding father:

> I revere the name of John Wesley as much as any man of history. "Great," exclaimed Dr. Whedon, "were Wesley's logical powers; greater his administrative powers; but greatest of all his intuitive powers." But should Mr. Wesley teach me a doctrine so repugnant to the common instincts of humanity as unconditional reprobation [referencing Calvin], I should vehemently reject its acceptance. He did teach me the doctrine of absolute prescience of future contingencies, but I unhesitatingly repudiate it with acclaims loud and clear.[41]

McCabe painstakingly argues that "divine nescience of future contingencies is a necessity." Nescience is "not-knowing" and the antonym of prescience. McCabe means it is necessary that God *not* know which events that *might* happen in the future actually will transpire. It is a denial of exhaustive definite foreknowledge. In discussing predestination, Wesley had said, "The sum of all is this: the almighty all-wise God sees and knows from everlasting to everlasting all that is, that was, and that is to come, through one eternal now."[42] McCabe's colorful response to this view:

> Deny the reality of time; chain me in a duration-less eternal now; rob God of all change; congeal him into the iceberg of indifference which prescience necessitates; prohibit him from changing in his feelings toward me, when from obduracy I turn and break in

---

40. McCabe, *The Foreknowledge of God*, 21–22.
41. McCabe, *Divine Nescience of Future Contingencies*, 256.
42. Sermon 58: "On Predestination" [1773] in Wesley, *Sermons II*, 420.

penitence at his feet; forbid him sympathizing with me in the perplexities of my way, and in the tragedies of my probation; and deny to him the interest, sympathy, and tenderness which alone can be born from a future unfixed and uncertain both for him and for me; and you fill my Bible with obscurity, my theology with paralyzing doubts, and you wrap in distressing gloom the glorious cross of Jesus Christ.[43]

McCabe is arguably the most significant middle point in the trajectory from John Wesley to open theism because of the diligence with which he argued the nescient position. That effort is exemplified by the structure and content of *Divine Nescience of Future Contingencies a Necessity*. In order for us to appreciate how far along McCabe was on the road to open theism, I will review the book chapter by chapter. The first chapter argues that God's freedom necessitates a non-deterministic universe or God would not be free to act except in a pre-determined way. There must, therefore, be a universe of contingencies—things that may or may not come to pass.[44] McCabe here makes a brilliant argument. We expect him to say *human* freedom requires a non-deterministic universe, but his point is that *God's* freedom requires it not to be locked into predetermined actions.

The second chapter argues humans must be free to act independent of God, or moral accountability is impossible.[45] If exhaustive divine foreknowledge is true, future events cannot be otherwise than they are known to God, and therefore human freedom is meaningless (in spite of assertions to the contrary).[46] By drawing the logical conclusion that the future is predetermined if it is known ahead of time in the mind of God, McCabe highlights a highly undesirable implication of the Augustinian system. Humans must be free to change the future, or they cannot in fairness be held accountable for their actions.

---

43. McCabe, *Divine Nescience of Future Contingencies*, 289.
44. Ibid., 15.
45. Ibid., 32.
46. Ibid., 39–41.

The third and fourth chapters argue that God's perfections—particularly his creative freedom—require he be free to do new things in the future, and not be locked into a system of necessity determined in eternity. The "tenderness of the infinite heart" of the divine parent requires a genuine nescience of the outcome of life's journey.[47] God's moral character requires nescience or God is implicated in wrong-doing.[48] God's candor requires divine nescience.[49] God's happiness as a creator necessitates nescience—how can he delight at the repentance of a sinner without it?[50] McCabe here makes convincing arguments based on the character of God. God would be a liar if he knew it wasn't true when he told Abimelech (Genesis 20:3), Hezekiah (Isaiah 38:1), and the Ninevites (Jonah 3:4) that they were going to die. John Calvin calls these instances a "threat" and would rather imply God is a liar than concede he could change his mind (as in Jonah 3:9–10).[51] McCabe is correct to stress God's truthfulness and candor and anticipates open theism in wanting to question a theological stance if it seems to be saying something negative about God's character or actions.

The fifth chapter asks why the Holy Spirit would persistently and tenderly work in someone for decades if he knows through foreknowledge that in the end that person will choose eternal ruin?[52] Chapter six argues that nescience provides a defense against the determinism of Spinoza's pantheism, subsequent deism, and the idealism of Hegel and Schelling. Chapters seven and eight argue that the hope of salvation and the fear of being lost are both undermined by belief in a fixed future.[53] McCabe here is addressing important pastoral and apologetic concerns of his day.

---

47. Ibid., 49.
48. Ibid., 50.
49. Ibid., 53–54.
50. Ibid., 55–56. "God's present feelings toward me are those of a Father. I am trying to obey him. There is now no shadow between him and my soul. Jesus Christ reigns in my heart; his blood is cleansing me, and the Holy Ghost is carrying forward the sublime work of my recreation in the divine image unto good works. But if God now knows that eventually I will apostatize, all such fatherly feelings would be utterly impossible." Ibid., 56–57.
51. Calvin, *Institutes*, 1:228, Book 1 ch. 17 §14.
52. McCabe, *Divine Nescience of Future Contingencies*, 62–64.
53. Ibid., 69–70.

Chapter nine discusses ways in which nescience is a benefit to biblical hermeneutics. Here McCabe follows Isaak Dorner's suggestion that God sometimes works through a kingdom of providence with his sovereign will and sometimes works through a kingdom of free grace where he is a coworker with free agents.[54]

Chapter ten argues that nescience is necessary for prayer to be comprehensible, real, and effective.[55] Chapter eleven takes notice of how nescience makes a consistent theodicy possible.[56] Chapter twelve argues that nescience is necessary to a doctrine of universal, rather than limited, atonement.[57] Chapter thirteen discusses the fate of the wicked, rejecting both Jonathan Edwards' lurid description of everlasting fiery torment on the one hand and annihilation of the wicked on the other.[58] Chapter fourteen attempts a harmonization of Calvinistic and Arminian theological schools. McCabe suggests that the Calvinist should give up election and reprobation and the Arminian should give up divine prescience.[59]

---

54. Ibid., 75–76. Unconditional prophecies pertain in the former kingdom and conditional prophecies which are dependent on voluntary compliance belong to the latter. Ibid., 76. John Sanders also mentions Isaak Dorner in *The God Who Risks*, 322 n. 126. Isaak August Dorner, *Divine Immutability: A Critical Reconsideration*, trans. Robert Williams and Claude Welch (Minneapolis, Minn.: Fortress, 1994), 149–53.

55. McCabe, *Divine Nescience of Future Contingencies*, 100.

56. Ibid., 101. "'It is certain,' said Bishop I. W. Wiley, who has read and thought widely upon such themes, 'that the construction of a theodicy is utterly impossible on the basis of either the dogma of predestination or that of absolute prescience.'... Divine nescience of future contingencies is the thought that turns into gold every thing and every element needed in the construction of a splendid divine theodicy.... By its power we can transmute every one of them into a pure crystal to adorn the walls of our construction. It illumines the genesis of sin, explains the existence of evils, and accounts for all suffering." Ibid., 105-06.

57. McCabe argues that prescience locks in those who are elect for salvation, and those who are not with the result that the atonement only accomplishes redemption for part of the human family. Nescience, on the other hand, means salvation is available to all. Jesus restored "the forfeited power of alternative choices." Ibid., 108.

58. Ibid., 114–15. McCabe argues that prescience necessitates an unacceptable view of God. "The creation of immortal beings foreknown to be wicked, and interminably wretched can never be justified by any process of thought, either human or divine." Ibid., 147. McCabe quotes Orville Dewey: "If sin is not repented of in this life, then its punishment must take place in a future world. Of all the unveiled horrors of a future state, nothing seems so terrific as the self-inflicted torture of a guilty conscience." *The Works of the Rev. Orville Dewey, D. D., Pastor of The Church of the Messiah, New York* (London: Simms and McIntyre, 1844), 388.

59. McCabe, *Divine Nescience of Future Contingencies*, 155, 256. This, by far the longest chapter, ends with a passage that is replete with open theist overtones. "But how the Scriptures teem with

II. WESLEY AND RENEWAL & OPEN THEIST PARADIGMS

Chapter fifteen deals with the nature of time. Here, he has several concerns. The first is to argue that space and time are concrete realities.[60] (He is writing, of course, before Newton's view of the absoluteness of time and space was challenged by developments in the study of physics, especially the theory of relativity.) Time must have the properties of duration, succession, anteriority, and subsequence.[61] For 'anteriority' and 'subsequence', he coins the terms 'beforeness' and 'afterness'. These two properties are consistent with both the A-theory and B-theory views of time. Duration and succession are associated with the A-theory. McCabe's interest in the nature of time again anticipates open theism.

McCabe also argues that God has both a subjective life and an objective life.[62] The subjective life is his interior experience of "absolute enjoyment of itself" which, if necessary, can be conceived of as unchanging and timeless.[63]

---

evidences that this world was created at a solemn venture! 'It grieved God at his heart that he had made man.' 'It repenteth me that I have set up Saul to be king, for he has not kept my commandments.' 'What could have been done more to my vineyard that I have not done in it? I fenced it, gathered out the stones thereof, planted it with the choicest vine. I built a tower in the midst of it, and also made a wine-press therein. Wherefore, when I looked that it should bring forth grapes, brought it forth wild grapes?' These words express grief, disappointment, amazement and indignation. 'Hear, O heavens, give ear, O earth. I have nourished and brought up children, and they have rebelled against me.' 'They vexed his Holy Spirit, therefore he was turned to be their enemy and fought against them.' 'When the Lord saw it, he abhorred them, and said, I will hide my face from them, and I will see what their end shall be, for they are children in whom is no faith.' If these passages do not express contingency, uncertainty, adventure in the creation of man, we may despair of ever finding out the feelings of God or the meaning of his messages to a lost world." Ibid., 276–77.

60. Here he is briefly engaging Immanuel Kant who wrote, "Now what are space and time? Are they actual entities [*wirkliche Wesen*]? Are they only determinations or also relations of things, but still such as would belong to them even if they were not intuited? Or are they such that they belong only to the form of intuition, and therefore to the subjective constitution of our mind, without which these predicates could not be ascribed to any things at all?" (*Critique of Pure Reason*, A23/B37–8). Quoted in Andrew Janiak, "Kant's Views on Space and Time," in *The Stanford Encyclopedia of Philosophy*, ed. Edward N. Zalta (2009), http://plato.stanford.edu/archives/win2012/entries/kant-spacetime/.

61. McCabe, *Divine Nescience of Future Contingencies*, 280.

62. McCabe, *The Foreknowledge of God*, 259.

63. McCabe, *Divine Nescience of Future Contingencies*, 282–83. Here he is following Dr. Borden Parker Bowne, Professor of Philosophy at Boston University. McCabe opened the chapter quoting Bowne in *Zion's Herald*, the Boston Methodist weekly (March 6, 1879), "We do not hesitate to call the doctrine of foreknowledge untenable, if it be assumed that time is real." Bowne was a prominent Methodist theologian and philosopher and the leader of the Boston personalism movement. He seems to have the distinction of being the only pastor or theologian to have gone through a heresy trial in the Methodist Episcopal church. (He was acquitted.) "Two Acquittals

But not so his objective life. "God's objective life, that is, his life, experience, interest and enjoyment, as they are projected into and modified by his created universe, must necessarily be contingent."[64] It is hard to conceive how it is the nature of God to be simultaneously in time and not in time. At this point in his argument, it would seem that McCabe is on the way to being an open theist but not yet there. His choice of language reveals which direction he is leaning: he implies the B-theory of time "*may* be necessary to maintain" God's subjective absoluteness.[65] But he implies the A-theory of time *must* be

for Prof. Borden P. Bowne: Exoneration of Original Charges Followed by a Second Set. East Conference Applauds: Rev. Dr. Buckley Declares the Professor's Accuser Liable to Prosecution in Courts," *New York Times*, April 9 1904. For a detailed account of the trial, see George Elliott, "Orthodoxy of Bowne," *Methodist Review* 105, no. 3 (May 1922): 399–413. Most of that issue of the *Methodist Review* is dedicated to Bowne. Even before that issue, Bowne had been the subject of three appreciations, contributed sixteen articles, and been the recipient of nine book reviews in the *Methodist Review*.

64. McCabe, *Divine Nescience of Future Contingencies*, 284. McCabe distinguishes the necessities associated with God's subjective life from the contingencies associated with God's objective life. "It is this constant binding up of necessities with contingencies that forms the great source of confusion in theology and philosophy. How much wiser, therefore, would it be to keep these incompatible things separate and distinct in all our contemplations of God?" Ibid., 285. McCabe quotes Isaak Dorner for support: "From his internal absoluteness, which elevates his being above extension and succession, God cannot decline. But if he cause a world to exist it is a logical necessity that he have a positive relation to time and space.... God cannot have an eternally similar relation to past, present, and future time. If to him longer and shorter durations are equivalent; if relative to him one thing is not past and another present and another future, but every thing collapses into one point of the present, then history is a mere semblance devoid of results.... He wills every thing in its season. Were God free from time and raised above time, he really would not be free. He possesses not only a transcendent existence in himself, but a transitive existence, an immanence in the world. He lives not merely an eternal life of love in himself, but a temporal becoming of his self-communication takes place." *A System of Christian Doctrine*, trans. Alfred Cave (Edinburgh: T&T Clark, 1880). This distinction is close to the one Augustine makes between the immanent and economic Trinity (see note above on p. 24). The difference is that for Augustine, in the economic Trinity, God doesn't have a transitive existence in the world, because that would involve change. For Augustine, the "energies of divine operations" flow from God in one direction so God remains unchanged. Dorner challenges Augustine at this point: "If, according to Augustine, God sees the past and the future as present, he would not see them as they are, and therefore he would not see them truthfully. There must be movement in the divine knowledge.... There are things which are not the effects of the divine will.... There is a mutation in the divine consciousness, and this mutation is reflected into the divine will." Quoted by McCabe, *Divine Nescience of Future Contingencies*, 287. Dorner in this passage at one point seems to been affirming exhaustive divine control ("He wills every thing in its season") but later in the same passage he clarifies that not everything that happens is God's will ("There are things which are not the effects of the divine will") so the first phrase must mean that God wills that things in general happen in their appropriate time, i.e. in a sequence, not all at once.

65. McCabe again quoting Borden Parker Bowne: "'A being which is in full possession of itself, so that it does not come to itself successively, would not be in time. Such a being can be conceived

true.[66] In the concluding paragraph of the chapter, he passes the tipping point, and ultimately rejects the B-theory of time and the associated language of the eternal now of God.[67]

In chapter sixteen, McCabe sums up by citing support for his view of divine nescience. He also addresses Isaak Dorner's momentary self-contradiction where he says that God could not limit himself in order to make space for human freedom because it might mean that his plan for the world could fail.[68] McCabe responds that Dorner's position would be more self-consistent if he allowed God to be sufficiently resourceful to accomplish his will, even when particular free agents cannot do their part.[69] McCabe concludes by advocating divine nescience of future contingencies as the cornerstone of theology.[70] He suggests this internally consistent and robust theology will lead to a unity and

---

as having a changeless knowledge and a changeless life. As such it would be without memory and without expectation, but would be in the absolute enjoyment of itself. For such a being the present alone would exist, and its *now* would be eternal. For those who can see the Infinite as such a being, the Infinite must have a strictly non-temporal existence. All change in the Infinite, as thus conceived, would not be a succession of different states, but a ceaseless conservation of the same state. There would be neither past nor future, but an abiding present.'" McCabe, *Divine Nescience of Future Contingencies*, 283.

66. "In God's subjective nature his consciousness may not be a process of becoming and of passing away. This view may be necessary to maintain his subjective absoluteness. But, then, God must have an objective life in the vast world of contingencies. And in that life there may be in his consciousness a becoming and a passing away without in the least affecting his subjective absoluteness." Ibid., quoting himself in *The Foreknowledge of God*, 259.

67. This is demonstrated in the passage already quoted above at p. 63 (emphasis added): "Deny the reality of time; *chain me in a duration-less eternal now*; rob God of all change; congeal him into the iceberg of indifference which prescience necessitates; prohibit him from changing in his feelings toward me, when from obduracy I turn and break in penitence at his feet; forbid him sympathizing with me in the perplexities of my way, and in the tragedies of my probation; and deny to him the interest, sympathy, and tenderness which alone can be born from a future unfixed and uncertain both for him and for me; and you fill my Bible with obscurity, my theology with paralyzing doubts, and you wrap in distressing gloom the glorious cross of Jesus Christ." McCabe, *Divine Nescience of Future Contingencies*, 289.

68. Ibid., 295.

69. Ibid., 294.

70. "The great thought which is here so confidently advocated, that of divine nescience of future contingencies, I am persuaded will ultimately be found to be the principle of unity which stands visibly, forcibly and lovingly related to all other truths of divine revelation. The incognoscibility of future contingencies is the central principle which illumes all Scripture with the morning stars of consistency, reasonableness and inspiration. It illumes, becalms and unifies all theological truths. It expels from theology all irritating dogmas and absurdities." Ibid., 301.

zeal in Christian mission in the world.[71] It could be that some open theists harbor this hope.

In summary, this section has highlighted Lorenzo Dow McCabe as a remarkable Methodist scholar in the eighteenth century. If the road from Wesley to open theism is thought of as a bridge, we can see McCabe as the central pillar supporting the structure.[72] McCabe, while thoroughly loyal to Wesley, makes a strong case for making modifications in his theological thought that would make it more self-consistent and a further departure from the Calvinist/Augustinian system. He realized that if God knows exhaustively all future events, then nothing can change, and we must live in a deterministic universe. However, if God does *not* know in advance which possible future events actually will transpire, some significant theological problems melt away. For example, God can genuinely make conditional promises and prophecies, as we see so often in the Old Testament. McCabe also saw that it does no good to say that God knows the future because he knows how we will choose. If that were the case, the future cannot be any other way than God has foreseen it and so choice is illusory. Further, by giving up exhaustive divine foreknowledge, McCabe helps with theodicy. If God does not know with certainty in advance, the choices that humans and spirit beings will make, it is more understandable why he doesn't act more often to prevent evils from occurring. Last, McCabe contributes significantly in an open theist direction by showing why the theory of divine timelessness undermines the biblical self-revelation of God. God must be in time in order to be in a loving relationship with us.

---

71. "But what do I see when Christendom agrees upon a corner-stone for the doctrines of Christianity which will necessitate no self-contradictions in our thinking, and no paralyses in our strivings to obey? I see a union of Christian effort in all the great world-reformations germane to the Church universal. I see a hearty co-operation of all Christians in the work of sound secular education, a work in every way inconceivable in its importance to the progress of humanity.... I see harmony reigning throughout all the branches of the true Church of Christ; each provoking all others to good works; all concentrating efforts in unselfish zeal wherever God is pouring out his Holy Spirit of awakening... co-operating in missionary operations in heathen climes, impressing profoundly the heathen world that Christianity has but one Lord, one faith, one baptism, one soul and one devout object—the present and eternal salvation of the human family." Ibid., 302–03.

72. Randy Maddox provides context and describes some of the responses to McCabe. "Seeking a Response-able God: The Wesleyan Tradition and Process Theology," in *Thy Nature and Thy Name Is Love: Wesleyan and Process Theologies in Dialogue*, ed. Bryan P. Stone and Thomas Jay Oord (Nashville: Kingswood, 2001), 131–36.

3. John Wesley and Politico-economic Power

Beyond the issue of the nature of time, another factor might obscure the perception of Wesley as a precursor of open theism. On the surface, it would appear that Wesley does not provide a precedent for certain expressions of open theism that are cautious about political and economic power, viewing them as counterproductive to living out the love ethic of Jesus.[73] This hesitation comes out of open theism's emphasis on divine love and the human freedom that is necessary to reciprocate it. Attempts to use political or economic power to coerce behavior consistent with the kingdom of God are not consistent with open theist views and Jesus' teaching.

Wesley, however, was remarkably loyal to both the monarchy and the Church of England. It is surprising Methodism thrived in America given Wesley's disapproval of the revolution. But Wesley's loyalty to the crown comes out of an appreciation for the freedom which he enjoyed in his context. We might draw an analogy with how the apostle Paul could take advantage of his rights as a Roman citizen. Wesley appreciated the opportunity to travel and preach throughout the realm and not be hindered by the civil strife of the previous century. He was not blind to the shortcomings of certain monarchs, but could use the legal and political systems to his advantage.

Where Wesley provides an antecedent to an open theistic economic-political analysis is in economics. He expected Methodist societies to be so oriented to helping the poor that entire communities would be radically changed. For him, it was an aspect of reflecting God's love into the world, and this is where the connection to open theism can be made.

4. John Wesley's View of Providence

Another way in which Wesley's thought does not seem to be pointed toward open theism is his view of providence. He comes right up to the precipice of saying God controls everything. He can say, "God orders all things: he makes

---

73. Open theism may not be initially associated with socio-economic or political issues but once God has been described as non-coercive and altogether loving, certain implications follow for how his emulators live their lives and make decisions. For example, Gregory A. Boyd, *The Myth of a Christian Religion: Losing Your Religion for the Beauty of a Revolution* (Grand Rapids: Zondervan, 2009).

the sun shine, and the wind blow, and the trees bear fruit. Nothing comes by chance: that is a silly word: there is no such thing as chance."[74] In saying God "orders" all things, from his examples he is not quite saying God "controls" all things. It is more like God is preparing the scene for the action to take place—providing a field, a ball, and a structured game for soccer players. He is not determining who wins the game.

The text where Wesley comes closest to inferring that God controls everything that happens is where he quotes Matthew 10:29–30 from the KJV: "Had he not himself told us so, we should not have dared to think that 'not a sparrow falleth to the ground' without the 'will of our Father which is in heaven'; and much less affirm that 'even the very hairs of our head are all numbered!'"[75] The Greek text reads, "οὐχὶ δύο στρουθία ἀσσαρίου πωλεῖται; καὶ ἓν ἐξ αὐτῶν οὐ πεσεῖται ἐπὶ τὴν γῆν ἄνευ τοῦ πατρὸς ὑμῶν. ὑμῶν δὲ καὶ αἱ τρίχες τῆς κεφαλῆς πᾶσαι ἠριθμημέναι εἰσίν." The KJV does Wesley a disservice here by inserting the word 'will'—the word is absent from the Greek—and quite changing the meaning of the passage. It just says the sparrow does not fall to the ground "without the Father." It is saying, God is there. In both the preceding and following verse, Jesus says, "Do not fear"—his point is to dispel fear and reassure of God's concern and presence. The passage does not say that God willed the sparrow to fall. Therefore, Wesley is pulled back from the precipice of saying that God controls everything that happens.

Wesley specifically denies that God treats humans as wooden puppets but as intelligent beings with real freedom:

> Whereas all the manifold wisdom of God (as well as all his power and goodness) is displayed in governing man as man; not as a stock or a stone, but as an intelligent and free spirit, capable of choosing either good or evil. Herein appears the depth of the wisdom of God in his adorable understanding, will, or liberty![76]

---

74. Sermon 95: "On the Education of Children" [1783] in Wesley, *Sermons III*, 353.
75. Sermon 118: "On the Omnipresence of God" [1788] in Wesley, *Sermons IV*, 43.
76. Sermon 67: "On Divine Providence" [1786] in Wesley, *Sermons II*, 541.

II. WESLEY AND RENEWAL & OPEN THEIST PARADIGMS

Because he is sensitive to the freedom of individuals to choose for or against God, Wesley chooses his language carefully when talking about God's providence. He prefers the language of 'governing', 'superintending' and 'influencing'. God is not determining every detail.

> God acts in heaven, in earth, and under the earth, throughout the whole compass of his creation; by sustaining all things, without which everything would in an instant sink into its primitive nothing; by governing all, every moment superintending everything that he has made; strongly and sweetly influencing all, and yet without destroying the liberty of his rational creatures.[77]

Similarly:

> On the contrary, we have the fullest evidence that the eternal, omnipresent, almighty, all-wise Spirit, as he created all things, so he continually superintends whatever he has created.... He governs all, not only to the bounds of creation, but through the utmost extent of space; and not only through the short time that is measured by the earth and sun, but from everlasting to everlasting.[78]

Wesley is reacting to deism which has God setting the world in motion but then leaving everything to "take its own course." There is no hint here of a predetermined future, or a future known exhaustively in advance. Clearly when he says God "governs" and "influences," Wesley is allowing significant room for human freedom and, in so doing, prepares for the view that the future is partially open and, to some degree, determined by human choices.

---

77. Sermon 118: "On the Omnipresence of God" [1788] in Wesley, *Sermons IV*, 42.
78. Sermon 120: "The Unity of the Divine Being" [1789] in ibid., 67.

B. PROTO-PENTECOSTAL/CHARISMATIC CONSIDERATIONS

1. John Wesley and Manifestations of the Holy Spirit

If we only had the early Wesley, we would be hard pressed to see a trajectory toward pentecostalism. For someone who is going to be so influential in the prehistory of the pentecostal movement, it comes as a bit of a surprise to hear the early John Wesley in Sermon 4: "Scriptural Christianity" (1744) talk about spiritual gifts. He is noncommittal whether the "extraordinary gifts of the Holy Ghost" were designed "to remain in the church throughout the ages" or whether they would be "restored at the nearer approach of the 'restitution of all things.'" Even in the early church, he thinks they were given sparingly. "Perhaps not one in a thousand" spoke in tongues or manifested the extraordinary gifts of the Spirit.[79]

Rather, Wesley wishes to emphasize the ordinary fruits of the Spirit as evidence of the infilling of the Spirit. Being filled with love, joy, peace, patience, gentleness, goodness, fidelity, meekness, and temperance produces an "inward change" that fulfills all "outward righteousness."[80] Wesley's interpretation here of being filled with the Spirit (Acts 4:31) is consistent with his sustained interest in sanctification—seeing a real transformation in the interior life of the believer which produces a change in outward actions. The change doesn't come with sweaty human moral effort, but through a cooperation between the believer and the Spirit. The Spirit produces the life of God in the believer. As we shall see in Chapter IV (p. 131), this emphasis on sanctification was a significant feature of early pentecostalism, and I'll include it in Chapter V (p. 167) as an element of an open theist renewal theology.

But the later Wesley is warmer to the charismatic gifts. In Sermon 89: "The More Excellent Way," (1787) he denies that they almost ceased because the world had been Christianized so they were no longer needed as had been "vulgarly supposed." Referring to the extraordinary gifts of the Holy

---

79. Sermon 4: "Scriptural Christianity" [1744] in Wesley, *Sermons I*, 60.
80. Ibid., 160–61.

Spirit (i.e. healing, prophesying, speaking in tongues, and interpretation) he says, "We seldom hear of them after that fatal period when the Emperor Constantine called himself a Christian, and from a vain imagination of promoting the Christian cause thereby heaped riches, and power, and honour, upon the Christians in the general; but in particular upon the Christian clergy."[81] Wesley says the gifts almost dried up because the love of Christians "waxed cold."[82] He continues, "This was the real cause why the extraordinary gifts of the Holy Ghost were no longer to be found in the Christian church—because the Christians were turned heathens again, and had only a dead form left."[83]

Several things are of interest here. First, he opposes Augustine's view that the patronage of the emperor was a good thing for the Christian church. It indicates Wesley's willingness to resist the church father where he believes him to be in the wrong. Second, he allows the gifts were "common" in the first two or three centuries, especially among teachers. This perceived frequency of their occurrence represents a change from the "sparing" in Sermon 4 (from 1744). Third, he locates the lack of spiritual gifts not in Jesus' unwillingness to dispense them but in human disinterest in things related to the Holy Spirit. This reasoning is incredibly significant because it suggests the possibility of creating favorable conditions for an outpouring of the Holy Spirit and his gifts through fervent prayer and love. This expectation of the Spirit to be active where willing prayerful human partners are found can be seen as part of a beginning of a trajectory to the holiness movement with its camp meetings and the pentecostal movement with its prayer meetings.

Manifestations of a distinctly supernatural character that would later also be found in pentecostalism were seen occasionally in Wesley's own ministry.[84] Daniel Jennings lists seventeen incidents involving spiritual warfare,

---

81. Sermon 89: "The More Excellent Way" [1787] in Wesley, *Sermons III*, 263.

82. Ibid., 264.

83. Ibid., 3:264.

84. Wesley also reports approvingly of people getting slain in the Spirit at the preaching of Whitefield. Whitefield and Wesley had just returned from Baptist Mills where Whitefield preached on the Holy Spirit. Wesley writes, "I had an opportunity to talk with him of those outward signs which had so often accompanied the inward work of God. I found his objections were chiefly grounded on gross misrepresentations of matter of fact. But the next day he had an opportunity of

sixteen miraculous healings (both people and horses), five occasions of an individual and twelve occasions of multiple people being slain in the Spirit, experiences of holy laughter (both genuine and demonic), fourteen accounts of unusual manifestations of the Holy Spirit, encounters with both genuine and false prophecy, thirty accounts of people having visions and dreams, some supernatural answers to prayer, and other experiences which Wesley interpreted as divinely guided.[85]

One incident can serve as a sign of how Wesley responded to these events. On April 30, 1739, he wrote from Bristol to James Hutton. He recounts how four days previously he had been preaching at Newgate. He gave out the text then invited God to confirm the preaching of the word with signs following.[86]

> Immediately the power of God fell upon us: one, and another, and another sunk to the earth; you might see them dropping on all sides as thunder-struck. One cried out aloud. I went and prayed over her, and she received joy in the Holy Ghost. A second falling into the same agony, we turned to her, and received for her also the promise of the Father. In the evening I made the same appeal to God, and almost before we called He answered.

The evidence is that John Wesley was remarkably bold in asking God for manifestations of the Holy Spirit and his power. He didn't just tolerate dramatic physical and verbal reactions to his preaching. He actively asked God

---

informing himself better. For no sooner had he begun (in the application of his sermon) to invite all sinners to believe in Christ, than four persons sunk down close to him, almost in the same moment. One of them lay without either sense or motion. A second trembled exceedingly. The third had strong convulsions all over his body but made no noise, unless by groans. The fourth, equally convulsed, called upon God with strong cries and tears. From this time, I trust, we shall all suffer God to carry on his own work in the way that pleaseth him." Entry for Saturday, July 7, 1739 in *Journal and Diaries*, 19:78–79.

85. Daniel R. Jennings, *The Supernatural Occurrences of John Wesley* (Oklahoma City, Okla.: Sean Multimedia, 2005, 2012).

86. The predestination controversy with Whitefield was heating up. "Thursday, 26th, preaching at Newgate on those words, 'He that believeth hath everlasting life,' I was led, I know not how, to speak strongly and explicitly of Predestination, and then to pray 'that if I spake not the truth of God, He would stay His hand, and work no more among us. If this was His truth, He would not delay to confirm it by signs following.'"

for signs following and believed he was answered when he saw people fall under the Holy Spirit's power.

2. The Maxfield–Bell Crisis

Considering Wesley as a source of twentieth and twenty-first century pentecostalism, it is instructive to look in some detail at his relationship to a charismatic revival in his own day, one led by Thomas Maxfield, George Bell, and others.[87] One can get the impression from some writers that he had grave misgivings about the entire episode and by implication the modern pentecostal movement. A sympathetic re-reading of the accounts leaves a different impression.

Thomas Maxfield had a powerful conversion experience when Wesley preached in Bristol, his hometown, in 1739.[88] Maxfield travelled with Charles Wesley for a year or two as he visited the societies. In the summer of 1739, Charles wrote to his brother John saying that the Moravians thought Maxfield was the only thing standing in the way of Charles's "conversion to stillness," a sign of Maxfield's influence even a year after his conversion.[89] John Wesley asked Maxfield to lead the prayers of the society at the Foundry, his London headquarters, while he was traveling. Maxfield, although not ordained, felt led to go beyond what was asked and began to preach. Many in attendance approved, including Susanna Wesley and Lady Huntingdon—who may have been an instigator.[90] John, perturbed by a complaint he had received of the unauthorized preaching by a lay person, returned to London and expressed his

---

87. Dayton, *Theological Roots of Pentecostalism*.

88. Richard P. Heitzenrater, *Wesley and the People Called Methodists* (Nashville: Abingdon, 1995), 115. Maxfield would later say he was converted under Whitefield's preaching earlier that same year.

89. Ibid. The Moravians of the Fetter Lane society had drifted into a quietism that opposed external activity. Wesley's opposition to it led to a severance from that society and his moving to the Foundry.

90. She wrote to Wesley, probably in 1741, "I never mentioned to you, that I have seen Maxfield. He is one of the greatest instances of God's peculiar favour, that I know.... How is God's power shewn in weakness. You can have no idea, what an attachment I have to him. He is highly favoured of the Lord. The first time I made him expound, expecting little from him, I sat over against him, and thought, what a power of God must be with him, to make me give any attention to him.... His power in prayer is very extraordinary." Quoted in Frank Baker, "Thomas Maxfield's First Sermon," *Proceedings of the Wesley Historical Society* 27, no. 1 (March 1949): 8–9.

dissatisfaction to his mother. Her response was, "Take care what you do with respect to that young man, for he is as surely called of God to preach, as you are. Examine what have been the fruits of his preaching, and hear him also for yourself."[91] Henry Moore, an early Wesley biographer, continues, "He did so. His prejudice bowed before the force of truth, and he could only say, 'It is the Lord: let him do what seemeth him good.'"[92] Maxfield thus became the first lay preacher for whom Wesley was solely responsible.[93] Wesley allowed this development reluctantly, out of a need for preachers and a recognition of Maxfield's gifts, but was conflicted by his high church sensibilities.[94] Twenty years later, Maxfield's willingness to go beyond what Wesley was comfortable with would again become evident.[95]

George Bell had been a Corporal in the King's Life-Guards.[96] He was converted in 1758 and became a friend of Thomas Maxfield. He also preached at the Foundry on occasion.

Bell developed a reputation as an extreme enthusiast.[97] 'Enthusiasm' was used pejoratively. Samuel Johnson's 1755 *Dictionary of the English Language* defines it in this way: "Enthusiasm is (a) A vain belief of private revelation; a vain confidence of divine favour; (b) Heat of imagination, violence of

---

91. Heitzenrater, *Wesley and the People Called Methodists*, 115. Heitzenrater is quoting Baker, "Thomas Maxfield's First Sermon," 8. Baker in turn quotes Henry Moore, *The Life of the Rev. John Wesley, A.M., Fellow of Lincoln College, Oxford; in Which Are Included, the Life of His Brother, the Rev. Charles Wesley, A.M., Student of Christ Church, and Memoirs of Their Family: Comprehending an Account of the Great Revival of Religion, in Which They Were the First and Chief Instruments* (London: J. Kershaw, 1824), 506.

92. Moore, *Life of the Rev. John Wesley*, 8.

93. Ibid., 7. Previously, John Cennick, a Moravian who later allied with the Calvinistic Methodists, had preached for Wesley in Bristol in 1739. Joseph Humphreys with Whitefield's recommendation had begun to preach at the Foundry in September of 1740 but remained aligned with Whitefield.

94. Ibid., 8.

95. In the meantime, John Wesley's journal entry for June 19, 1745, describes in some detail how Maxfield had been press-ganged and Wesley's attempts to use the legal system to get him freed. But for a sympathetic warrant server (Mr. Eustick), Wesley would have been conscripted himself. Eustick seems to have procrastinated in delivering Wesley until a time the magistrate would be absent (he was at church,) and so executing the summons in a way that Wesley was free to go. Wesley, *Journal and Diaries*, 20:69–70.

96. Kenneth G. C. Newport, "George Bell, Prophet and Enthusiast," *Methodist History* 35, no. 2 (January 1997): 95.

97. Ibid., 96.

passion; (c) Elevation of fancy, exaltation of ideas."[98] Published critiques of Methodism in the eighteenth century clustered around three issues: "enthusiasm, anti-clericalism and doctrinal divergence."[99] The prominence of this theme in the anti-Methodist rhetoric suggests that Bell was not an aberration but part of a noticeable segment of the Methodist revival. A decade before, in 1750, Wesley had preached and later published in 1755 a sermon on enthusiasm.[100] "Wesley turned the tables on his critics, so to speak, in this sermon by arguing that enthusiasm or fanaticism, rightly understood, is the heady false confidence that emerges among those 'who imagine they have the grace which they have not.'"[101] He also warned against a second enthusiasm where people think they have gifts from God which they do not. He ends with an encouragement to grow and seek God's gifts:

> Use every means which either reason or Scripture recommends as conducive (through the free love of God in Christ) either to the obtaining or increasing any of the gifts of God. Thus expect a daily growth in that pure and holy religion which the world always did, and always will, call enthusiasm; but which to all who are saved from real enthusiasm—from merely nominal Christianity—is the wisdom and God and the power of God, the glorious image of the Most High, righteousness and peace, a fountain of living water, springing up into everlasting life![102]

The term 'enthusiast' at the time may have been derisive but a re-reading of the source materials from a renewalist perspective produces a more

---

98. Susan I. Tucker, *Enthusiasm, A Study in Semantic Change* (Cambridge: Cambridge University Press, 1972), 33ff.

99. W. Stephen Gunter, *The Limits of 'Love Divine': John Wesley's Response to Antinomianism and Enthusiasm* (Nashville: Kingswood, 1989), 267.

100. Sermon 37: "The Nature of Enthusiasm" [1750] in Wesley, *Sermons II*, 44–60.

101. *The Sermons of John Wesley: A Collection for the Christian Journey*, ed. Kenneth J. Collins and Jason Vickers (Nashville: Abingdon, 2013), 214. The sermon quote is from Wesley, *Sermons II*, 50.

102. Wesley, *Sermons II*, 59–60. He argues similarly in Sermon 119: "Walking by Sight and Walking by Faith" [1788] in Wesley, *Sermons IV*, 57–58.

sympathetic interpretation. Even Stephen Gunter, who is trying to counter a hagiographic approach to Wesley, can put a favorable spin on the term. He concedes it "was specifically applied to the Methodists because of their claims to extraordinary communications from the Holy Spirit, special vocation and spiritual accomplishments, unusual piety and distinctive doctrinal emphases."[103] Although there are differences in the details, it just doesn't sound that different from renewal movements in the twentieth and twenty-first centuries.

George Bell was fervent in prayer, sought to exercise a prophetic gift, encouraged speaking in tongues, had a healing ministry, and even attempted to raise the dead.[104] There were, however, some elements of his theology which were problematic. He and Maxfield took Wesley's teaching on sanctification in a perfectionistic direction, claiming a sinlessness that Wesley never intended when he advocated "Christian perfection."[105] Bell read the Book of

---

103. Gunter, *The Limits of 'Love Divine'*, 267. Gunter also clarifies how Wesley himself could be considered an enthusiast: "Wesley wanted to have it both ways. He did not wish to be identified with the typical enthusiasts who were viewed as 'religious madmen.' Those people were deluded and deceived; they were worse than fools. 'Proper enthusiasts' deprecated reason to such an extent that they simplistically ran into excesses with which Wesley wished to have no part. However, Wesley did want to maintain the essential concepts usually identified with 'proper enthusiasm,' namely, instantaneous conversion, the direct witness of the Spirit, and experiential proof of conversion. The crucial difference was that whereas 'proper enthusiasts' maintained these concepts in an 'unreasonable' manner, Wesley proposed a more respectable form of 'reasonable enthusiasm,' namely, an 'improper enthusiasm' based on revelation but guided by the proper application of reason.... It was the proper application of this concept of reason which Wesley felt justified his position on 'improper enthusiasm,' despite his conforming to the majority of headings in Johnson's definition of 'proper enthusiasm.'" ibid., 136.

104. Newport, "George Bell, Prophet and Enthusiast," 101.

105. Ibid., 96. Albert Outler summarizes: "A Christian might be endued, by grace, with the power not to sin willfully—which is all Wesley ever really claimed for his doctrine of perfection." Wesley, *Sermons I*, 65. As Wesley put it, "Christian perfection therefore does not imply (as some men seem to have imagined) an exemption either from ignorance or mistake, or infirmities or temptations. Indeed, it is only another term for holiness. They are two names for the same thing." Sermon 40: "Christian Perfection" [1741] in Wesley, *Sermons II*, 104. Vinson Synan adds, "The perfection Wesley taught was a perfection of motives and desires. Total 'sinless perfection' would come only after death. In the meantime the sanctified soul, through careful self-examination, godly discipline, and methodical devotion and avoidance of worldly pleasures, could have a life of victory over sin. This perfection, Wesley taught, could be attained instantly as a 'second work of grace' although it was usually preceded and followed by a gradual 'growth in grace.'" *The Holiness-Pentecostal Tradition: Charismatic Movements in the Twentieth Century*, 2nd ed. (Grand Rapids: Eerdmans, 1997), 6–7. Wesley's letter to Dorothy Furly of September 15, 1762 from St. Ives is perceptive: "I want you to be all love. This is the perfection I believe and teach. And this perfection is consistent with a thousand nervous disorders, which that high-strained perfection is not. Indeed, my judgement is that (in this case particularly) to overdo is to undo, and that to set

Revelation in a way that gave it a contemporary fulfillment. This led to him setting a date for the end of the world. Kenneth Newport observes that committing to a specific date was not only a factual but a strategic mistake; it gave Bell's opponents an opportunity to discredit him decisively.[106]

By 1762, Bell was co-leading large meetings with Maxfield in London's Beech Lane.[107] In December of that year, Wesley heard Bell again and concluded that he could no longer be permitted to pray or speak at the Foundry.[108] But Wesley still did not break off fellowship and was criticized for acting too indecisively. Maxfield and Bell chose to leave the Society with a small group of others before February 8, 1763.[109] This was about three weeks before the February 28, 1763 date that Bell had set as the end of the world.

Wesley's specific concerns with the Maxfield–Bell situation are revealing. He didn't dismiss out of hand the proto-pentecostal impulses or expel those who were seeking experiences with the Holy Spirit. After all, when later forming the Methodists into a denomination in the United States, Wesley's ideal was the primitive church immediately after Pentecost.[110] In dealing with Maxfield and Bell, Wesley seemed more interested in quality control and using common sense to prevent excesses rather than making a theological issue of seeking manifestations of the Holy Spirit.[111]

---

perfection too high (so high as no man that we ever heard or read of attained) is the most effectual (because unsuspected) way of driving it out of the world."

106. Newport, "George Bell, Prophet and Enthusiast," 103.

107. Ibid., 97.

108. Ibid., 99. See Wesley's journal entry for December 26, 1762, *Journal and Diaries*, 21:400–01. Wesley's early biographer Robert Southey quotes Wesley on December 26, 1760 [although he omits the source of the publication and it does not appear to be the *Journal* or the *Letters*] affirming that Mary Special had been instantaneously healed of pain and lumps in her breasts when Bell prayed for her. *Life of Wesley*, 153. In Wesley's view, Bell's gift of healing was genuine, but his false prophecy and teaching were problematic.

109. John's letter to Charles of February 8, 1763, reports that Maxfield refuses to come up to see him. John relays the substance of Maxfield's reply to his request as, "You take too much upon you. We *will not* come up."

110. Wood, *The Meaning of Pentecost in Early Methodism*, 174. Sermon 102: "Of Former Times" [1787] in Wesley, *Sermons III*, 448.

111. Judging by the change of tone in his letters, Wesley was wounded by the defection of Maxfield and Bell and by the criticism of colleagues Whitefield, Madan, Haweis, and Berridge concerning his open-minded response to the crisis. In a letter to Lady Huntingdon after the fact he writes, "As to the prophecies of those poor, wild men, George Bell and half a dozen more, I

A couple of months before the break, on November 2, 1762, Wesley wrote a letter to Maxfield clearly detailing his concerns. He lays them out in three sections: doctrine, spirit, and outward behavior. In each section, he first affirms what is good in the Maxfield–Bell approach. The doctrinal issues are unrelated to prophecy and charismatic emphases but center on the nature of sanctification. Wesley begins, "I like your doctrine of Perfection, or pure love; love excluding sin; your insisting that it is merely by faith; that consequently it is instantaneous (though preceded and followed by a gradual work), and that it may be now, at this instant." Then he has five rebukes. (1) Maxfield's definition of perfection goes too far, saying a person can be not just free from willful sin but absolutely perfect, infallible and beyond temptation. Maxfield claims "the moment he is pure in heart he cannot fall from it." Wesley would affirm, by contrast, that in this lifetime we never lose our need for forgiveness for unintentional and negligent sins. (2) Maxfield is claiming that the discovery of sanctification is only two or three years old (when it became real

---

am not a jot more accountable for them than Mr. Whitefield is; having never countenanced them in any degree, but opposed them from the moment I heard them. Neither have these extravagances any foundation in any doctrine which I teach." (Letter of John Wesley to the Countess of Huntingdon undated but marked "Received at Brighthelmstone, March 21, 1763." *Letters of John Wesley*, 4:205–06.)

The letter to Lady Huntingdon needs to be read alongside the one Wesley had written two months prior to the newspaper to voice his objection to Bell's prophecy: To the Editor of the *London Chronicle* from Windmill Hill, January 7, 1763. "Sir,—When I returned to London two or three months ago, I received various accounts of some meetings for prayer which had lately been held by Mr. Bell and a few others. But these accounts were contradictory to each other. Some highly applauded them, others utterly condemned; some affirmed they had done much good, others that they had done much hurt. This convinced me it was requisite to proceed with caution and do nothing rashly. The first point was to form my own judgement, and that upon the fullest evidence. To this end I first talked with Mr. Bell himself, whom I knew to be an honest, well-meaning man. Next I told him they were at liberty for a few times to meet under my roof. They did so, both in the Society room at the Foundery and in the chapel at West Street. By this means I had an opportunity of hearing them myself, which I did at both places. I was present the next meeting after that, which is mentioned by Mr. Dodd and Mr. Thompson in the *Public Ledger*. The same things which they blame I blame also; and so I told him the same evening: and I was in hopes they would be done away, which occasioned my waiting till this time. But, having now lost that hope, I have given orders that they shall meet under my roof no more. What farther steps it will be necessary for me to take is a point I have not yet determined.—I am, sir, Your humble servant." Ibid., 4:200. The *London Chronicle* letter (the facts of which would likely have been known to Lady Huntingdon) indicates that Wesley was not at all distant from Bell, even to the extent of providing him a venue. Describing him as an "honest, well-meaning man" rather than a fanatic demonstrates how gentle was Wesley's approach to the crisis. Certainly, his accountability for Bell ended when he left the Society, but his attempts to personally dissuade Bell suggest he earlier did feel a sense of responsibility.

to him), while the Wesley brothers have been teaching it for twenty years. Wesley says, "I dislike the saying, 'This was not known or taught among us till within two or three years.' I grant you did not know it. You have over and over denied instantaneous sanctification to me." Wesley is concerned about this because Maxfield is undermining his teaching and authority. Wesley's intuition on this was borne out a few months later when people in Society meetings dismissed his teaching on sanctification as inadequate in comparison with Maxfield's. Wesley thought setting the bar too high made holiness unattainable for anyone except Jesus, thus making sanctification a purely theoretical teaching rather than a lived experience. (3) Maxfield was teaching that only fully sanctified individuals were saved. Wesley's response is, "I dislike your directly or indirectly depreciating justification, saying a justified person is not in Christ, is not born of God, is not a new creature, has not a new heart, is not sanctified, not a temple of the Holy Ghost, or that he cannot please God or cannot grow in grace." Wesley's issue here is that Maxfield was collapsing the *ordo salutis* in a problematic way.[112] (4) The fourth critique is, "I dislike your saying that one saved from sin needs nothing more than looking to Jesus; needs not to hear or think of anything else; believe, believe is enough; that he needs no self-examination, no times of private prayer; needs not mind little or outward things; and that he cannot be taught by any person who is not in the same state." Wesley thinks that naked faith is not enough for the sanctified believer, but that continued growth in the capacity to love requires the spiritual disciplines. Further, not being willing to learn from others who don't happen to hold precisely the same views lacks humility and leads to an unhealthy narrowness of thought. (5) The fifth point concerns their defensive attitude

---

112. Kenneth J. Collins, "A Hermeneutical Model for the Wesleyan *Ordo Salutis*," *Wesleyan Theological Journal* 19, no. 2 (Fall 1984): 23–37. Collins emphasizes that justification and sanctification are processes with a parallel structure, both dependent on faith. In simplified form, Wesley's *ordo salutis* involves prevenient grace, i.e. the Holy Spirit working to make faith possible, conversion/justification, sanctification, and restoration. Albert Outler goes into a little more detail: "The order of salvation, as Wesley had come to see it, is an organic continuum: conscience, conviction of sin, repentance, reconciliation, regeneration, sanctification, glorification. All of these are progressive stages in the divine design to restore the image of God in human selves and society." Wesley, *Sermons I*, 80. Theodore Runyon concurs: "Justification and regeneration inaugurate a process of sanctification, the aim of which is the full restoration of the image of God in humanity." *The New Creation: John Wesley's Theology Today* (Nashville, Tenn.: Abingdon, 1998), 57.

towards people who teach different versions of sanctification. "I dislike your affirming that justified persons in general persecute them that are saved from sin; that they have persecuted you on this account; and that for two years past you have been more persecuted by the two brothers than ever you was by the world in all your life." Maxfield seems to have felt persecuted by John and Charles Wesley and others who while justified didn't claim to be free from sin without qualification.[113] This point leads to Wesley's next section.

In the second section of Wesley's letter on November 2, 1762, to Maxfield, the focus is on his attitudes. Again, Wesley begins with an affirmation: "As to your spirit, I like your confidence in God and your zeal for the salvation of souls." Then follows four rebukes. (1) The first concerns a lack of humility and sense of superiority over other Methodist preachers.[114] That attitude is corrosive to the camaraderie so essential to a voluntary organization. (2) The issue of enthusiasm is raised.[115] Wesley is concerned that feelings and "inward impressions" are being overvalued at the expense of "reason, knowledge, and wisdom." Wesley is not saying that trying to be sensitive to the leading of the Spirit is illegitimate, only that a balance is needed with rational thought. The part of the critique of enthusiasm with some bite is the one concerning discernment. They were "mistaking the mere work of imagination for the voice of the Spirit." Bell's false prophecy of the upcoming end of the world on February 28, 1763, may be in view but there could have been other instances as well. Wesley trusted the inner witness of the Spirit concerning

---

113. "As early as 1760, he encouraged 'the select band in London... who professed to be entirely sanctified,' who saw visions and 'began to have a contempt for those who had not.' At the conference of 1761 Maxfield silenced his accusers (Wesley, *Works*, iii. 120)." Gerald le Grys Norgate, "Maxfield, Thomas (d.1784)," in *Dictionary of National Biography*, Vol. 37 (London: Smith, Elder & Co., 1885–1900).

114. "But I dislike something which has the appearance of pride, of overvaluing yourselves and undervaluing others, particularly the preachers: thinking not only that they are blind and that they are not sent of God, but even that they are dead—dead to God, and walking in the way to hell; that they are going one way, you another; that they have no life in them. Your speaking of yourselves as though you were the only men who knew and taught the gospel; and as if not only all the clergy, but all the Methodists besides, were in utter darkness." Letter of John Wesley to Thomas Maxfield from Canterbury dated November 2, 1763, Wesley, *Letters of John Wesley*, 4:193.

115. "I dislike something that has the appearance of enthusiasm, overvaluing feelings and inward impressions: mistaking the mere work of imagination for the voice of the Spirit; expecting the end without the means; and undervaluing reason, knowledge, and wisdom in general." Ibid.

such claims and was getting no such confirmation. (3) Where God's grace is emphasized, antinomianism is a risk.[116] A concern for holiness and "tenderness of conscience" was being played off against faith. (4) Wesley's fourth and biggest attitudinal concern was lack of love for the brothers. Wesley could see it was leading to a separation from the Society.[117]

The third section of Wesley's letter to Maxfield on November 2, 1762, concerned behaviors. Once again, it began with an encouragement: "I like the general tenor of your life, devoted to God, and spent in doing good." Later he affirms, "As to your more public meetings, I like the praying fervently and largely for all the blessings of God; and I know much good has been done hereby, and hope much more will be done." He expresses a similar evaluation that much good had been done in the meetings in his letter to his brother Charles from London on December 11, 1762.[118] The concerns John mentions to Maxfield in the third section were numerous, though. The first several clustered around how meetings were conducted. (1) Wesley felt Maxfield was too indifferent to the rules of the Society which encouraged members to meet together regularly.[119] He was also concerned that Maxfield's frequent prayer meetings meant members had to neglect either work or attendance at

---

[116]. "I dislike something that has the appearance of Antinomianism, not magnifying the law and making it honourable; not enough valuing tenderness of conscience and exact watchfulness in order thereto; using faith rather as contradistinguished from holiness than as productive of it." Ibid.

[117]. "But what I most of all dislike is your littleness of love to your brethren, to your own Society; your want of union of heart with them and bowels of mercies toward them; your want of meekness, gentleness, longsuffering; your impatience of contradiction; your counting every man your enemy that reproves or admonishes you in love; your bigotry and narrowness of spirit, loving in a manner only those that love you; your censoriousness, proneness to think hardly of all who do not exactly agree with you: in one word, your divisive spirit. Indeed, I do not believe that any of you either design or desire a separation; but you do not enough fear, abhor, and detest it, shuddering at the very thought. And all the preceding tempers tend to it and gradually prepare you for it. Observe, I tell you before. God grant you may immediately and affectionately take the warning!" Ibid., 4:193–94.

[118]. "Examining the Society, I found about threescore persons who had been convinced of sin and near fourscore who were justified at these meetings. So that on the whole they have done some hurt and much good. I trust they will now do more good, and no hurt at all." Ibid., 4:196.

[119]. "But I dislike your slighting any, the very least rules of the bands or Society, and your doing anything that tends to hinder others from exactly observing them. Therefore—

"I dislike your appointing such meetings as hinder others from attending either the public preaching or their class or band, or any other meeting which the Rules of the Society or their office requires them to attend.

required band and society meetings. (2) In the more public meetings themselves, Wesley mentioned several points of protocol.[120] He disapproved of praying only to God the Son and neglecting the Father. He didn't care for more than one thing going on at a time (for example, several people speaking or praying at once). He objected to prayer being an occasion to magnify themselves instead of making their needs known to God. Then there a few stylistic objections: using "poor, flat, bald hymns," never kneeling for prayer, making inappropriate gestures, screaming in prayer to the point of not being understandable. (3) Wesley objects to a forerunner of "name it and claim it" theology.[121] Maxfield was trying to take on a performative role in justification and sanctification. Wesley wanted to see genuine faith by the recipient in response to the Holy Spirit and not just acquiescence to a preacher's exhortation. (4) Wesley dislikes Maxfield's lack of love, defensiveness, and his willingness to attack those who question his teachings.[122]

While Wesley raises significant concerns in this letter to Maxfield, it is important to notice what he does not say. There is no hint of cessationism in Wesley's comments. He affirms God is at work in the meetings. Wesley does not say it is inappropriate to pray for the fullness of the Spirit but affirms praying fervently for the blessing of God. Wesley raises no objection to the exercise of the more supernatural spiritual gifts. He requires careful discernment

---

"I dislike your spending so much time in several meetings, as many that attend can ill spare from the other duties of their calling, unless they omit either the preaching or their class or band. This naturally tends to dissolve our Society by cutting the sinews of it." Ibid., 4:194.

120. "(1) The singing or speaking or praying of several at once: (2) the praying to the Son of God only, or more than to the Father: (3) the using improper expressions in prayer; sometimes too bold, if not irreverent; sometimes too pompous and magnificent, extolling yourselves rather than God, and telling Him what you are, not what you want: (4) using poor, flat, bald hymns: (5) the never kneeling at prayer: (6) your using postures or gestures highly indecent: (7) your screaming, even so as to make the words unintelligible." Ibid.

121. By "name it and claim it" theology I'm referring to the version of the "prosperity gospel" popularized in the Word of Faith movement and the teaching of Kenneth E. Hagin and Kenneth Copeland. The basic idea is that health and wealth can be yours through positive confession. Wesley says, "(8) Your affirming people will be justified or sanctified just now: (9) the affirming they are when they are not: (10) the bidding them say, 'I believe.'" ibid.

122. "(11) The bitterly condemning any that oppose, calling them wolves, &c.; and pronouncing them hypocrites, or not justified." Ibid.

of prophecy through reason and inward witness and asks: Is what is being said indeed from God?

The Maxfield–Bell crisis provides a unique window on Wesley's relationship to charismatic communities. His handling of the affair was brilliant given he had little precedent to draw on. He was appropriately tentative. He took time for observation and evaluation before deciding on a course of action.[123] He didn't shut it down but worked on an interpersonal level to correct mistakes. He didn't move in and take over but had the humility to allow other gifted preachers room to have a significant ministry. He wanted relationships to be characterized by love and was deeply concerned by attitudes of pride and superiority that would lead to division. He insisted on faithfulness to the theological core of the Methodist movement—sanctification through the power of the Holy Spirit where lives were visibly changed—but did not want to stand in the way of a powerful move of God.

Wesley's subsequent letter to Maxfield late in January 1763 (with Bell's end of the world date only about a month away) is also important. It reiterates that Wesley's main concern was Maxfield's version of the doctrine of sanctification and not the charismatic manifestations or even Bell's false prophecy (which are not mentioned).[124]

In conclusion, Wesley's relationship to charismatic phenomena and 'enthusiasm' is open to reinterpretation. The Maxfield-Bell controversy demonstrates that the situation was more complicated than sometimes presented. It

---

123. John Wesley opened his letter to his brother Charles on December 11, 1762, with: "For eighteen or twenty days I heard with both ears, but rarely opened my mouth. I think I now understand the affair at least as well as any person in England." Ibid., 4:196.

124. John Wesley to Thomas Maxfield from London, January 26, 1763. "MY DEAR BROTHER,— For many years I and all the preachers in connexion with me have taught that every believer may and ought to grow in grace. Lately you have taught, or seemed to teach, the contrary. The effect of this is, when I speak as I have done from the beginning, those who believe what you say will not bear it—nay, they will renounce connexion with us; as Mr. and Mrs. Coventry did last night. This breach lies wholly upon you. You have contradicted what I taught from the beginning. Hence it is that many cannot bear it; but when I speak as I always have done, they separate from the Society. Is this for your honour or to the glory of God?

O Tommy, seek counsel, not from man, but God; not from Brother Bell, but Jesus Christ!—I am Your affectionate brother." Ibid., 4:201.

was not a case of Wesley's trying to quash enthusiasm. Wesley was trying to encourage experiences with the Holy Spirit while keeping the focus on growth in sanctification. If early Methodism could with some justification be attacked as being a fertile ground for enthusiasm, it is hardly surprising that Wesleyan developments should produce the pentecostal movement.

CHAPTER III
John Wesley and John Fletcher Initiate a Trajectory toward Open Theism

In the previous chapter, I investigated several problematic areas that had the potential to undermine the argument of this chapter and the next. I looked at John Wesley's understanding of the relation of God with time and the nature of divine foreknowledge. I highlighted Lorenzo Dow McCabe as a remarkable eighteenth-century Methodist scholar who recognized this point of weakness in Wesley's thought. McCabe sought to remedy this weak point by demonstrating the many advantages of affirming, as open theists do now, that God does not know exhaustively and definitely the future choices of free creatures. I looked at the tension in Wesley's view of providence and his interest in affirming human free will. Turning to Wesley's attitude toward proto-pentecostal manifestations, we saw how he became more open. The Maxfield-Bell affair was a defining moment, evidencing, on the one hand, Wesley's engagement with enthusiasm and, on the other hand, his concern to protect the unity of the movement and its teaching on sanctification.

This chapter traces John Wesley's (and John Fletcher's) connection with open theism. Five theological themes that indicate Wesley is moving in a direction toward open theism are explored: (1) soteriology and God's grace, (2) human freedom and God's omnipotence, (3) God's omniscience and omnipresence, (4) God's capacity for feeling and suffering, and (5) divine love. The second half of the chapter looks at Wesley and Fletcher's engagement with the English Calvinists. Those debates are at least analogous to the current open theism debates and are possibly the genesis of those debates. I give particular attention to John Fletcher's *Five Checks to Antinomianism* because they were persuasive in moving many towards Wesley's position.

Wesley planted the garden in which open theism grows. He chose the plants to be nourished—human freedom, divine love as the core of theology, and divine-human partnership for the restoration of creation.[1] He also identified weeds to be gently uprooted whenever they sprouted—Augustinian/Calvinistic determinism, predestination, and a monergistic view of grace.

Clark Pinnock wrote of John Wesley:

> What I want to lift up in his work is the transforming vision of God that lies at the heart of his reform and to urge his heirs to keep the vision alive.... In Wesley, one finds the vision of the sovereign God freely creating human beings capable of experiencing his love, opening the way for them to enter reciprocal relationships with God and fellow creatures.[2]

Using the *Sermons* as indicative of this theological thinking, the next section indicates significant ways in which Wesley's impulses are toward open theism.

A. THEOLOGICAL THEMES POINTING TO OPEN THEISM

1. Soteriology and God's Grace

Before noticing ways that Wesley's soteriology points in a distinctively openness direction, I will identify its quintessential character. His soteriology has both christological and pneumatological emphases. This passage captures the

---

[1]. Sanctification, the Holy Spirit, and concern for the poor are also very significant seedlings. Sanctification and the Holy Spirit are being considered in our discussion of the pentecostal-charismatic trajectory. Concern for the poor is an expression of God's love reflected through believers who have been recipients of that love.

[2]. Clark H. Pinnock, "The Beauty of God: John Wesley's Reform and Its Aftermath," *Wesleyan Theological Journal* 38, no. 2 (2003): 58–59.

III. WESLEY AND FLETCHER INITIATE A TRAJECTORY

dual emphases: "The righteousness of Christ is the whole and sole *foundation* of all our hope. It is by faith that the Holy Ghost enables us to build on this foundation. Follow the way of love and eagerly desire spiritual gifts, especially the gift of prophecy."[3] In an intuition that N. T. Wright has corroborated, Wesley identifies the righteousness (or faithfulness) of Christ as the basis of salvation.[4] Then, through the Holy Spirit, sanctification is made real through a life of love and the exercise of charismatic gifts.

Wesley stressed God's grace at work through the Holy Spirit, even before the moment of justification. He also emphasized human participation. Albert Outler noted that the Calvinists "had stressed the Father's elective will.... Wesley tilted the balance the other way because of his sense of the importance of the Holy Spirit's prevenient initiative in all the 'moments' of the *ordo salutis*. He could thus make room for human participation in reaction to the Spirit's activity and for human resistance as well—yet always in a very different sense from any Pelagian, or even 'Semi-Pelagian', doctrine of human initiative."[5] Outler also observed, "In Wesley's soteriology 'therapeutic metaphors tend to outweigh the forensic ones that had dominated Western traditions since Anselm.'"[6] Wesley lays the base for a synergistic theological enterprise. Taking soteriology in a direction away from Calvinism in this way is consistent with open theism. Open theism's nondeterministic approach to soteriology is congruent with Wesley's.[7]

Further, open theism depends on an enlarged view of God's grace. In the open view, God, out of his love for humanity, gives up exhaustive control of everything that happens in order for there to be room in the created order for truly free creatures. Even though this is not his own view of providence,

---

[3]. Sermon 20: "The Lord Our Righteousness" [1765] in Wesley, *Sermons I*, 459.

[4]. N. T. Wright, *Justification: God's Plan & Paul's Vision* (Downers Grove: InterVarsity, 2009).

[5]. Wesley, *Sermons I*, 81.

[6]. Ibid., 80.

[7]. For example, Clark Pinnock writes, "The truth is, although humankind can do no good apart from grace, grace is given to all and calls for a response. As persons, we cooperate with the grace of God because it is part of our very being. Scripture upholds the primacy of grace and the inability of human nature to do good, but it also teaches that it is the responsibility of the person to respond to God's gift." Pinnock, *Most Moved Mover*, 164. Then in a note he adds, "This lies at the heart of Wesley's theology. It is an important way in which he took the Reformation further." Ibid., 164 n. 23.

Wesley made this claim credible by stressing both the grace of God to humanity and by insisting that humans have real freedom to choose for or against God rather than being subject to preordained elective decrees. Although Wesley does not express the thought in the same terms as open theists, we can view it as a logical corollary of his view that humans have real freedom and God is omnipotent. There must be some explanation for how that is possible and open theism provides it.

2. Human Freedom and God's Omnipotence

Wesley discusses how God is omnipotent in his sermon series on the Sermon on the Mount.

> The Lord God omnipotent then reigneth, when he is known through Christ Jesus. He taketh unto himself his mighty power, that he may subdue all things unto himself. He goeth on in the soul conquering and to conquer, till he hath put all things under his feet, till "every thought" is "brought into captivity to the obedience of Christ."[8]

A cursory reading may lead one to conclude that Wesley is merely affirming God's omnipotence. On close reading, the passage is somewhat subversive. This precedes it:

> In order that the name of God may be hallowed, we pray that his kingdom, the kingdom of Christ, may come. This kingdom then comes to a particular person when he "repents and believes the gospel;" when he is taught of God not only to know himself but to know Jesus Christ and him crucified. As "this is life eternal, to know the only true God, and Jesus Christ whom he hath sent," so it is the kingdom of God begun below, set up in the believer's heart. The Lord God omnipotent then reigneth....[9]

---

8. Sermon 26: "Upon Our Lord's Sermon on the Mount, VI" [1748] in Wesley, *Sermons I*, 581–82.
9. Sermon 26: "Upon Our Lord's Sermon on the Mount, VI" [1748] in ibid., 581.

III. WESLEY AND FLETCHER INITIATE A TRAJECTORY

Wesley is saying the freedom of humanity to choose for or against God's kingdom conditions the idea of God's omnipotence. He is using the word 'omnipotent' but in a way that precludes God exerting absolute control.[10] It is also significant that Wesley affirms, "He goeth on *in the soul* conquering and to conquer." God conquers through love. This understanding of omnipotence is far from the Calvinistic notion of God controlling everything that happens. David Naglee provides some elucidation.

> On the rational side of Wesley's understanding of divine omnipotence, he relied heavily upon Samuel Clarke's *Discourse Concerning the Unchangeable Obligations of Natural Religion and the Truth and Certainty of the Christian Revelation*. In particular, proposition seven of this work treats God's almighty power in three dimensions: (1) as a creative power; (2) as a power of beginning motion; and (3) as a power of free will.[11]

Naglee quotes Wesley: "God's omnipotent power was given to man in a small degree to allow him to be a moral agent, without which 'he could not be a moral agent, any more than a tree or a stone.'"[12] Further, "Wesley believed that divine omnipotence was placed under a principle of self-restriction by God in reference to the extension of his power to man, making man a free moral agent. This self-restriction, by God, was necessary because without it man is not in the image of God...."[13]

This self-restriction by God in order to give humans some real freedom and power is illustrated in a passage that occurs a little later in the sermon just quoted.

---

10. The late Wesley does not always avoid speaking of God as almighty, but it is interesting he corrects "Almighty" to "All-sufficient" in translating *El Shaddai*. Sermon 118: "On the Omnipresence of God" [1788] in Wesley, *Sermons IV*, 47 n. 45.

11. Naglee, *From Everlasting to Everlasting*, 107.

12. Ibid., 108. Naglee cites *Works* (Zondervan) VI, 222, 318; X, 229, 232, 362.

13. Ibid., 109.

> When therefore we pray that the "will of God" may "be done on earth as it is in heaven," the meaning is that all the inhabitants of the earth, even the whole race of mankind, may do the will of their Father which is in heaven as *willingly* as the holy angels; that these may do it *continually,* even as they, without any interruption of their willing service. Yea, and that they may do it *perfectly*....[14]

For Wesley, free will is not an illusion but a gift that is given in order that obedience to the will of God may be voluntary and not coerced.

Pinnock connects human freedom and God's self-giving:

> God has chosen to self-limit for the sake of human freedom. It was something that God chose to do and not anything that was imposed on him. And gloriously too, kenosis brings with it a pleroma as well. Kenosis is more than just self-giving. By self-limiting, God obtains new sorts of values that would not otherwise be obtainable. The kenosis is also a gain, a self-realization, a way in which God realizes possibilities eternally present in the divine being but not yet experienced by God. For example, by giving up total control, God can enjoy real relations with finite creatures. If God were to give up on exhaustive foreknowledge, he could enjoy forms of creativity. God may limit the divine properties in order that free creatures might exist, but he thereby realizes new possibilities for himself. Therefore, we can speak of both kenosis and pleroma. In short, the reform of classical theism is well under way and in the basic directions which Wesley indicated.[15]

By insisting on the reality of human freedom and the possibility of working with God for good, Wesley laid the groundwork for coming to a better

---

14. Sermon 26: "Upon Our Lord's Sermon on the Mount, VI" [1748] in Wesley, *Sermons I*, 584. Italics are Wesley's.
15. Pinnock, "The Beauty of God," 64–65.

understanding of how God chooses to use his omnipotence—by self-giving and self-limiting.

3. God's Omniscience and Omnipresence

Chapter two looked at how Wesley's view of God's omniscience was subject to a mid-course correction by Lorenzo Dow McCabe and others. This section examines how Wesley's own thought prepared the way for that development. The middle Wesley commenting of the Lord's Prayer talks about the nature of God:

> "Hallowed be thy name."… The name of God is God himself—the nature of God so far as it can be discovered to man. It means, therefore, together with his existence, all his attributes or perfections—his eternity, particularly signified by his great and incommunicable name Jehovah….[16]
>
> His "fullness of being," denoted by his other great name, "I am that I am;" his omnipresence;—his omnipotence;—who is indeed the only agent in the material world, all matter being essentially dull and inactive, and moving only as it is moved by the finger of God. And he is the spring of action in every creature, visible and invisible, which could neither act nor exist without the continued influx and agency of his almighty power;—his wisdom, clearly deduced from the things that are seen, from the goodly order of the universe; his Trinity in Unity and Unity in Trinity….—his essential purity and holiness;—and above all his love, which is the very brightness of his glory.[17]

Several things are of interest here. (1) He emphasizes the relational aspect of God by saying he is known in his names. (2) Wesley speaks of the divine omnipotence by which he means God uses his power to give life and energy to the world. When Wesley says that all things are "moved by the finger of

---

16. Sermon 26: "Upon Our Lord's Sermon on the Mount, VI" [1748] in Wesley, *Sermons I*, 580.
17. Sermon 26: "Upon Our Lord's Sermon on the Mount, VI" [1748] in ibid., 581.

God" he is saying he gives them the impulse to move. He is not saying God controls everything, i.e., where or how they will move. (3) Wesley says that the name Jehovah is incommunicable. We only know of God what he chooses to reveal to us. It is interesting, though, that Wesley goes on to emphasize the communicable attributes of God—his wisdom, purity, holiness, and love. In another place, Wesley even asserts that God's eternity is communicable.[18] (4) Lastly, it is significant that Wesley places divine love above all the other divine attributes.[19] For Wesley, God's love is really his defining characteristic. God's glory is not so much his power as his outshining, burning love.

The late Wesley makes a fascinating theological move, which is remarkable from an open theist perspective. As he discusses God's omniscience, we would expect him to explain it based on the stasis theory of time as he did in his younger days as we saw in chapter two—God knows everything because he sees everything in time and space at once, in one eternal now. But in "On the Omnipresence of God" (1788) he argues that God's omniscience is a consequence of his omnipresence.[20] He argues similarly in "The Unity of the Divine Being" (1789): "The omniscience of God is a clear and necessary consequence of his omnipresence. If he is present in every part of the universe, he cannot but know whatever is, or is done there."[21] Argued this way, God's omniscience does not extend to every event in the future. It is completely consistent with all the usual open theist options. Open theists affirm that God knows everything about the past (because he was there) and everything about

---

18. "[Eternity] is not an incommunicable attribute of the great Creator; but he has been graciously pleased to make innumerable multitudes of his creatures partakers of it. He has imparted this not only to angels, and archangels, and all the companies of heaven, who are not intended to die, but to glorify him and live in his presence for ever, but also to the inhabitants of the earth who dwell in houses of clay.... Indeed all spirits, we have reason to believe, are clothed with immortality; having no inward principle of corruption, and being liable to no external violence." Sermon 54: "On Eternity" [1786] in Wesley, *Sermons II*, 361.

19. We'll look at divine love in more detail in §5 below.

20. Sermon 118 in Wesley, *Sermons IV*, 44. Similarly, Wesley explained God's omniscience on the basis of his omnipresence two years earlier. "Now it must be that he knows everything he has made, and everything he preserves from moment to moment. Otherwise he could not preserve it: he could not continue to it the being which he has given it. And it is nothing strange that he who is omnipresent, ... who is in every place, should see what is in every place, where he is intimately present." Sermon 67: "On Divine Providence" [1786] in Wesley, *Sermons II*, 538.

21. Sermon 120 in Wesley, *Sermons IV*, 62.

III. WESLEY AND FLETCHER INITIATE A TRAJECTORY

the present (because he is everywhere). Most open theists are of the opinion that the future does not yet exist, so God is not there.[22] The future, therefore, is only knowable to God to the extent that he knows how he is going to act, and to the extent that near-term future events can be extrapolated from a complete knowledge of the present. The rest is possibilities, all of which God knows in their unimaginable complexity.[23] Pinnock summarizes the significance of this point:

> The future is not fixed in every respect. God is even now working with us to bring it about. This is the basis of our having "say so" in the unfolding of history. It is central to the Wesleyan conviction that we are able to make a difference. In this matter, we see God knowing the past and present exhaustively, as well as that part of the future which is determined either by God's plan or by other considerations. And we believe that God also knows all the possibilities of what humans might do and could do and even are likely to do, but lacks absolute certainty about what we will actually do with the freedom he gave us. This is important because it is a question of whether or not we possess real freedom to affect anything. God invites us to collaborate with him to bring the as-yet open parts of the future into being.[24]

Attending to the late Wesley allows us to see him moving by stages toward open theism. Holiness was a lifelong passion for Wesley because he intuited knowing God should make a difference in how we live. He believed God gave

---

22. "The 'future' is not an ontological reality (a thing) that already exists." John Sanders, *The God Who Risks: A Theology of Providence* (Downers Grove: InterVarsity Press, 1998), 15.

23. A God with present knowledge "knows those events that will be future that are determined (i.e., not contingently free) either because God specifically determines the event or because God knows that present causal factors will determine the event. In other words, though the future does not exist, God knows some events will happen (certain possibilities will become actualities). That part of the future that is indefinite is known by God as possibilities and probabilities. God is not caught off-guard since God knows everything that can possibly happen and the precise probability that something will happen." Sanders, "Open Theism: A Radical Revision or Miniscule Modification of Arminianism?," 83. Sanders goes on to reference Boyd, *Satan and the Problem of Evil*, 127–132.

24. Pinnock, "The Beauty of God," 66.

humans the power to make significant choices and have influence for good through working synergistically with the Holy Spirit. Open theism makes that logically coherent by removing the determinism implicit if God knows the future exhaustively.

4. God's Capacity for Feeling and Suffering

Wesley's critique of the doctrine of God's impassibility makes way for open theism in a remarkable way. Impassibility is the view that God cannot be affected by anything external, and particularly that he cannot suffer. It comes out of Plato's commitment to the idea of God's immutability and through Augustine into Calvinism. If God cannot change, then he cannot have feelings which change. Wesley is not convinced.

> Is he an Epicurean god? Does he sit at ease in the heaven, without regarding the poor inhabitants of earth? It cannot be.... On the contrary, he hath expressly declared that as his "eyes are over all the earth"; [Pss. 34:15; 83:18] so he "is loving to every man, and his mercy is over all his works." Consequently he is concerned every moment for what befalls every creature upon earth; and more especially for everything that befalls any of the children of men.[25]

For Wesley, the biblical witness of God's compassion trumps the traditional understanding.

What may have triggered this break with Augustinian theism beyond the issues of election and predestination? When Wesley is writing on God's attributes in 1748, he remarkably does not mention divine immutability or impassibility, either to affirm or deny them.[26] But by 1786, he is vocal in opposition to divine impassibility in the passage just quoted beginning, "Is he an Epicurean god?" It is probable that the reason for the shift is that Wesley had given up trying to accommodate the Calvinists and was seeking to make his own theology self-consistent and true to his reading of the Bible. In 1765

---

25. Sermon 67: "On Divine Providence" [1786] in Wesley, *Sermons II*, 539–40.
26. Sermon 26: "Upon Our Lord's Sermon on the Mount, VI" in Wesley, *Sermons I*, 581.

III. WESLEY AND FLETCHER INITIATE A TRAJECTORY

he had preached Sermon 20, "The Lord Our Righteousness" which clearly differentiated his soteriology from that of the Calvinists. In 1770, there was the controversy over the Conference minutes and Lady Huntingdon's opposition. Wesley's meeting with Thomas Maxfield in 1773 is revealing. Maxfield had published a pamphlet accusing Wesley of turning Whitefield's followers against him while he was in America. Wesley writes, "I had much conversation with Thomas Maxfield. He said his printing that wretched book against me was owing to the pressing instances of Mr. Whitefield and Lady Huntingdon. I cannot tell how to believe it; but if it was, they might have been better employed."[27] His subsequent letter to Maxfield on February 14, 1778, refutes the charges. Wesley mentions the literary attacks of Richard Hill, Rowland Hill, and Augustus Toplady. He signs the letter, "Your injured yet still affectionate brother."[28] These exchanges suggest that the Calvinistic and Wesleyan Methodists were on two distinctly different tracks. Wesley would have felt there was nothing to be gained by minimizing their differences, and so felt free to publish his opposition to divine impassibility.

Wesley's stance on God's passibility is very significant to open theism. If God is passible, then he is necessarily not immutable. If God's inner experience can change, then he is not immutable. Therefore, Wesley here makes two important corrections to the tradition in an open theist direction.[29]

But the implications of Wesley's rejecting divine impassibility do not stop there. "A thing changes, even extrinsically, only if different things are true of it at different times. Perhaps, then, defending DDI [the doctrine of divine

---

27. Entry for February 4, 1773 in Wesley, *Journal and Diaries*.

28. Wesley, *Letters of John Wesley*, 6:300–306.

29. See above at p. 25 for Pinnock's view. Wesley doesn't expressly deny divine immutability but mentions it only three times and with qualifications. For example, he speaks of Christ's "immutable holiness." Sermon 20: "The Lord Our Righteousness" [1765] in Wesley, *Sermons I*, 452. Quoting Hebrews 6:17, he speaks of God's faithfulness and mentions the "immutability of his counsel." Sermon 23: "Upon Our Lord's Sermon on the Mount, III" [1748] in ibid., 516. The only other explicit reference to divine immutability in the *Sermons* is from the middle Wesley: "But although man was made in the image of God, yet he was not made immutable. This would have been inconsistent with that state of trial in which God was pleased to place him. He was therefore created able to stand, and yet liable to fall." Sermon 45: "The New Birth" [1760] in Wesley, *Sermons II*, 189. By 'immutable' here Wesley means not capable of moral failure.

immutability] requires commitment to divine timelessness."[30] By implicitly giving up divine immutability, Wesley no longer needs to subscribe to divine timelessness.[31] Divine timelessness is required to make sense of God not being able to change or be affected by his creation. But how could God know everything and not know what his own experience of compassion feels like in response to events as they become real in time? God must be in time to make sense of how he can experience compassion or relate to human beings.

By rejecting divine impassibility, Wesley implicitly relinquishes divine immutability with respect to God's thinking and feeling (but not his character). If God is not immutable then it is no longer consistent for him to be timeless because change requires time. The logical consequence of Wesley's position is the affirmation that God is in time. If God is in time, then the possibility that he does not know the future exhaustively becomes a real option. If he does not know the future exhaustively, then we are freed from the determinism of being locked into a future that is known by God. By denying divine impassibility, and by implication divine immutability and divine timelessness, Wesley opens a path to open theism.

5. Divine Love

Divine love was central to John Wesley's conception of who God is. David Naglee emphasizes this point: "Of the revealed attributes of God, none was as important and vital to Wesley as divine love."[32] The recognition that God's most defining characteristic is love was programmatic. It meant that Wesley was not preoccupied, as some theologians are, with issues of God's power and sovereignty. That left him free to emphasize the real freedom that God has allowed to humans. It meant that Wesley was not preoccupied with divine

---

30. Brian Leftow, "Immutability," in *The Stanford Encyclopedia of Philosophy*, ed. Edward N. Zalta (2011), http://plato.stanford.edu/archives/win2012/entries/immutability/. The quote is from the last two sentences of the article.

31. Wesley doesn't actually take this step but he is on the threshold. He prefers to speak of God being 'everlasting' rather than 'eternal'. 'Everlasting' is something that continues to exist forever within time. "A second essential attribute of God is eternity. He existed before all time. Perhaps we might more properly say, he *does* exist from everlasting to everlasting." Sermon 69: "The Imperfection of Human Knowledge" [1784] in Wesley, *Sermons III*, 570.

32. Naglee, *From Everlasting to Everlasting*, 1:120.

III. WESLEY AND FLETCHER INITIATE A TRAJECTORY

justice and judgment. That left him free to emphasize God's grace. Wesley prioritizes the human response to divine love, first in love toward God, then in love to neighbor.

Wesley says, "The Circumcision of the Heart," (1733) was "the first of all my writings which have been published," showing the early priority he gave this theme.[33]

> Yet lackest thou one thing, whosoever thou art, that to a deep humility and a steadfast faith hast joined a lively hope, and thereby in a good measure cleansed thy heart from its inbred pollution. If thou wilt be perfect, add to all these charity: add love, and thou hast the "circumcision of the heart."[34]

In "A Plain Account of Christian Perfection," Wesley quotes this very sermon which he had preached at Oxford thirty-three years earlier and picks up immediately after the passage just quoted. Here, he makes clear what is the essence of Christian perfection—the most distinctive of his teachings and probably the one he expended the most energy defending.

> "Love is the fulfilling of the law," "the end of the commandment." …
> It is not only "the first and great command," but … all the commandments in one. "Whatsoever things are just, whatsoever things are pure, … if there be any virtue, if there be any praise, they are all comprised in this one word—love. In this is perfection, and glory, and happiness. The royal law of heaven and earth is this, "Thou shalt love the Lord thy God with all thy heart, and with all thy soul, and with all thy mind, and with all thy strength."[35]

---

[33]. John Wesley, *Doctrinal and Controversial Treatises II*, ed. Paul Wesley Chilcote and Kenneth J. Collins, The Works of John Wesley (Nashville: Abingdon, 2013), 13:139. This theme even predated his Aldersgate experience.

[34]. Sermon 17 in Wesley, *Sermons I*, 1:407.

[35]. "A Plain Account of Christian Perfection" [1766] in Wesley, *Doctrinal and Controversial Treatises II*, 13:138. Ellipses indicate Wesley's abridgement of the original. The sermon continues: "Not that this forbids us to love anything besides God: it implies that we 'love our brother also.'"

In one word, Christian perfection is *love*—loving God and loving your neighbor. *Love* still expressed what Wesley meant by sanctification or perfection fifty-one years later: "This is the sum of Christian perfection: it is all comprised in that one word, love. The first branch of it is the love of God: and as he that loves God loves his brother also, it is inseparably connected with the second."[36]

For Wesley, an experience of God's love was at the core of what it means to be a Christian. For example, he speaks of someone who might have authentically believed as a result of the preaching of the Apostle Peter: "This then was the very essence of his faith, a divine ἔλεγχος [evidence, conviction] of the love of God the Father, through the Son of his love, to him a sinner, now 'accepted in the beloved.'"[37] He continues:

> "The love of God" was also "shed abroad in his heart by the Holy Ghost which was given unto him." Because he was a son, God had sent forth the Spirit of his Son into his heart, crying Abba, Father!" And that filial love of God was continually increased by the "witness he had in himself" of God's pardoning love to him, by "beholding what manner of love it was which the Father had bestowed upon him, that he should be called a child of God."[38]

For Wesley, the love of God is not simply absorbed by the human recipient. Humans can reflect it into the world. In reflecting on the image of God, he writes in an early sermon:

> Man was what God is, Love. Love filled the whole expansion of his soul; it possessed him without a rival. Every movement of his heart was love; it knew no other fervor. Love was his vital heat; it was the genial warmth that animated his whole frame. And the flame of it

---

36. Sermon 76: "On Perfection" [1784] in Wesley, *Sermons III*, 74.
37. Sermon 4: "Scriptural Christianity" [1744] in Wesley, *Sermons I*, 161–62. This was his last sermon to the university at Oxford.
38. Sermon 4: "Scriptural Christianity" [1744] in ibid., 162–63.

III. WESLEY AND FLETCHER INITIATE A TRAJECTORY

was continually streaming forth, directly to him from whom it came, and by reflection to all sensitive natures....[39]

This reflected love of brother and sister can be costly. There is a root of pacifism in Wesley derivative from love of neighbor. Speaking of the prototypical Christian: "It was impossible for him knowingly and designedly to do harm to any man."

There is a deep concern for the poor:

He "gave all his goods to feed the poor." He rejoiced to labour or to suffer for them; and whereinsoever he might profit another, there especially to "deny himself." He counted nothing too dear to part with for them, as well remembering the word of his Lord, "Inasmuch as ye have done it unto one of the least of these my brethren, ye have done it unto me."[40]

Wesley's theological interest in divine love that is absorbed then reflected to God and radiated out to others comes, of course, out of Jesus' teaching. For example, Matthew 22: 36–40.

"Teacher, which commandment in the law is the greatest?" He said to him, "'You shall love the Lord your God with all your heart, and with all your soul, and with all your mind.' This is the greatest and first commandment. And a second is like it: 'You shall love your neighbor as yourself.' On these two commandments hang all the law and the prophets."

Wesley, in preaching on the Sermon on the Mount, fleshes out what love of neighbor is:

---

[39]. Sermon 141: "The Image of God" [1730] in Wesley, *Sermons IV*, 294–95.
[40]. Sermon 4: "Scriptural Christianity" [1744] in Wesley, *Sermons I*, 164–65.

Charity, or love (as it were to be wished it had been rendered throughout, being a far plainer and less ambiguous word), the love of our neighbor as Christ hath loved us, "suffereth long," is patient toward all men.... And it suffers all this, not only for a time, for a short season, but to the end: still feeding our enemy when he hungers; if he thirst, still giving him drink; thus continually "heaping coals of fire," of melting love, "upon his head."

And in every step toward this desirable end, the "overcoming evil with good," "love is kind" (χρηστεύεται, a word not easily translated)—it is soft, mild, benign. It stands at the utmost distance from moroseness, from all harshness or sourness of spirit; and inspires the sufferer at once with the most amiable sweetness and the most fervent and tender affection.[41]

He identifies both attitudinal aspects (for example, "tender affection") but also actions that can come at a cost: "feeding our enemy" and "overcoming evil with good."[42]

Howard Snyder summarizes well: "Love was the key dynamic in Wesley's whole life and theology. The Christian's life was to be one of active faith—faith working by love."[43] It was at the core of Wesley's theology just as it is at the core of open theism's theological concern.

B. CONTROVERSY WITH CALVINISM

Clark Pinnock identified the problematic issues that Wesley engaged. Referring to Augustine, he writes:

---

41. Sermon 22: "Upon Our Lord's Sermon on the Mount, II" [1748] in ibid., 499–500.

42. I noted in the Introduction that Thomas Jay Oord defines love in this way: "To love is to act intentionally, in sympathetic/empathetic response to God and others, to promote overall well-being." *Nature of Love,* 17.

43. Howard A. Snyder, *The Radical Wesley and Patterns for Church Renewal* (Downers Grove: InterVarsity, 1980), 88.

III. WESLEY AND FLETCHER INITIATE A TRAJECTORY

In his response to Pelagius, he [Augustine] mapped out a monergistic doctrine in which God predestined the fall of men and angels and stands behind every sin and evil in a comprehensive plan. Augustine's obsession with the absolute and unconditional power of God makes him the absolute ruler of the universe whose will directs every event in creation, regardless of the consequences that flow from it. It cannot be said that Augustine affirms the unqualified goodness of God because he found it impossible to conceive of a self-limitation of God's power such that God could allow free creatures to act against his own perfect will. We can say that, according to Augustine, God is *great*, but not (I believe) that God is *good*. If God dominates the world completely, then his goodness is in serious doubt. Wesley saw this clearly. He saw that the sovereign God gives power to others, and that control is not the highest form of power. Power can also be expressed when God empowers others to choose to love him or not.[44]

It was the Calvinist doctrine of absolute predestination which Wesley found troubling enough to risk a break with Whitefield. Susanna Wesley wrote, "The doctrine of predestination, as maintained by the rigid Calvinists, is very shocking, and ought utterly to be abhorred; because it directly charges the most h[igh] God with being the author of sin. And I think you reason very well and justly against it."[45] She says that some are elect based on God's prescience or foreknowledge.

Augustus M. Toplady was the most prolific of Wesley's Calvinist opponents. Wesley summarizes his *Doctrine of Absolute Predestination*, ch. 5 §9: "The sum of all is this: One in twenty (suppose) of mankind are *elected;* nineteen in twenty are *reprobated*. The *elect* shall be saved, do what they will. The *reprobate* shall be damned, do what they can. Reader, believe this, or be damned. Witness my hand, A[ugustus] T[oplady]."[46]

---

44. Pinnock, "The Beauty of God," 60.
45. Wesley, *Sermons II*, 413.
46. Sermon 55: "On The Trinity" [1775] in ibid., 373. Toplady complained that Wesley had not quoted him accurately: "In almost any other case, a similar forgery would transmit the criminal to

Wesley unconstricts the narrowness of Calvinism's predestination, where salvation is entirely about God's elective choices. Wesley affirms the choice of salvation as a human response: "Yet 'grace would much more abound,' yea, and that to every individual of the human race, unless it was his own choice."[47] From God's perspective, salvation is an open door and potentially universal.[48]

Sermon 20, "The Lord Our Righteousness" [1765] is "Wesley's clearest statement of the essential differences between his own soteriology and that of the English Calvinists."[49] He affirms, "Our justification comes freely of the mere mercy of God."[50] This emphasis on God's extravagant love and mercy is foundational for open theism. Legalism, self-righteous arrogance, or preoccupation with God's wrath does not take you there.

Allan Coppedge helpfully summarizes the nature of Wesley's debates with the Calvinists:

> Wesley's dispute with the Calvinists was not a static one or a constant one. The free-grace controversy with Whitefield concentrated on election, perseverance, and perfection; then in the late 1750s and

---

Virginia or Maryland, if not to Tyburn." A. B. Toplady, Vicar of Broad-Hembury, Augustus, *The Doctrine of Absolute Predestination Stated and Asserted: Translated in Great Measure from the Latin of Jerom Zanchius, with Some Account of His Life Prefixed, and An Appendix Concerning the Fate of the Ancients; Also A Caveat Against Unsound Doctrine, to Which Is Added, A Letter to the Rev. John Wesley* (New York: George Lindsay, 1811 [rprt. from 1772 original]), 275. In actuality, Wesley's summation is not a direct quote, but it does beautifully capture the essence of Toplady's book.

47. Sermon 59: "God's Love to Fallen Man" [1782] in Wesley, *Sermons II*, 424.

48. Salvation is open to all: "The sum of all is this: the God of love is willing to save all the souls that he has made. This he has proclaimed to them in his Word, together with the terms of salvation revealed by the Son of his love, who gave his own life that they believe in him might have everlasting life. And for these he has prepared a kingdom from the foundation of the world. But he will not force them to accept of it. He leaves them in the hands of their own counsel." Sermon 127: "On the Wedding Garment" [1790] in Wesley, *Sermons IV*, 148.

Wesley has a remarkably broad perspective. Speaking of God's providential care of creation: "'Is he the God of the Jews', says the Apostle, 'and not of the Gentiles also?' [2 Tim. 2:19] And so we may say, Is he the God of the Christians, and not of the Mahometans and heathens also? Yea, doubtless of the Mahometans and heathens also. His love is not confined: 'The Lord is loving unto every man, and his mercy is over all his works.'" Sermon 67: "On Divine Providence" [1786] in Wesley, *Sermons II*, 542.

49. Albert Outler in Wesley, *Sermons I*, 42.

50. Ibid., 456.

III. WESLEY AND FLETCHER INITIATE A TRAJECTORY

early 1760s, Wesley argued with Hervey over imputed righteousness. In the clash with Toplady, the focus of debate was on free will. Though the Minutes controversy began over the question of how faith and works related to justification, its center shifted in midstream, converging on election and perfection. The wheel had come full circle. Many points were discussed and rediscussed, but the hub of disagreement was centered on tension between predestination and holiness.[51]

This last observation indicates why John Fletcher's *Five Checks to Antinomianism* were so significant. They address the question: if you are elect, why would it matter how you live? For that matter, if you are *not* elect, why would it matter how you live? The Calvinists were saying that only faith was decisive in salvation or final judgment. Wesley argued, "The imagination that faith *supersedes* holiness is the marrow of antinomianism."[52] Wesley individually edited and published Fletcher's Five Checks as they were written in the years 1771–75. The *First Check* opens by reprinting the circular letter signed by Walter Shirley on behalf of Lady Huntingdon and others disapproving of Wesley's 1770 Conference Minutes, calling them a "dreadful heresy."[53] It goes on to reprint the minutes then provide a defense of Wesley's view of "holiness of heart and life," or "full sanctification," or "Christian perfection."[54] The *Second Check* particularly defends free agency and addresses antinomianism. His foil is Dr. Tobias Crisp (1600–43), antinomian author of *Christ*

---

51. Allan Coppedge, *Shaping the Wesleyan Message: John Wesley in Theological Debate* (Nappanee, Ind.: Francis Asbury Press, 1987, 2003), 226. Hervey stressed imputed righteousness. "Wesley advocated, instead, the scriptural phrase 'faith reckoned for righteousness,' a righteousness he saw as both inherent and imputed. God really did work righteousness and holiness in believers. Wesley did not agree that God counted men righteous without actually making them so." Ibid., 121. Wesley was concerned that a stress on imputed righteousness would lead to antinomianism. The 1770 Conference Minutes contained a controversial doctrinal section that began "We said in 1744, 'We have leaned too much toward Calvinism.' Wherein?" The minutes argued that works matter, not as producing merit for earning salvation, but as a way of pleasing God through "the whole of our present inward tempers and outward behavior." Ibid., 168.
52. Sermon 127: "On the Wedding Garment" [1790] in Wesley, *Sermons IV*, 148.
53. Fletcher, *Five Checks to Antinomianism*, 2.
54. Ibid., 9, 11.

Alone Exalted.[55] The *Third Check* responds to five letters of Richard Hill (author of *Pietas Oxoniensis* and *Goliath Slain* which look into the expulsion of six Calvinist Methodist students from Oxford). It looks at inconsistencies in Calvinism, refutes objections to Wesley's position, and revisits problems with antinomianism. The *Fourth Check* addresses thirteen letters of Richard Hill and Roland Hill. Fletcher is particularly interested in defending justification by works (not in initial justification at conversion which is by faith, but at final justification in the last day) and the Book of James. He is also arguing against Tobias Crisp's view of "finished salvation" and Calvin's interpretation of imputed righteousness. The first half of the *Fifth Check* responds to Richard Hill's "Finishing Stroke" by further discussing antinomian themes:

> The point we debate is not whether Christ's blood "cleanses from all sin," but whether it actually cleanses from all guilt an impenitent backslider, a filthy apostate; and whether God says to the fallen believer, that commits adultery and murder, "Thou art all fair, my love, my undefiled, there is no spot in thee." This you affirm in your fourth letter: and this I expose, as the very quintessence of ranterism, antinomianism, and Calvinistic perseverance.[56]

Fletcher's counterargument is along these lines: "Now whence arises the fallacy of this argument? Is it not from overlooking the Mediator's law, the law of Christ?"[57] He continues:

---

55. A representative passage from Crisp: "Let me therefore tell you, suppose a member of Christ, a free-man of his should happen to fall, not only by a failing or a slip; but also by a gross failing, a heavy failing; nay, a scandalous falling into sin; Christ making a person free, disannuls, frustrates, and makes void every curse and sentence that is in the law, that is against such a transgressor; that this member of Christ is no more under the curse when he hath transgressed than he was before he transgressed. Thus I say, Christ has conveyed him beyond the reach of the curse; it concerns him no more than if he had not transgressed." John Gill, ed. *Christ Alone Exalted, in the Perfection and Encouragement of the Saints, Notwithstanding Sins and Trials: Being the Complete Works of Tobias Crisp... Containing Fifty-two Sermons, on Several Select Texts of Scripture*, 7th ed. (London: John Bennett, 1832), 130–31. Though the elect transgress "there is nothing to be laid to their charge; no curse can come against them, nor be executed upon them; there is no clapping them in gaol for their transgression." Ibid., 132.

56. Fletcher, *Five Checks to Antinomianism*, 205–06.
57. Ibid., 207.

III. WESLEY AND FLETCHER INITIATE A TRAJECTORY

Christ is neither an Eli, nor a Nero; neither a dolt, nor a tyrant; but a priestly king, a Melchisedec. If he is a king, he has a law; his subjects may, and the disobedient shall, be condemned by it. If he is a priestly king, he has a gracious law; and if he has a gracious law he requires no absolute impossibilities. Thus the covenant of grace keeps a just medium between the relentless severity of the first covenant, and the antinomian softness, or the covenant trumpeted by some Calvinists.[58]

The second half of the *Fifth Check* is a response to John Berridge (1716–1793). In *The Christian World Unmasked* Berridge writes, "Final justification by faith is the capital doctrine of the gospel. Faith being the term of salvation, &c., must utterly exclude all justification by works." And he writes of "an absolute impossibility of being justified in any manner by our works."[59] Fletcher makes the case for holiness of life flowing from God's gracious declaration of provisional justification at conversion which is confirmed at the final judgment by the evidence of a changed life and merciful works. He draws on scriptures such as Romans 2:13, 16, "For it is not the hearers of the law who are righteous in God's sight, but the doers of the law who will be justified… on the day when, according to my gospel, God, through Jesus Christ, will judge the secret thoughts of all;" and James 2:24, "You see that a person is justified by works and not by faith alone."[60] Fletcher ends with a gracious invitation to Berridge, his opponent in controversy, to preach in his pulpit.[61]

Fletcher's *Five Checks* established him as Wesley's definitive vindicator and had a remarkable effect. The *Checks* "helped significantly to reduce the number of adherents to Calvinism."[62] Fletcher made a significant Wesleyan contribution to the eighteenth-century theological debates.

---

58. Ibid., 208.

59. John Berridge, *The Christian World Unmasked*, 2nd ed. (London: Edward and Charles Dilly, 1773), 170–71, 26. The second quote is found at p. 20 of the 1854 Boston edition. The first quote has been editorially deleted.

60. Fletcher, *Five Checks to Antinomianism*, 252.

61. Ibid., 284.

62. Wood, *The Meaning of Pentecost in Early Methodism*, 209.

AN OPEN THEIST RENEWAL THEOLOGY

In the contemporary theological debate, there are a handful of biblical texts which seem to support Calvinism and are an apparent problem for open theists. Probably the most difficult is Romans 8:29-30.[63] Wesley's exegesis is brilliant although it requires reading the passage with new ears:

> The more frequently and carefully I have considered it, the more I have been inclined to think that the Apostle is not here (as many have supposed) describing a chain of causes and effects (this does not seem to have entered into his heart) but simply showing *the method in which God works*—*the order* in which the several branches of salvation constantly follow each other.[64]

To put it another way, God has decided ahead of time that "all who believe in the Son of his love shall be conformed to his image, shall be saved from all inward and outward sin into all inward and outward holiness."[65] The shift simply requires noticing the plurals in the passage. The passage is not talking about select individuals, but groups identified by their stage of salvation.

The ideas provided by Wesley and Fletcher to open theism are significant, but so too is the model he offered in energetically refuting the excesses of Calvin and his followers. Wesley and Fletcher cared passionately about these issues and a similar intensity of conviction can be detected in the open theism debates.

It is probably the case that John Wesley was sometimes the instigator of theological conflict.[66] This is to be expected in someone who cared passion-

---

63. The NRSV reads, "For those whom he foreknew he also predestined to be conformed to the image of his Son, in order that he might be the firstborn within a large family. And those whom he predestined he also called; and those whom he called he also justified; and those whom he justified he also glorified." Eugene Peterson's translation in *The Message* is consistent with Wesley's approach: "God knew what he was doing from the very beginning. He decided from the outset to shape the lives of those who love him along the same lines as the life of his Son. The Son stands first in the line of humanity he restored. We see the original and intended shape of our lives there in him."

64. Sermon 58: "On Predestination" [1773] in Wesley, *Sermons II*, 416.

65. Sermon 58: "On Predestination" [1773] in ibid., 418.

66. He did not hold back in telling it as he saw it, especially when those who emphasized holiness or co-working with God were slandered. With respect to that minority in church history who worshiped God in Spirit and truth: "I have often doubted whether these were not the very persons

III. WESLEY AND FLETCHER INITIATE A TRAJECTORY

ately about theology and the salvation of men and women. His manner of argumentation is worthy of emulation and has been a model for open theists. In the Preface to *Sermons on Several Occasions* he writes:

> 9. Are you persuaded you see more clearly than me? It is not unlikely that you may. Then treat me as you would desire to be treated yourself upon a change of circumstances. Point me out a better way than I have yet known. Show me it is so by plain proof of Scripture. And if I linger in the path I have been accustomed to tread, and am therefore unwilling to leave, labour with me a little, take me by the hand, and lead me as I am able to bear. But be not displeased if I entreat you not to beat me down in order to quicken my pace. I can go but feebly and slowly at best—then, I should not be able to go at all. May I not request of you, farther, not to give me hard names in order to bring me into the right way? Suppose I was ever so much in the wrong, I doubt this would not set me right. Rather it would make me run so much the farther from you—and so get more and more out of the way.
>
> 10. Nay, perhaps, if you are angry so shall I be too, and then there will be small hopes of finding the truth. If once anger arise ἠύτε καπός ['like a puff of smoke'] (as Homer somewhere expresses it), this smoke will so dim the eyes of my soul that I shall be able to see nothing clearly. For God's sake, if it be possible to avoid it let

---

whom the rich and honourable Christians, who will always have number as well as power on their side, did not stigmatize from time to time with the title of 'heretics'.... Nay, I have doubted whether that arch-heretic, Montanus, was not one of the holiest men in the second century. Yea, I would not affirm that the arch-heretic of the fifth century (as plentifully as he has ben bespattered for many ages) was not one of the holiest men of that age, not excepting St. Augustine himself—a wonderful saint! As full of pride, passion, bitterness, censoriousness, and as foul-mouthed to all that contradicted him as George Fox himself. I verily believe the real heresy of Pelagius was neither more nor less than this, the holding that Christians may by the grace of God (not without it; that I take to be a mere slander) 'go on to perfection'; or, in other words, 'fulfil the law of Christ.'... 'But St. Augustine says'—When St. Augustine's passions were heated his word is not worth a rush. And here is the secret. St. Augustine was angry at Pelagius. Hence he slandered and abused him (as his manner was) without either fear or shame." Sermon 68: "The Wisdom of God's Counsels" [1784] in ibid., 555–56.

us not provoke one another to wrath.... For how far is love, even with many wrong opinions, to be preferred before truth itself without love?[67]

Wesley and Fletcher both found it necessary to engage in controversy with their Calvinist brothers and sisters. However, they did all they could to preserve loving relationships amid the discussions, and in so doing have provided a model for open theists.

It is the judgment of Randy Maddox that Wesley might well affirm open theism.[68] Maddox says, "If he [Wesley] had possessed a more nuanced hermeneutic for dealing with such passages [as Acts 15:18], he might have decided that a 'self-limiting God' was consistent with his general convictions about how God works."[69] The later Wesley was clearly wrestling with the questions that open theism addresses: "We know, the Lord is loving unto every man, and that his mercy is over all his works. But we know not how to reconcile this with the present dispensations of his providence. At this day is not almost every part of the earth full of darkness and cruel habitations?"[70] This admission of cognitive dissonance from the later Wesley suggests he was open to rethink his understanding of divine providence. Wesley and Fletcher's passionate opposition to Reformed doctrines such as absolute predestination puts the spirit of their theology on the path to open theism.

In this chapter I looked at theological themes important to both Wesley and open theism and examined Wesley and Fletcher's debates with the English Calvinists. The evidence clearly suggests that the later Wesley and Fletcher were moving theologically in the direction of what would later become open theism.

---

67. Wesley, *Sermons I*, 107.
68. Pinnock, "Open Theism: 'What Is This?'," 49.
69. Randy L. Maddox, *Responsible Grace: John Wesley's Practical Theology* (Nashville: Kingswood, 1994), 53.
70. Sermon 69: "The Imperfection of Human Knowledge" [1784] in Wesley, *Sermons II*, 578–79.

CHAPTER IV

Open Theism in Another Wesleyan Trajectory—Pentecostalism

*T*he previous chapter explored ways that John Wesley and John Fletcher can be seen as on a continuum with open theism. This chapter describes first how Wesley and Fletcher can be seen as at the beginning of a trajectory toward pentecostalism. The second half of the chapter explores ways that early pentecostalism emphasized themes important to open theism, and so indicate how the two trajectories might come together.

To provide context, a little needs to be said about pentecostalism. The pentecostal charismatic renewal is a world-wide phenomenon with perhaps six hundred fourteen million followers as of 2010, including 94,383,000 classical Pentecostals, 206,579,000 mainline charismatics, and 313,048,000 neo-charismatics.[1] The movement's origins may be diverse.[2] However, one of

---

1. Todd Johnson and Kenneth R. Ross, eds., *The Atlas of Global Christianity 1910–2010* (Edinburgh: Edinburgh University Press, 2009), 102. Cited in Vinson Synan, ed. *Spirit-Empowered Christianity in the Twenty-First Century* (Lake Mary, Fla.: Charisma House, 2011), 543. Allan Anderson points out that Johnson's figures might be somewhat inflated. *An Introduction to Pentecostalism: Global Charismatic Christianity*, 2nd ed. (Cambridge: Cambridge University Press, 2014), 3. For example, Johnson categorizes African Independent Churches as pentecostal although not all would be encompassed by the definition adopted above at p. 44. Anderson mentions Jason Mandryk's more conservative figure of 426 million 'Renewalists" (including 178 million Pentecostals) in 2010. Jason Mandryk and Patrick Johnstone, *Operation World*, 7th ed. (Colorado Springs, Colo.: Biblica, 2010).

2. The late Nigerian-born scholar Ogbu Kalu argued, "African Pentecostalism did not originate from Azusa Street and is not an extension of the American electronic church." *African*

the most identifiable starting points is the Azusa Street revival of 1906–1908 led by William Seymour. Even Allan Anderson, who champions a polycentric view of the origins of pentecostalism, can concede: "In a real sense, the Azusa Street revival marks the beginning of classical Pentecostalism and as we will see, from there the revival reached to many other parts of the world."[3]

Part of Azusa Street's prehistory is found in the Bible schools of the former Methodist, Charles Fox Parham (1873–1929) in Topeka, Kansas and Houston, Texas. On December 31, 1900, at the turn of the century, one of his students, Agnes Ozman, asked Parham and the other students to pray for her to receive the baptism of the Holy Spirit and she spoke in tongues. What had been possible in theory in Parham's teaching was experienced by him and among his students.

William J. Seymour (1870–1922) was also briefly one of Parham's students. Seymour was the son of former slaves. Born in Louisiana, he moved to Indianapolis in 1895 and worked as a waiter at high end hotels. He was converted there in a black Methodist Episcopal church and here "undoubtedly gained his appreciation for the teachings of John Wesley, the founder of Methodism."[4] Seymour moved to Cincinnati and probably studied at a Bible school run by the holiness preacher Martin Wells Knapp and his wife. While visiting Chicago, Seymour had occasion to have conversations with John G. Lake, the holiness healing evangelist and later founder of the Apostolic Faith Mission of South Africa (which planted over 700 churches) and with the

---

Pentecostalism: An Introduction (Oxford: Oxford University Press, 2008), 8. Clifton Clarke's homage to Kalu mentions several scholars of like mind. Clarke quotes Allan Anderson: "Historians of Pentecostalism have often reflected a bias interpreting history from a predominately white American perspective, neglecting (if not completely ignoring) the vital and often more significant work of Asian, African, African American and Latino/a Pentecostal pioneers." Allan Anderson, *An Introduction to Pentecostalism: Global Charismatic Christianity* (Cambridge: Cambridge University Press, 2004), 166. Clarke notes three other scholars with whom Kalu is in agreement that pentecostalism is a "global phenomenon with multiple access points." Clifton R. Clarke, "Ogbu Kalu and Africa's Christianity: A Tribute," *Pneuma* 32 (2010): 115. Clarke mentions: J. Kwabena Asamoah-Gyadu, *African Charismatics* (Leiden and Boston: Brill, 2005), 6 ; Paul Pomerville, *The Third Force in Missions: A Pentecostal Contribution to Mission Theology* (Peabody, Mass.: Hendrickson, 1985), 23 ; and Douglas Peterson, *Not by Might Nor by Power* (Oxford: Regnum Books International, 1996), 45.

3. Anderson, *Introduction to Pentecostalism (2nd ed.)*, 43–44.

4. Robeck, *The Azusa Street Mission and Revival*, 28.

IV. OPEN THEISM IN A PENTECOSTAL TRAJECTORY

healing evangelist John Alexander Dowie of Zion, Illinois.[5] He felt a call to ministry and moved to Houston in 1903. He worshiped at a black holiness church pastored by Lucy Farrow who supplemented her income as a cook for Charles Parham's ministry school in Houston. Farrow asked Seymour to pastor the church while she worked for Parham in Kansas as a nanny. She received the baptism of the Holy Spirit and the gift of tongues after overhearing Parham's interactions with his students.[6]

With Farrow's encouragement, Seymour became a student of Parham's for six weeks in Houston beginning in January 1906. Because of segregation laws and Parham's racism, he sat in the hallway listening through a half-open door instead of in the classroom with the white students. Seymour became convinced of Parham's teaching that speaking in tongues is the "initial evidence" of being baptized in the Holy Spirit.[7]

Seymour was invited to Los Angeles to become the pastor of a small holiness church on Santa Fe Street by its founder, Julia Hutchins, who hoped to be freed up to do mission work in Africa. Seymour began preaching there on February 24, 1906, but by March 4, Hutchins had decided she couldn't accept Seymour's view on the baptism in the Spirit and locked him out. Edward and Mattie Lee invited him to stay with them and they began a prayer meeting and Bible study that met each evening. Attendance at the meeting grew, so they moved it to 214 North Bonnie Brae Street, the home of Richard and Ruth Asberry. Seymour asked Lucy Farrow to come from Houston to help. "On April 9, 1906, this Bible study was visited by a move of the Holy Spirit in which people began to speak and sing in tongues."[8] Eight people, including Seymour, "fell to the floor in a religious ecstasy, speaking in tongues."[9] Growth in numbers forced them again to move, this time to a former African Methodist Episcopal church on Azusa Street. It became known as the Apostolic Faith Mission and came to public notice in the *Los Angeles Daily*

---

5. Ibid., 35.
6. Ibid., 44.
7. Hollenweger, *Pentecostalism*, 21–22.
8. Robeck, *The Azusa Street Mission and Revival*, 5.
9. Synan, *The Holiness-Pentecostal Tradition*, 96.

Times on April 18, 1906, the same day as the devastating San Francisco earthquake. The revival was marked both by a remarkable sense of God's presence and a breaking down of racial and social barriers.[10] Over the next three years, thousands of people visited the mission from all over the world seeking to be a part of what God was doing there.

Whether it is Parham or Seymour who should be identified as the founder of classical American pentecostalism is debated. The distinctive teaching about the gift of tongues came from Parham. However, the Assemblies of God New Testament scholar Russ Spittler writes, "The doctrine of speaking in tongues as the initial physical evidence of the baptism of the Holy Spirit can be labeled the distinctive teaching of the pentecostal churches. But it is misguided to confuse that which *distinguishes* pentecostalism with its *essence*."[11] The eminent historian of pentecostalism, Walter Hollenweger, argues that it is Seymour who captures that essence. "In the final analysis the choice between Parham and Seymour is not an historical but a theological one. Where does one see the decisive contribution of Pentecost: in the religious experience of speaking in tongues as seen by Parham, or in the reconciling Pentecostal experience of Pentecost as seen by Seymour (which of course includes glossolalia and gives it an important role)?"[12] In a way, Parham disqualifies himself by his resistance to the racial integration at Azusa Street. While both Parham and Seymour are connected to John Wesley and John Fletcher as holiness preachers, it is Seymour who follows Wesley and Fletcher in seeing love as the decisive criterion for evaluating spirituality.

---

10. Robeck, *The Azusa Street Mission and Revival*, 13–16.

11. Russell P. Spittler, "Glossolalia," in *The New International Dictionary of Pentecostal and Charismatic Movements*, ed. Stanley M. Burgess and Eduard M. van der Maas (Grand Rapids: Zondervan, 2003), 675.

12. Hollenweger, *Pentecostalism*, 23.

IV. OPEN THEISM IN A PENTECOSTAL TRAJECTORY

A. WESLEY AND FLETCHER INITIATE A TRAJECTORY TOWARD PENTECOSTALISM

In what ways can the work of Wesley and Fletcher be seen as the beginning of a trajectory toward pentecostalism?[13] The first point that should be made is that the affinity between Wesley's ideas and pentecostalism is not just a question of borrowed language or historical progression. The affinity goes much deeper than that, to the core of Wesley's theological concerns. Albert Outler observes:

> He learned much more from Eastern spirituality than liturgy. He found there a distinctive pneumatology.... Here is the font of Wesley's most distinctive ideas about prevenient grace and human freedom and, most crucially, of his peculiar doctrine of perfection as τελείωσις (perfecting perfection) rather than *perfectus* (perfected perfection).... This distinctive view of the person and work of the Holy Spirit provides us with many a clue to aspects of Wesley's thought that are otherwise puzzling.... It is this pneumatology that lies at the heart of Wesley's visions of perfection; and it helps explain why his version of this doctrine was so readily misunderstood by persons long accustomed to the forensic orientations in Latin soteriology.[14]

Wesley's theology is pneumatological at its core, hence having a natural compatibility with pentecostalism and its interest in the Holy Spirit.[15] The com-

---

13. Walter Hollenweger traces five roots of pentecostalism. Four of the five (catholic, critical, evangelical, and ecumenical) originate in Wesley (who he indicates was influenced by Catholicism and the Reformation), and go through the holiness movement, to pentecostalism. (The fifth root is the black oral root). Ibid., 2.

14. Wesley, *Sermons I*, 74–76.

15. Albert Outler, in locating Wesley's main theological interests, highlights his dominant role for the Holy Spirit: "Wesley brought to this complex heritage [of the English Reformation] two new elements: the first, a distinctive stress on the primacy of Scripture (not merely as 'standing revelation' [Offspring Blackall] but as a 'speaking book'); and, second, an insistence upon the personal assurance of God's justifying, pardoning grace (which is what he always meant by such terms as 'experience', 'experimental', 'heart religion'.) The constant goal of Christian living, in his view, is sanctification ('Christian perfection' or 'perfect love'); its organizing principle is always the *order*

patibility may well derive from the genetic relationship. To be more exact, the core of Wesley's theology is both pneumatological and christological just as pentecostalism has a heightened interest in both Jesus and the Holy Spirit.[16]

Another way to evaluate Wesley's proto-pentecostal propensity is to listen to one of his critics. Joseph Butler, philosopher and the bishop of Bristol, complained to Wesley about Whitefield on August 18, 1739, saying, "Sir, the pretending to extraordinary revelations, and gifts of the Holy Ghost is a horrid thing—a very horrid thing."[17] Wesley's response was, "My Lord, for what Mr. Whitefield says, Mr. Whitefield, and not I, is accountable. I pretend to no *extraordinary* revelations, or gifts of the Holy Ghost: None but what every Christian may receive, and ought to expect and pray for."[18] He seems to say that charismatic gifts should be the expectation of every follower of Jesus.

Wesley's openness to charismatic spirituality is also indicated by his sympathetic evaluation of Montanus and the prophetic movement he originated in the late second century. Wesley says, "As to the heresies fathered upon Montanus, it is not easy to find what they were."[19] He felt an affinity with the Montanists' high standards of holiness.

Wesley's strongest affinity with the pentecostal movement is seen in his anticipation of it in this prophecy: "The grand Pentecost shall 'fully come,' and 'devout men in every nation under heaven,' however distant in place from each other, shall 'all be filled with the Holy Ghost.'"[20] He could see a time when what God had begun to do in the Methodist revival would go worldwide.

Laurence Wood's *The Meaning of Pentecost in Early Methodism* describes how John Fletcher has a "legacy of 'pentecostalizing' Wesley's theology of

---

of salvation; the divine agency in it all is the Holy Spirit. Thus it was that Wesley understood prevenience as the distinctive work of the Holy Spirit and as the primal force in all authentic spirituality. This perspective was expounded in unsystematic forms, and yet it was inwardly coherent and relatively consistent in its development. And it is this basic viewpoint that is to be looked for in all the sermons: early, middle, and late." Ibid., 1:56–57.

16. Wood, *The Meaning of Pentecost in Early Methodism*, 140 n. 54.

17. Moore, *Life of the Rev. John Wesley*, 1:464. Quoted by Outler in Wesley, *Sermons II*, 1.

18. Moore, *Life of the Rev. John Wesley*, 1:464. Butler tried to ban Wesley from preaching in his diocese but Wesley reminded him that as an ordained priest and Oxford fellow he was free to preach anywhere within the Church of England. Ibid., 1:465.

19. Sermon 61: "The Mystery of Iniquity" [1783] in Wesley, *Sermons II*, 461.

20. Sermon 63: "The General Spread of the Gospel" [1783] in ibid., 494.

IV. OPEN THEISM IN A PENTECOSTAL TRAJECTORY

Christian perfection" and how Wesley himself adopted his interpretation.[21] Here he is challenging Donald Dayton's view that Wesley disliked the approach, and it was marginalized until given new life by Phoebe Palmer.[22] For Fletcher, the power of the Holy Spirit was not only a theological motif but the desire of his heart:

> O, for that pure baptismal flame! O, for the fulness of the dispensation of the Holy Ghost: pray, pray, pray for this: this shall make us all of one heart and of one soul: pray for gifts—for the gift of utterance; and confess your royal Master! A man without gifts is like the king in disguise: he appears as a subject only.[23]

Fletcher exhorted his friends to "spread the flame of love."[24] Fletcher's intentional prayer for the Holy Spirit with his gifts and the "flame of love" he engenders became prototypical for the early pentecostal movement.

Probably the strongest evidence that early pentecostalism was on a trajectory from Wesley and Fletcher is seen in its teaching. Most particularly, Seymour follows Wesley in identifying justification as the first work of grace and sanctification as the second.[25]

---

21. Wood, *The Meaning of Pentecost in Early Methodism*, 1–2.

22. Ibid., xvi. Persuasive is the fact that either Charles or John Wesley, or both, read and/or edited virtually everything Fletcher wrote. John Wesley then published and approved Fletcher's work.

23. Hester Ann Rogers, *Life and Correspondence of Mrs. Hester Ann Rogers: With Corrections and Additions, Comprising an Introduction by Thomas O. Summers* (Nashville: Publishing House of the M. E. Church, South, 1855, rprt. 1870), 344. Quoted by Wood, *The Meaning of Pentecost in Early Methodism*, 149.

24. Rogers, *Life and Correspondence of Mrs. Hester Ann Rogers*, 337, 341. Quoted by Wood, *The Meaning of Pentecost in Early Methodism*, 148.

25. William J. Seymour, *The Doctrines and Discipline of the Azusa Street Apostolic Faith Mission of Los Angeles, California*, ed. Larry Martin (Joplin, Mo.: Christian Life Books, 2000), 42. In attempting to rebut the Holiness equation of Spirit baptism with sanctification, the early pentecostals could go too far by denying Spirit baptism was a work of grace. "The baptism of the Spirit, or immersion in the Holy Ghost, can hardly be called a work of grace, for by it we are neither saved nor sanctified." Hattie M. Barth, "Justification, Sanctification and Baptism of the Holy Ghost," *The Bridegroom's Messenger* 1, no. 6 (January 15, 1908): 2. Cited in Kimberly Ervin Alexander, "Boundless Love Divine: A Re-evaluation of Early Understandings of the Experience of Spirit Baptism," in *Passover, Pentecost and Parousia: Studies in Celebration of the Life and Ministry of R. Hollis Gause*, ed. Steven Jack Land, Rickie D. Moore, and John Christopher Thomas (Blandford Forum, Dorset, UK: Deo, 2010), 151. That Spirit baptism should not be

Seymour, following Charles Parham, extended the Wesleyan teaching. Wesley equated sanctification with the baptism of the Holy Spirit. Wood observes, "In the sermon, 'Of the Church,' it is significant that Wesley says the Holy Spirit 'in a lower degree is given to all believers.' This is because Wesley is linking the full baptism with the Holy Spirit with those believers who have received a higher degree of the Spirit in full sanctifying grace."[26] Seymour came to see the baptism of the Holy Spirit as a distinct experience subsequent to sanctification.[27] This distinguishing of the Holy Spirit's work of sanctification from the Holy Spirit's empowerment of the believer came out of Seymour's life experience.[28] He and his Wesleyan followers had ex-

---

seen as a work of grace is problematic in light of the pentecostal understanding that the baptism of the Holy Spirit is the occasion of charismatic gifting, such as receiving the gift of tongues. The biblical word for 'charismatic' gifts, χαρίσματα, comes from the Greek word for χάρις or 'grace, favor; gratitude; gift'.

Kimberly Alexander writes: "This brief survey of doctrinal statements and discourse regarding the purpose and function of Spirit baptism in the early Pentecostal movement reveals that leaders felt a necessity to differentiate the experience from the prerequisite experience of sanctification. This context of animosity produced an apologetic which placed Spirit baptism outside of the *via salutis*. However, more thoughtful reflection, even within the earliest period, produced explanations regarding the significance of the experience that identify it as transformational and as a part of the *via salutis*. At least two leaders, Tomlinson and King, speak of the experience as deepening the relationship with God, or of revealing more of God." Ibid., 157–58.

26. Wood, *The Meaning of Pentecost in Early Methodism*, 175. He mentions Sermon 74 [1785] in Wesley, *Sermons III*, 50.

27. Steven J. Land argues, "Thus, the point of Pentecostal spirituality was not to have an experience or several experiences, though they spoke of discrete experiences. The point was to experience life as part of a biblical drama of participation in God's history." Steven Jack Land, *Pentecostal Spirituality: A Passion for the Kingdom* (Cleveland, Tenn.: CPT, 2010), 74–75. Speaking in tongues was thought to be indicative of an outpouring of God's Spirit in the last days. This point is discussed in Alexander, "Boundless Love Divine," 146.

28. "It is probable, therefore, that William J. Seymour worshipped with these people [the Evening Light Saints, who became the Church of God (Anderson, IN)] during his time in Indianapolis, and that while he came to faith in a Methodist Episcopal Church of some sort, he went on to be further converted and/or 'sanctified' while attending services offered by the Evening Light Saints." Robeck, *The Azusa Street Mission and Revival*, 29. Seymour on the subject of the baptism of the Holy Spirit had been persuaded by the teaching of Charles Parham. Seymour was a student for six weeks at Parham's Apostolic Bible Training School in Houston before being called to Los Angeles. Ibid., 47–50. "At first Seymour had his doubts about Parham's message. Like many holiness people, Seymour believed that he had been baptized in the Spirit when he had been sanctified. But Lucy Farrow convinced him that if he simply sought God, he would also receive what she had received. It would prove his earlier holiness understanding of baptism in the Spirit wrong.... He finally concluded that Parham's position on baptism in the Holy Spirit with the Bible evidence of speaking in other tongues made sense as the best interpretation of the biblical facts." Ibid., 46.

IV. OPEN THEISM IN A PENTECOSTAL TRAJECTORY

perienced sanctification but were convinced that there was more of the Holy Spirit's power available by analogy with the experience of the disciples on the day of Pentecost. An experience subsequent to regeneration and sanctification is reported from the first column of the first page of the first issue of *The Apostolic Faith* newspaper: "It would be impossible to state how many have been converted, sanctified, and filled with the Holy Spirit."[29] The inclusion of sanctification puts it clearly in the Wesleyan stream of influence.[30]

The holiness movement had developed the thought of Wesley and Fletcher in describing the baptism of the Holy Spirit as an enduement of power. For Seymour, this baptism of the Holy Spirit is also a flood of love.[31]

> The baptism in the Holy Ghost and fire means to be flooded with the love of God and power for service, and a love for the truth as it is in God's word. So when we receive it, we have the same signs to follow as the disciples received on the day of Pentecost.[32]

It is distinct from the grace of sanctification but does not supersede it.[33] A testimony on the first page of the first issue of *The Apostolic Faith* newspaper similarly characterizes the baptism of the Holy Spirit as one of divine love:

---

29. William J. Seymour, ed., *The Azusa Street Papers: A Reprint of The Apostolic Faith Mission Publications, Los Angeles, California (1906–1908)* (Foley, Ala.: Together in the Harvest, 1906–1908 [reproduction 1997]).

30. A Wesleyan understanding of sanctification carries over into open theism as well. "The open view also makes sense of the experience of sanctification, since growth in grace illustrates the personal character of salvation. Again, God gives us everything we need for life and godliness but it is up to us to make use of the provisions (2 Pet. 1:3–4). God wants us to pursue holiness but his will for us can be frustrated by our unwillingness to cooperate. Holiness cannot be attained without the Spirit but the Spirit cannot sanctify us without cooperation. The open view makes sense of the call to holiness as something that does not happen automatically but as something we have to attend to." Pinnock, *Most Moved Mover*, 167.

31. Kimberly Alexander makes the point that for some of the early pentecostals, Spirit baptism was not perceived as only providing power for service: "In reading the more thoughtful reflections of Pentecostals, and especially in reading the testimonies of those receiving the experience, even in the earliest months of the revival, one is made aware that this experience did more than just 'equip'. These testimonies, and the theological reflection written in light of the experience, reveal that this was a transformative crisis experience." Alexander, "Boundless Love Divine," 167.

32. Seymour, *Doctrines and Disciplines*, 42.

33. "Too many have confused the grace of sanctification with the enduement of power, or the baptism with the Holy Ghost." Ibid., 43.

A Nazarene brother who received the baptism with the Holy Ghost in his own home in family worship, in trying to tell about it, said, "It was a baptism of *love*. Such abounding *love*! Such compassion seemed to almost kill me with its sweetness! People do not know what they are doing when they stand out against it. The devil never gave me a sweet thing; he was always trying to get me to censuring people. This baptism fills us with *divine love*."[34]

The early pentecostals, while aware they were innovating, were cognizant of being on a trajectory from Wesley. Laurence Wood shows that "a self-understanding of Pentecostalism goes back behind the Wesleyan-Holiness movement to Wesley himself."[35]

B. OPEN THEISM IN EARLY PENTECOSTALISM

In order to demonstrate the plausibility of the project of the next chapter—to fuse renewal emphases and open theism—it will be useful to identify an open theist theme in early pentecostalism. In what ways does *The Apostolic Faith* and Seymour's only book (*The Doctrines and Discipline of the Azusa Street Apostolic Faith Mission of Los Angeles, California*) highlight impulses important to open theism?

The theme that holds together Wesley, pentecostalism, and open theism is love. Wesley could say, "Nothing is higher than this but Christian love—the love of our neighbour flowing from the love of God."[36] Pinnock defines open theism in terms of love.[37] The theme was central for William Seymour and the beginnings of the pentecostal movement as well.

---

34. Italics mine. William J. Seymour, ed., *The Azusa Street Papers: The Apostolic Faith: The Original 13 Issues* (San Bernardino, Calif.: PentecostalBooks.com, 1906–1908; reprint 2013), 1, no. 1 (September 1906): 1 [in the section "The Old-Time Pentecost," (1997): 10; (2013): 10].

35. Wood, *The Meaning of Pentecost in Early Methodism*, xv.

36. Sermon 91: "On Charity" [1784] in Wesley, *Sermons III*, 300.

37. The open view of God "expresses two basic convictions: *love* is the most important quality we attribute to God, and *love* is more than care and commitment; it involves being sensitive and responsive as well. These convictions lead the contributors to this book to think of God's relation to the world in dynamic rather than static terms. This conclusion has important consequences.

IV. OPEN THEISM IN A PENTECOSTAL TRAJECTORY

The importance of love to the early pentecostal movement is evidenced in the original fifteen issues of *The Apostolic Faith*, the newspaper of the Azusa Street mission (and later the Portland offshoot). The word *love* occurs 290 times, *beloved* ninety-four times, *loved* forty-seven times, and *loves* or *loveth* seven times. In contrast, words associated with Calvinism—*predestination, predestine, predestinate, sovereignty, sovereign,* or *election*—are noticeable in their absence.[38] *Elect* occurs just once in a theological sense, in an allusion to Matthew 24:24.[39]

Love was at the core of the Azusa Street Mission experience and identity. Seymour writes: "We are not fighting men or churches, but seeking to displace dead forms and creeds and wild fanaticisms with living, practical Christianity. '*Love*, Faith, Unity' are our watchwords...."[40] These watchwords had an experiential reality to them: "The work at Azusa Mission is growing deeper and more powerful than ever.... The spirit of unity, *love* and power is manifest."[41] In passing it is worth noting that the concern for "living, practical Christianity" is reminiscent of John Wesley.[42] The idea of advocating for a

---

For one thing, it means that God interacts with his creatures. Not only does he influence them, but they also exert an influence on him. As a result, the course of history is not the product of divine action alone. God's will is not the ultimate explanation for everything that happens; human decisions and actions make an important contribution too. Thus, history is the combined result of what God and his creatures decide to do. Another consequence of this conviction concerns God's knowledge. As an aspect of his experience, God's knowledge of the world is also dynamic rather than static. Instead of perceiving the entire course of human existence in one timeless moment, God comes to know events as they take place." Pinnock et al., *The Openness of God*, 15–16, italics mine.

38. There is just one occurrence and it is non-theological: "God does not make the husband the tyrant or cruel *sovereign* over the wife, neither does He make the wife to exercise tyranny over the husband, but He makes both one" in 1, no. 12 (January 1908): 3 [in the section "To the Married," (1997): 60; (2013): 343, italics mine].

39. "Satan is making his last dreadful fight; for he knows his time is short. He would deceive the very *elect* if it were possible but thank God, it is not possible." Vol. 1, no. 9 (June–Sept 1907): 4 [in the section "Type of the Coming of Jesus," (1997): 49; (2013): 279, italics mine]. (There are also two instances of *elected* referring to political elections.)

40. Seymour, *The Apostolic Faith*, 1, no. 1 (September 1906): 2 [in the section "The Apostolic Faith Movement," (1997): 11; (2013): 12, italics mine]. The paragraph is reprinted in issues no. 2, 10, 12, and 13.

41. Ibid., 1, no. 6 (March 1907): 1 [in the section "Pentecost Both Sides of the Ocean," (1997): 30; (2013): 157–58, italics mine].

42. For example, "Why has Christianity done so little good in the world?" Sermon 122: "Causes of the Inefficacy of Christianity" [1789] in Wesley, *Sermons IV*, 86.

theology that gives preference to divine love is held in common with open theism and other relational theologies.[43]

There is other evidence that love was William Seymour's primary experience of knowing God. For example, in addressing other Christians, he doesn't characteristically call them "dear Spirit-baptized ones," "dear sanctified ones," "dear saved ones," "dear justified ones," "dear redeemed," or "dear freed ones." He calls them "dear loved ones" (occurs nineteen times in the issues of *The Apostolic Faith*, most in passages attributable to Seymour), "dear beloved" (fourteen times), "dearly beloved" (once in vol. 1 no. 4 and six times in vol. 1 no. 5), "O/Oh, beloved" (twenty-eight times), or simply "beloved" (thirty-two times). The phrase "dear loved ones" also occurs in *Doctrines and Disciplines*, which is attributed to William Seymour.[44]

Seymour, in alignment with most open theists, saw love as God's primary descriptor:

> It is sweet to have the promise of Jesus and the character of Jesus wrought out in our lives and hearts by the power of the Blood and the Holy Ghost, and to have that same *love* and that same meekness and humility manifested in our lives, for His character is *love*. Jesus was a man of *love*.... Yes, He was a man of *love*. He was the express image of the Father, God manifest in the flesh.
>
> Dear *loved* ones, we must have that pure *love* that comes down from heaven, *love* that is willing to suffer loss, *love* that is not puffed up, not easily provoked, but gentle, meek, and humble.[45]

---

43. For example, Thomas J. Oord writes of relational theologians, "Many think God's primary attribute is love, and many believe God's chief desire is that people love others as themselves. Most think God relates within Trinity, and Jesus Christ best reveals God's relational love. Most think God and creatures are genuinely free, at least to some degree." Oord, "Relational Theology," 2.

44. For example, "Dear loved ones, God's promises are true." Seymour, *Doctrines and Disciplines*, 42.

45. While not a signed article by Seymour, it is not attributed to anyone else thus represents the editorial view of the paper. Seymour, *The Apostolic Faith*, 1, no. 3 (November 1906): 4 [in the section "The Character of Love," (1997): 21; (2013): 79, italics mine]. Mel Robeck observes that Clara Lum "took primary editorial responsibility, editing the paper and undoubtedly writing many of the articles (though always anonymously). Robeck, *The Azusa Street Mission and Revival*, 99. The phrase "Dear loved ones" does hint, though, that Seymour was the author of this section.

IV. OPEN THEISM IN A PENTECOSTAL TRAJECTORY

For Seymour, love defines God's character. God *is* love. Of the Holy Spirit, the editor of *The Apostolic Faith* writes, "His character is *love*."[46] Jesus *loved* people. As his followers, self-sacrificial love was to be their way of life.

Human love expressed in imitation of Jesus is characteristically self-sacrificial. Divine love, too, wasn't just a theological construct but was known experientially. For example, as the first calendar year of the revival ended *The Apostolic Faith* reports, "And as the New Year was announced, such a wave of glory, *divine love* and unity came over us."[47]

Five additional considerations reinforce the impression of Azusa Street's compatibility with open theism. One is the view of the future that is expressed. I can find no place where the future is said to be determined or known, with one possible exception.[48] There is no suggestion of God comprehensively determining the future.

A second consideration is the efficacy of personal agency that is asserted. Of the eleven occurrences of 'determine' or 'determined', one is a quote of Paul in 1 Cor. 2:2 saying, "For I am determined not to know anything among you save Jesus Christ and Him crucified." One occurrence is a reference to the intent of evil forces: "It seemed that all the powers of darkness were determined to prevent me from obtaining the priceless blessing."[49] The remaining nine occurrences are all instances of people making up their minds to pursue a course of action. The impression one receives from *The Apostolic Faith* is that people have the freedom to make real efficacious choices.

---

46. Seymour, *The Apostolic Faith*, 2, no. 13 (May 1908): 2 [in the section "Character and Work of the Holy Ghost," (1997): 63; (2013): 361].

47. Ibid., 1, no. 5 (January 1907): 1 [at the beginning of the section "Beginning of World Wide Revival," (1997): 26; (2013): 119, italics mine].

48. This passage comes in a sermon on the Book of Revelation. "John was permitted to see from the beginning of the church age on down to the white throne judgment, the final winding up of the world.... John saw things past, things present, and things in the future." Ibid., 1, no. 11 (January 1908): 3 [in the section "Christ's Messages to the Church," (1997): 56; (2013): 317–18]. Seymour may have been aware that when a biblical prophet "sees" he is usually giving God's perspective on a present situation with a view to changing people's behavior, not necessarily giving a preview of the next reel of history's movie. Given the difficulties in interpreting Revelation, we wouldn't want to make too much of this one instance where Seymour is exegeting scripture rather than expressing his own thoughts.

49. Ibid., 1, no. 5 (January 1907): 4 [in the section "A Business Man's Testimony of Pentecost," (1997): 29; (2013): 153].

The Azusa Mission's posture of humility suggests A third consideration. "This is a humble work in a humble place and we are glad that it is."[50] Seymour was known for his genuine humility.[51] Seymour believed Jesus intended the church to practice three ordinances: baptism, the Lord's supper—and foot washing.[52] Foot washing requires unaccustomed humility and resonates with the open theist theme of God's condescension in giving up some power and control in order that reciprocated love might be a real possibility. Because foot washing emulates an act of Jesus, it serves to focus us on how God is perfectly revealed in Jesus.

> Three ordinances Christ Himself instituted in His Church. First, He commands His minsters to baptize in water in the name of the Father and the Son and the Holy Ghost.... Second, foot washing is an ordinance that Jesus Himself instituted in His church and we, His followers, should observe it. For He has commanded us to observe all things that He has commanded us to teach. So we find we will have to recognize these three ordinances.
>
> We believe in foot washing; we believe it to be an ordinance. Jesus said, in John 13:13–17, "Ye call me Master and Lord, and ye say well, for so I am. If I then, your Lord and Master, have washed your feet, ye also ought to wash one another's feet for I have given you an example, that ye should do as I have done to you...."[53]

The humility exemplified by William Seymour is of a very different character than the self-abnegation that can be found in places like the Keswick

---

50. Ibid., 1, no. 2 (October 1906): 2 [in the section "Marks of Fanaticism," (1997): 15; (2013): 41].

51. "Seymour's demeanor was unusual for a Christian leader in the holiness movement at that time. Many holiness leaders seemed to thrive on conflict and confrontation. William J. Seymour seems to have taken the opposite tack—one of gentleness, humility, weakness, and graciousness.... Frank Bartleman observed that 'Brother Seymour generally sat behind two empty shoe boxes, one on top of the other [which served as the mission's pulpit]. He usually kept his head inside the top one during the meeting, in prayer. There was no pride there.'" Robeck, *The Azusa Street Mission and Revival*, 92–93.

52. Seymour, *Doctrines and Disciplines*, 40.

53. Ibid.

IV. OPEN THEISM IN A PENTECOSTAL TRAJECTORY

movement. A Calvinist assertion of human depravity can lead to a ' self" theology.[54] It is an expression of consecration that is an alternative to Wesleyan sanctification.[55] It bypasses the love of God. Instead of the Holy Spirit revealing sin to the conscience and it being renounced in the light of God's love, self-hatred can be encouraged with an introspective searching for sin of all kinds. It doesn't lead to living completely committed to the reality that God loves you and the healing and hope which that brings. When Jesus said, "If any want to become my followers, let them deny themselves and take up their cross and follow me" (Mark 8:34) he meant putting an end to self-centeredness, self-absorption, and self-indulgence. He meant taking action in the physical world (not self-hating introspection) and following his lead. He meant walking with him and following his teaching. Instead of a joyful co-working between God and humans in Keswick teaching you sometimes hear Calvinist denials of the possibility of humans doing any good—it is all God. That view is dispiriting to an active participation with God in expressing his compassion and love to the world.[56]

---

54. For example, Roy and Revel Hession *The Calvary Road* (Fort Washington, Pa.: Christian Literature Crusade, 1950).

55. For example, Jessie Penn-Lewis, *The Cross of Calvary and Its Message* (London: Marshall Bros., 1903).

56. The historical context of these two ways of viewing sanctification are summarized in David Bundy's remarkable bibliographic essay on the Keswick movement: "The Holiness-Keswick debate focused on two issues: original sin and the nature of sanctification. Holiness Movement clergy in the Methodist-Wesleyan context emphasized the instantaneous removal of original sin by an instantaneous act of grace; viz, entire sanctification. Keswick maintained a Reformed view of sin and a gradual process of sanctification. The categories became 'eradicationist' (Keswick term for the Holiness position) versus 'suppressionist' (Holiness Movement term for the Keswick position). Suppression described the Keswickian goal of 'uniform sustained victory over known sin.' There was agreement regarding the need for sanctification." David D. Bundy, *Keswick: A Bibliographic Introduction to the Higher Life Movements* (Wilmore, Ky.: B. L. Fisher Library, Asbury Theological Seminary, 1975), 43. Both of these terms were caricatures and misrepresented the core of their respective positions. The goal of sanctification in the Keswick view as expressed by Jessie Penn-Lewis was a daily dying to self. For example, she writes: "How clearly the Greek words used bring out the position basis of having 'died out' in Christ's death, and the progressive 'putting to death' perpetually which must of necessity be done day by day." Jessie Penn-Lewis, *The Centrality of the Cross*, 4th ed. (Dorset, England: Overcomer Book Room, 1920), 11. Similarly, "eradication" was a mischaracterization of the Wesleyan view of sanctification which claimed through the Holy Spirit an instantaneous freedom from the compulsion to commit deliberate sin but expected an ongoing process of sanctification and growth in love.

A fourth consideration is the personal and highly relational way attenders of the Azusa Street mission interacted with Jesus in prayer. For them the common theme, "Jesus Christ the same yesterday, and today, and forever" (Hebrews 13:8) cannot have been understood in metaphysical terms. That would be a denial of the pre-incarnate Word which changed to become incarnate as a human baby. That baby didn't stay the same but grew to be an adult human who was God incarnate. That human underwent change when he was executed by crucifixion. And then he underwent a radical change when God raised him from the dead. For Azusa Street, "Jesus Christ the same yesterday, and today, and forever" meant that what Jesus did through the power of the Holy Spirit in his earthly ministry (teaching, healing, exorcism) he is still doing today through his church in the power of the Holy Spirit.

A fifth consideration is the propensity of the Apostolic Faith Mission to use biblical terminology rather than Greek philosophical terms in describing God. In explaining its doctrine, Seymour mostly writes in his own words and for the most part develops themes that are compatible with open theism. Here, there is no mention of Greek philosophical categories or any description of God as omnicontrolling. Seymour is preoccupied with salvation in the broader sense (justification and sanctification), followed by the baptism of the Holy Spirit. Eight pages into the chapter on doctrine, he reproduces the Methodist Episcopal *Articles of Religion* (modified by Wesley from the *Thirty-nine Articles of Religion* of the Church of England) with only three changes. Most substantive is the change from two sacraments to three with the addition of foot washing.[57] Then after the *Articles of Religion* you have a page describing attributes of God without any comment from Seymour but with supporting scriptures. It seems out of place. It turns out the list is virtually identical to one published in 1876 by Foote and Rand in the *Bible Student's Companion*.[58] Seymour either used Foote and Rand or had access to some common third source. Of the thirty-one original attributes of God, Seymour deletes seven

---

57. Seymour, *Doctrines and Disciplines*, 49. Incidentally, Seymour also deleted a sentence on the baptism of children (p. 50) and a reference to "the rulers of the United States" (p. 51).

58. William C. Foote and William Wilberforce Rand, *Bible Student's Companion: Containing Bible Text-Book, Concordance, Table of Proper Names, Twelve Maps, Indexes, Etc.* (New York: American Tract Society, 1876), 67.

IV. OPEN THEISM IN A PENTECOSTAL TRAJECTORY

(light, heart-searching, glorious, and the four last ones: long-suffering, jealous, compassionate, a consuming fire) and adds none. Seymour's list says God is Spirit, invisible, incorruptible, eternal, immortal, omnipotent, omnipresent, omniscient, immutable, only wise, incomprehensible, unsearchable, most high, love, perfect, holy, just, true, upright, righteous, good, great, gracious, faithful, and merciful.[59] The lack of original commentary and the minimal nature of the redaction suggests Seymour invested little time or thought in this list. That the descriptors with Greek philosophical origin (omnipotent, omnipresent, omniscient, immutable, and incomprehensible) appear rarely in *The Apostolic Faith* is telling.[60]

To summarize, the compatibility of open theism with early pentecostalism is evidenced in the issues of *The Apostolic Faith* and Seymour's *The Doctrines and Discipline of the Azusa Street Apostolic Faith Mission of Los Angeles, California*. A deterministic view of the future is almost entirely absent. People have genuine free will. Humility, as evidenced in foot washing, resonates with God's condescension in granting humans real freedom and

---

59. Seymour, *Doctrines and Disciplines*, 67. He retains the original scripture citations with just two deletions, one addition, and one emendation (Psalm 139:7 becomes Psalm 139:7–10). He deleted as support for God's omnipotence Exod. 6:3, "I appeared to Abraham, Isaac, and Jacob as God Almighty, but by my name 'The Lord' I did not make myself known to them." Of the first four items in the list, he moves three to a subsequent position (including "love" to a position just before "perfect," and "unsearchable" to just after "incomprehensible."

60. 'Omnipotent' occurs only three times, always in the phrase, "Hosanna to His omnipotent name." The phrase is probably an echo of Rev. 19:6 where the KJV that Seymour used translates παντοκράτωρ 'omnipotent'. Interestingly, three paragraphs after one of these cases, Seymour says, "We must be *coworkers* with Him, partakers of the Holy Ghost." Seymour, *The Apostolic Faith*, 1, no. 9 (June–September 1907): 3 [in the section "The Holy Spirit Bishop of the Church," (1997): 48; (2013): 269]. By 'omnipotent' Seymour cannot mean 'omnicontrolling' or it would make no sense to speak of us as 'coworkers'.

'Omnipresent' occurs just once and is consistent with an open view. It has the poignancy of being in a letter sent from Africa: "Our hearts rejoice in the omnipresent God this morning. We thank Him as never before. His loving presence is with us." Ibid., 1, no. 6 (March 1907): 5 [in the section "On the Way to Africa," (1997): 34; (2013): 182].

Most significantly for compatibility with open theism, 'omniscient', 'omniscience', and 'all-knowing' do not occur. Neither does 'immutable', 'immutability' or 'unchangeable' (although an unidentified sister testifies, "I am rejoicing in His unchangeableness." Ibid., 1 no. 7 (April 1907): 2 [in the section "Azusa Mission, Thursday Evening, May 1," (1997): 39; (2013): 215].) 'Incomprehensible' does not occur. That is significant for relational theologies because it is difficult to see how relationship is possible with an unknowable being. One of the claims of the New Testament is that God has chosen to reveal himself and is therefore to that extent knowable.

in becoming incarnate. The theological emphasis is not on an immovable, unchanging, impassible deity but on how God is active in the world through justification, sanctification, and the baptism of the Holy Spirit. And above all, the theme of divine love flowing from God and then through people to others, links open theism compellingly with Wesleyan pentecostalism.

CHAPTER V

A Convergence of the Two Trajectories

This chapter will describe a Wesleyan renewal theology with an open theist identity. Yong, Archer, Pinnock, and Boyd have indicated this as a possibility but have not explicitly worked it out in that way. (1) Wesley and Fletcher's emphasis on God's love and grace rather than judgment or control, (2) Seymour's description of the baptism of the Spirit as an outpouring of love, and (3) open theism's view of God's nature as defined by love; these suggest an emerging theme—God's love—which is poured out, transforms individuals and communities, then is reflected into human relationships.[1]

While it would be inappropriate to make any predictions, there is potential here for a movement on a global scale. Jeremy Rifkin in 1979 wrote, "If the Charismatic and evangelical strains of the new Christian renewal movement [today] come together and unite a liberating energy with a new covenant vision for society, it is possible that a great religious awakening will take place, one potentially powerful enough to incite a second Protestant reformation."[2] Recovering from Wesley and Fletcher a passion for both personal and social change, absorbing from the pentecostal-charismatic movements a dependence on the power of the Holy Spirit with a willingness be Jesus' hands, feet, and

---

1. A similiar approach is found in Pinnock, *Flame of Love*. Pinnock's pneumatology is inspiring but more needs to be said in the light of ongoing challenges from neo-Calvinists.
2. Jeremy Rifkin, *The Emerging Order: God in the Age of Scarcity* (New York: G. P. Putnam's Sons/Ballantine, 1979, rprt. 1983), xi. He is quoted in Howard A. Snyder, "The Church as Holy and Charismatic," *Wesleyan Theological Journal* 15, no. 2 (Spring 1980): 26.

voice, and incorporating the ability of open theism to respond to pressing intellectual issues, and to be a catalyst through its emphasis on the openness of the future—these three elements together create the possibility of a new global renewal movement. They suggest, at least, a way forward.

A. TOWARDS AN OPEN THEIST RENEWAL THEOLOGY

I will develop this synthesis of open theism and renewal theology under two headings: theology and praxis. In order to give some coverage to the major themes of theology, only an outline will be suggested due to space and time limitations. Two topics, anthropology and pneumatology will, however, be developed in a little more detail because here are found themes which are emphasized in open renewal theology.

1. God in Open Renewal Theology

Theology here describes a radically loving and self-giving God who chose to give real freedom to creatures then lives with us in a non-deterministic universe. (a) God created all things and sustains the universe with his power. (b) He is engaged in a cosmic conflict with spiritual beings who oppose him. (c) Renewalist open theism emphasizes God's immanence rather than transcendence.[3] God is present in time and knows everything that is knowable.[4] God is everywhere in space—he is especially near to those who seek him. (d) God is in community within the Trinity and desires community with people.[5] (e) He is humble and condescends to communicate and meet us where we are—supremely in the incarnation of his Son. (f) He suffers with

---

[3]. God's transcendence is easily intuited. One only needs to stand under a clear night sky away from city lights and be in awe. That God should come near and risk interacting with humans is much more surprising. That God is revealed to be at his core, love, is amazing. That the love of God is accessible to humans is astonishing.

[4]. From an open theist point-of-view the future does not exist yet as predetermined events so it is open to the extent that God has not decided ahead of time what he intends to do.

[5]. Genesis begins with God and humans relating naturally in the garden. The Wesleyan vision of restoration is not just going back to the garden, but a deeper relationship on a renewed earth that comes out of many choices in a Godward direction.

and rejoices with those he has created. (g) In this vision, God is passionate, responsive, and, above all, loving beyond our capacity to imagine. (h) He is the source of all beauty and the only deserving recipient of our worship.

2. Christology in Open Renewal Theology

Christology in open renewal theology is formed around (1) the conviction that Jesus perfectly reveals what God is like, (2) Jesus' teaching of the kingdom of God with its radical love, and (3) Jesus' self-giving sacrifice which is love at the extreme.

The assertion that Jesus says everything there is to say about what God is like comes from Colossians 1:15–19, "He is the image of the invisible God.... In him all the fullness of God was pleased to dwell." Jesus perfectly reveals God. Where biblical material, especially from the Old Testament, seems discordant it is a procedural misstep to try to form a synthesis between the two perceptions. God hasn't changed, but the Bible is progressive in its revelation of who he is.

A second distinctive of open renewal christology is that it takes seriously what Jesus actually taught, not just who he is.[6] Jesus' teaching about the kingdom of God is often marginalized in evangelical preaching. For example, one rarely hears an ethic of nonviolence preached. An open renewal christology would seek to prioritize Jesus' ideas.

A third distinctive is the centrality of Jesus' supreme act of love. Love is nowhere more evident than the Son of God giving his life for us on the cross. An open renewal christology revolves around this event which so clearly reveals the heart of God for us, together with Jesus' vindication by the Father raising him from the dead.

[6.] Brian Zahnd may or may not self-identify as an open theist or charismatic theologian, but his books are remarkably instructive on this point. Brian Zahnd and Miroslav Volf, *Unconditional?* (Lake Mary, Fla.: Charisma House, 2010); Brian Zahnd, *Beauty Will Save the World* (Lake Mary, Fla.: Charisma House, 2012); Brian Zahnd, *A Farewell to Mars: An Evangelical Pastor's Journey Toward the Biblical Gospel of Peace* (Colorado Springs, Colo.: David C. Cook, 2014). Incidentally, Tom Wright in a recent interview ("Tom Wright—The Man Behind the Theology," Nomad Podcast 85, June 25, 2015) when asked what one book (other than ones he had written) which every Christian should read replied that "One of the most amazing books of the twenty-first century" is Miroslav Volf, *Exclusion and Embrace: A Theological Exploration of Identity, Otherness, and Reconciliation* (Nashville: Abingdon, 1996).

These three elements form the basis of open renewal christology: Jesus reveals God, Jesus' teaching matters, and the cross and resurrection are theology's center of gravity.

3. The Church in Open Renewal Theology

The Church in renewalist open theism is communities of those who (1) follow Jesus, (2) worship God, (3) celebrate the sacraments, (4) exercise spiritual gifts, (5) depend on the Holy Spirit, and (4) reflect God's love into a hurting world. While the Church can be just two individuals who are meeting intentionally in the presence of Jesus, Wesley's class, band, and society meetings set a remarkable precedent for sustaining healthy and accountable spiritual relationships.

As a student of Luke–Acts, Roger Stronstad has a view of the Church which is consonant with this definition.

> The Church is to be a community of prophets. But from the post-apostolic period to the present it has not functioned as a prophetic community which is powerful in works and word. In fact, in too many places the Church views itself as a didactic community rather than as a prophetic community, where sound doctrine is treasured above charismatic action. Indeed, the preaching and teaching of the word displaces Spirit-filled, Spirit-led, and Spirit-empowered ministry. The Spirit of prophecy has been quenched and the gifts of the Spirit have been sanitized and institutionalized.[7]

This definition of the Church captures the activism of a Wesleyan renewal ecclesiology. To incorporate an open theistic element would involve simply emphasizing a radical openness of the future which invites a response to prophetic calls creatively to live out the kingdom of God.

---

[7]. Roger Stronstad, *The Prophethood of All Believers: A Study in Luke's Charismatic Theology* (Cleveland, Tenn.: CPT, 2010), 121.

V. A CONVERGENCE OF THE TWO TRAJECTORIES

4. Eschatology in Open Renewal Theology

Eschatology in a renewalist open theist perspective actually has more to say than might be expected from a position that denies the existence of the future. There will be a future even if it is not currently accessible to us. Even though he is not necessarily an open theist, Frank Macchia annunciates an understanding of eschatology that draws together open renewal themes. Eschatology involves the "realization of the kingdom of God in history."[8] He writes, "The kingdom of God gains its substance as a historical dynamic from the expanding presence and victory of God's love in both purity and power especially in the church but also throughout the world, both implicitly and explicitly through the church's missionary arm."[9]

While we could develop an open renewal eschatology in several directions, following the lead of John Wesley is attractive. Wesley saw beyond heaven to a renewed earth with the goal of salvation as the restoration of all things, including the image of God in humans.

5. Anthropology in Open Renewal Theology

Anthropology in a renewalist open theist perspective acknowledges (1) that humanity has gone awry in its alienation from God. (2) However, by conditioning his own omnipotence, God has chosen to give humans some real freedom. (3) Human free will can be used or abused. (4) Christ-followers work synergistically with God to bring the kingdom into present reality.

In describing a relational anthropology, Frank Macchia provides a basis for an open renewal understanding of anthropology.[10] "'Relation'" he says "is not a human luxury or an addendum to human existence. There is something about relationships that is 'ontological,' or essential to human existence or that mode of being we call 'human' and 'creaturely.'"[11] An open renewal understanding of anthropology is relational and focused on relationships.

---

8. Frank D. Macchia, *Baptized in the Spirit: A Global Pentecostal Theology* (Grand Rapids: Zondervan, 2006), 44.

9. Ibid., 45–46.

10. Ibid., 168–178. Open theism is relational theology and Macchia writes as a Pentecostal.

11. Ibid., 168.

(1) Humanity Gone Awry

In describing humanity's root problem, Jesus rarely used legal metaphors.[12] Rather, sin has made us sick.[13] We have become assimilated to the world and alienated from God. By contrast, a person who has developed psychologically in a healthy way has appropriate barriers and bridges: "A healthy self is lived in a creative and constructive interplay of distinction and connection."[14] Instead, "We waffle between alienation and assimilation, both of which are signs of a fallen reality as well as that which distorts our souls or inner sense of self. This fallen reality is essentially relational, as are the symptoms of destruction and oppression that we feel in the midst of it."[15] According to Genesis 2–3, this relational chaos results from human distrust of God incited by Satan, and the subsequent disobedience and alienation from God.

God found a way to turn around the disaster of human rebellion. In the person of his Son, he died for humanity's sins on the cross and broke the power of sin and death. An open renewal theology has natural affinities with the Christus Victor interpretation of this atonement.[16] John Wesley, many early Pentecostals, and some open theists (particularly Greg Boyd) discuss the reality of Satan.[17] In the Christus Victor understanding, the atonement, above all, represents the defeat of Satan and the ransoming of humanity from his control.

---

12. E.g., the only time in the Synoptic Gospels he uses the term 'guilty' is: "Whoever blasphemes against the Holy Spirit can never have forgiveness, but is guilty of an eternal sin" Mark 3:29. Jesus does extend forgiveness (e.g., Luke 5:20, 7:28) but that is more relational than forensic.

13. E.g., in Mark 2:17, Jesus says, "It is not the healthy who need a doctor, but the sick. I have not come to call the righteous, but sinners."

14. Macchia, *Baptized in the Spirit*, 170.

15. Ibid., 169.

16. Gustaf Aulén, *Christus Victor: An Historical Study of the Three Main Types of the Idea of Atonement*, trans. A. G. Hebert (New York: Macmillan, 1969).

17. E.g., Sermon 72: "Of Evil Angels" [1783] Wesley, *Sermons III*, 15–29. "Satan is making his last dreadful fight; for he knows his time is short." Seymour, *The Apostolic Faith*, Vol. 1, no. 9 (June–Sept 1907): 4 [in the section "Type of the Coming of Jesus," (1997): 49; (2013): 279]. For Greg Boyd references, see above at p. 32.

V. A CONVERGENCE OF T...

(2) Human Freedom

The usual historic Arminian view is tha...
This knowledge creates a soft determinisr...
can change because God's knowledge is...
view, what can be known about the future i...
This distinction is of great practical signific...
termined does not invite Spirit-led proactive...
down in the way a future that is open does...
day seem to be in a kind of stand-off, with J... ...aiting patiently for God to act (because to take the initiative might seem like trying to earn your salvation through works) and God waiting for people to respond to the prompting of his Spirit and exercise their freedom to move in compassion.

In the open renewal view, human freedom is a gift that costs God something. John Polkinghorne quotes the British philosopher John Lucas discussing how God must feel when human freedom is abused: "Faced with a dilemma of either a God who withdraws the gift of freedom or a God who is frustrated by the gift of freedom, Lucas opts for the latter as 'the cross on which God has chosen to be impaled.... It is a corollary of caring; that one should be vulnerable, and a God who cares infinitely will be infinitely vulnerable.'"[19]

Human freedom is essential to God's project of renewing the world as the kingdom of God. Without the freedom to obey or not obey, to love or not to love, allegiance means nothing because it is coerced and not chosen. Our love and allegiance are among the very few things we can give to God that he would not otherwise have and demonstrate the ideal expression of human freedom.

(3) Human Free Will

Open theists are not in agreement on whether God overrides human free will. Some think God can and does.[20] Probably most think God *can* but typically

---

18. This implicit determinism was mentioned above at p. 98.

19. John R. Lucas, *Freedom and Grace* (London: SPCK, 1976), 29. Cited in Polkinghorne, *Science and Providence*, 79.

20. The supporters of this view usually cite the Exodus passages which say the Lord "will harden" or "hardened" Pharaoh's heart (4:21, 7:3, 8:15, 8:32, 9:12, 9:34, 10:1, 20, 27, 11:10). But then

...[21] John Polkinghorne and Thomas Jay Oord are of the ...cannot override human free will.[22] This position helps explain ...oes not prevent evil people from exercising their free will. Thomas ...rd argues from biblical texts that it is contrary to God's nature to over-...de human free will.[23] It seems safe to say that God, at least normatively, achieves his purposes through persuasion.

What about when one person's free will impinges on that of another? God's non-coercive normal mode of acting through influence provides an important rationale for a commitment to human nonviolence. This non-coercive open theist view of God's action provides a significant model for humans as we work with God to achieve his purposes.

(4) Humans Work Synergistically with God

A Wesleyan anthropology differs significantly from a Calvinist anthropology. The latter is so concerned to protect the free and unmerited character of salvation that the depravity of the human condition is overemphasized. Wesley is no less clear on the unmerited nature of salvation but insists that salvation entails more than a onetime not-guilty declaration. The process of salvation entails people working synergistically with God. Albert Outler observes, "The essence of Wesley's synergism; every human action is a reaction to prevenient grace."[24] Wesley: "First, God works; therefore you *can* work. Secondly, God works; therefore you *must* work."[25]

---

in Exodus 12:31, Pharaoh changes his mind and lets the Israelites go, even after his heart has been "hardened." (God does "harden" his heart again in 14:4, 8, 17). "Harden" does not seem to entail an overriding of free will so much as a locking in of a decision already made.

21. This would be John Sanders' position. Sanders, *The God Who Risks*, 225–242.

22. John C. Polkinghorne, *Belief in God in an Age of Science* (New Haven, Conn.: Yale University Press, 1998), 14. Tom Oord, "20th Anniversary of Book, *The Openness of God*" session at the American Academy of Religion annual meeting (San Diego: November 23, 2014).

23. Thomas Jay Oord, *The Uncontrolling Love of God: An Open and Relational Account of Providence* (Downers Grove: IVP Academic, forthcoming 2015).

24. Wesley, *Sermons III*, 208 n. 60.

25. Sermon 85: "On Working out Our Own Salvation" [1785], ibid., 206.

V. A CONVERGENCE OF THE TWO TRAJECTORIES

What does it mean to work synergistically with God? One approach would be to start where Jesus is already at work, among the poor and oppressed. Clark Pinnock wrote prophetically in 1977:

> Latin American and Black theologians are pressing for a radical understanding of what it means to *do* the truth in a situation of oppression and suffering.... We are summoned to enter into the same struggle, to hear the Word of God ourselves in a world of poverty and dire distress.... The "theology of liberation" is in reality God's instrument for the refinement of our own commitment to the gospel, and has been leading many to reflect on the need for the liberation of North American Christians.... All believers in Jesus Christ have been summoned to a life of radical discipleship, oriented to his cross (Mark 8:34).[26]

Pinnock laments, "To put it most mildly, we are insensitive to the cries of the world's poor.... A serious attempt to assist the world's poor has not been made except by a very few, and we stand condemned as pretty indifferent to the problem."[27] Besides this call for work in relief and development, Pinnock raises the bigger issue of economic justice:

> To this relative absence of tender-heartedness must be added a shocking lack of justice and fair play. That we control a disproportionately large share of the world's real wealth is partly because of our domination of "world trade," a new economic colonialism by which we have repatriated large profits from countries which have only some basic raw material to sell and a large supply of cheap labor. In every way they are disadvantaged in relation to our superior economic leverage and technical development. We are rather like the fat sheep in Ezekiel's pathetic picture which "push and thrust

---

26. Clark H. Pinnock, "A Call for the Liberation of North American Christians," in *Evangelicals and Liberation*, ed. Carl E. Armerding (Nutley, N.J.: Presbyterian and Reformed, 1977), 128.
27. Ibid., 130.

at the weak until they are scattered abroad" (Ezek. 34:21). We, the wealthy six percent of the earth's population, cluster around the well of the earth's resources and drink deeply from it, while the vast majority of peoples are shunted aside, lapping up the trickles that spill from our cups.[28]

This call for working with God for economic justice precedes by almost two decades Pinnock's interest in open theism, but the two concerns have this common impetus from the Hebrew prophets.[29] They both come from the same conviction that God is passionately involved in the world he has made. One seeks to emphasize God's love for the poor. The other emphasizes that God is wholly loving in both his being and actions.

Working synergistically with God is possible in other spheres of influence as well. It works wherever we have freedom to take action and can sense the anointing of God's Spirit. Because the future is in measure open to us, we may work in partnership with God, either through his direct initiative, or remarkably, through ours.

From an open theist renewal perspective, anthropology acknowledges human alienation from God, highlights the freedom with which God has gifted humans, suggests that the example of divine non-coercive persuasion models a nonviolent ethic, and describes how humans work synergistically with God to bring the kingdom into present reality.

---

28. Ibid., 131.

29. In the interim, Pinnock wrote a critique of the Marxist assumptions of most liberation theologies of the time. "I am troubled at the way in which our proper Christian concern for the poor has been unwisely routed along the tracks of collectivist economics." Clark H. Pinnock, "The Pursuit of Utopia," in *Freedom, Justice, and Hope: Toward a Strategy for the Poor and Oppressed*, ed. Marvin Olasky (Westchester, Ill.: Crossway, 1988), 66. He affirmed a pragmatic approach: "We need to see reality: Facts are facts, and facts dictate that any society with a social conscience should adopt a market approach, with whatever refinements its citizens wish to introduce along the way." Ibid., 82. Pinnock didn't have occasion to return to writing on political theology as he worked out a more Wesleyan approach. If he had, he could have found a basis for a radical critique of materialism and consumerism in Wesley's objection to the ideas of his contemporary, the Scottish philosopher Adam Smith, who pioneered Political Economy. *The Wealth of Nations* was first published in 1776. Albert Outler comments: "One might guess that what Wesley has in mind here was the huge popularity of Adam Smith's case for economic self-interest and the lack of an adequate current critique from clergy and other opinion-makers." Sermon 87: "The Danger of Riches" [1781] in Wesley, *Sermons III*, 229 n. 3.

V. A CONVERGENCE OF THE TWO TRAJECTORIES

6. Pneumatology in Open Renewal Theology

Pneumatology begins with (1) creation and the hovering Spirit (here Wesley's curiosity about the created world and open theism's interest in science have something to say), (2) describes the Spirit at work everywhere drawing people to God (Wesley's understanding of prevenient grace comes into play here), (3) describes how the Spirit indwells the believer at the point of coming to faith in Jesus, (4) explains how the Spirit is poured out in empowerment for service and holiness, (5) explores the Spirit's work in the world, and then (6) discusses how the Spirit continues to progressively sanctify and provoke love in people. That soteriology has been subsumed under pneumatology will not have escaped your notice. An open theist renewal pneumatology will now be developed a little further by looking at these six ways the Spirit is at work.

(1) Pneumatology and Creation

The Spirit of God appears early in the Bible. The second verse tells us that the Spirit was instrumental in creation:

> In the beginning, God created the heavens and the earth. ² Now the earth was formless and empty, darkness was over the surface of the deep, and the Spirit of God was hovering over the waters (NIV).

Greg Boyd suggests that the Spirit here is performing a restraining function—subduing the forces of chaos—as becomes clear when Genesis is compared with other Ancient Near Eastern creation accounts.[30] If this is the case, then Genesis describes a re-creation of the earth after some cosmic disaster, perhaps related to the rebellion of Satan and his followers.[31] The Spirit of God in this scenario is engaged in spiritual warfare from the first page of the Bible. Because we experience the Spirit as a gentle, loving, indwelling advocate, it is easy for us to forget the immense power he possesses. That power is clear in the Spirit's role in the universe's creation and in ongoing evolutionary processes.

---

30. Boyd, *God at War*, 84–85, 104-108.
31. Ibid., 103–113.

Ralph Winter, probably the foremost mission strategist of our generation, argued that the Holy Spirit was not alone in influencing the direction of evolution.[32] This minority view has tremendous explanatory power and deserves our attention. Winter writes, "Nature has been pervasively distorted into violence by Satan."[33] He observes that Genesis 1:29–30 describes plants as food, not animals. Winter notes that predatory life first appeared in the Cambrian period (roughly 541–485 *million years ago*). To Satan, not to God, should be attributed the violence found in nature.[34]

The Spirit continues his creative work in the world and continues to restrain evil. Polkinghorne writes: "The scientific recognition of the evolutionary character of the universe has encouraged theological recognition of the immanent presence of God to creation and of the need to complement the concept of *creatio ex nihilo* by a concept of *creatio continua*. Continuous creation has been an important theme in the writings of scientist-theologians."[35]

---

32. In assuming theistic evolution, I'm following the lead of Clark Pinnock whose view was that we've spent enough time debating evolution versus creationism. "We are held back by creationism and intelligent design. We're bugged by people who won't let us start. We have to just start." "Theology After Darwin" session at the Open Theology and Science Conference (Azusa, Calif.: April 11, 2008). The issue of spiritual warfare came up at the same session and Pinnock's view was that open theism could go either way: "Openness theology could put more or less emphasis on spiritual warfare. Greg [Boyd] puts a lot of weight on the importance of spiritual warfare. You also have [William] Hasker who doesn't." In my view, without the insights of the warfare perspective there are too many unanswered theodicy questions.

33. Winter, "The Most Precarious Mission Frontier," 168.

34. He quotes Bruce McLaughlin: "According to Scripture, the universe was originally good and the glory of God is still evident in it (Rom. 1:20). But something else—something frightfully wicked—is evident in it as well. Of their own free will, Satan and other spiritual beings rebelled against God in the primordial past and now abuse their God-given authority over certain aspects of creation. Satan, who holds the power of death (Heb. 2:14), exercises a pervasive, structural, diabolic influence to the point that the entire creation is in bondage to decay. The pain-ridden, bloodthirsty, sinister and hostile character of nature should be attributed to Satan and his army, not to God. Jesus' earthly ministry reflected the belief that the world had been seized by a hostile, sinister lord. Jesus came to take it back." Bruce McLaughlin, "From Whence Evil?," *Perspectives on Science and the Christian Faith: Journal of the American Scientific Affiliation* 56, no. 3 (September 2004): 237–238.

35. John C. Polkinghorne, ed., *The Work of Love: Creation as Kenosis* (Grand Rapids: Eerdmans, 2001), 95. He cites three books including his own *Science and Creation: The Search for Understanding* (Philadelphia: Templeton Foundation, 1988, 2006), ch. 4. Ian G. Barbour, *Issues in Science and Religion* (London: SCM, 1966), ch. 12. Arthur R. Peacocke, *Creation and the World of Science: The Re-shaping of Belief* (Oxford: Oxford University Press, 1979, 2004), chs. 2 and 3.

V. A CONVERGENCE OF THE TWO TRAJECTORIES

Jürgen Moltmann expresses similar thoughts on the immanence of the Spirit of God in creation:

> The immanence of the transcendent Spirit is also the foundation and driving power of the *history of life* into ever richer and more complex forms and syntheses. The so-called "self-organization of the universe" is nothing other than the resonance of the universe as it responds to the immanence of the divine Spirit that drives it.[36] Why else should life organize itself? Why else its torment of chaos and death, if there is not something present in all things which desire to endure and not pass away, which wills to live and not die? Why the struggle for survival if life does not promise more than it can give?...
> In everything that is, the eternal Being manifests itself. Everything living is a resonance responding to the living God. Through his creative Spirit, God is already present in all things....
> God's Spirit in all things makes the world in which we live a *spiritual* world. Our human spirituality must adapt itself to it.... It will become a pentecostal spirituality of the wakened senses and the attentive heart.[37]

This intuition that the earth is inherently spiritual meshes with Boyd's spiritual warfare motif except that Boyd would identify spirits both malevolent and those serving God besides the Holy Spirit.

Besides stressing the immanence and activity of the Spirit in the world, Moltmann with Polkinghorne is also emphasizing the kenotic nature of creation:

> Moltmann argues that the theology of kenosis has focused predominantly on the outward trinitarian act of self-limitation and

---

36. *The Self-Organizing Universe: Scientific and Human Implications of the Emerging Paradigm of Evolution* was written in 1980 by the Austrian astrophysicist Erich Jantsch.

37. Jürgen Moltmann, "Sighs, Signs, and Significance: Natural Science and a Hermeneutics of Nature," in *Divine Grace and Emerging Creation: Wesleyan Forays in Science and Theology of Creation*, ed. Thomas Jay Oord (Eugene: Wipf & Stock, 2009), 121.

self-emptying, but has overlooked God's immanent limitation. "God is nowhere greater than in his humiliation.... God is nowhere more divine than when he becomes man."[38] In Trinitarian "self-limitation" which is in reality "self-realization," God limits himself and determines to withdraw his omnipotence in order to "concede space" for a finite creation.[39] The "primordial kenosis" in the inner trinitarian relations of God, the self-surrender of the triune persons to one another in perichoretic penetration, is the expression of boundless love flowing outward in creation, reconciliation, and eschatological transformation.[40] Divine self-limitation likewise involves a restriction of omniscience, not that God does not know all things, but in the sense that "God doesn't know everything in advance because he doesn't will to know everything in advance. He waits for the response of those he has created, and lets their future come."[41] In Moltmann's theology, omnipresence is maintained in that the Spirit is immanent in creation as the source that undergirds all life, but omnipotence and omniscience have been limited through an intra-trinitarian and extra-trinitarian act of kenosis.[42]

What Moltmann and Polkinghorne write in Europe, characterized as kenotic theology, has many affinities with what in North America we mostly discuss

---

38. Jürgen Moltmann, *Trinity and the Kingdom: The Doctrine of God*, trans. Margaret Kohl (Minneapolis, Minn.: Fortress, 1993), 119.

39. Jürgen Moltmann, *Science and Wisdom*, trans. Margaret Kohl (Minneapolis, Minn.: Fortress, 2003), 62.

40. Ibid., 57.

41. Ibid., 64.

42. Peter Althouse, "Implications of the Kenosis of the Spirit for a Creational Eschatology: A Pentecostal Engagement with Jürgen Moltmann," in *The Spirit Renews the Face of the Earth: Pentecostal Forays in Science and Theology of Creation*, ed. Amos Yong (Eugene: Wipf & Stock, 2009), 157–58. It should be noted that Moltmann does go places theologically that I would rather not go. For example, he elaborates divine kenosis in a way that has the Father abandoning the Son on the cross (as is usual in Reformed theology) in what I believe is a misreading of Mark 15:34 and parallels. Jesus is describing his experience, not the ontological reality. How could a wholly loving father abandon his son in his hour of greatest need?

as open theism. A compelling case can be made for seeing the creator Spirit as humbly and lovingly engaged in the world.[43]

(2) The Work of the Spirit in Prevenient Grace

Albert Outler notes that John Wesley "could speak of 'the beautiful gradations of love' in faith's progress from its first assurance of God's pardoning grace all the way to its 'plerophory'."[44] Even before that assurance, Wesley saw the Holy Spirit as working persuasively to draw people to God preveniently, in what he calls "preventing grace."[45]

The Holy Spirit is always working actively to bring people to God through faith and repentance—a turning from self-sufficiency and self-interest to depending on the Spirit of Jesus for life, love, identity, and meaning.

In this concept of the Spirit working to draw people to God we have a remarkable point of confluence between Wesleyan pentecostal and open theist theology. Wesleyan prevenient grace meets the open theist emphasis that God primarily works through persuasion.[46] This vision of God as actively seeking to draw us by love is highly characteristic of open renewal theology.

---

43. In addition to the books edited by Yong and Oord just cited which have pentecostal and Wesleyan emphases respectively, a third volume making a significant contribution from an open theism perspective is Thomas Jay Oord, ed., *Creation Made Free: Open Theology Engaging Science* (Eugene, Ore.: Wipf & Stock, 2010).

44. Wesley, *Sermons I*, 81.

45. E.g., Sermon 85: "On Working out Our Own Salvation" [1785] in Wesley, *Sermons III*, 199. Salvation begins with prevenient grace, the "beginning of a deliverance from a blind, unfeeling heart, quite insensible of God and the things of God. Salvation is carried on by 'convincing grace', usually in Scripture termed 'repentance', which brings a larger measure of self-knowledge, and a farther deliverance from the heart of stone. Afterwards we experience the proper Christian salvation, whereby 'through grace' we 'are saved by faith', consisting of those two grand branches, justification and sanctification. By justification we are saved from the guilt of sin and restored to the favour of God: by sanctification we are saved from the power and root of sin, and restored to the image of God." Ibid., 204.

46. E.g., "In my view, the almighty God wins our hearts through the weakness of the cross and the power of the resurrection. God has made us to love, and love does not force its own way on the beloved." Sanders, *The God Who Risks*, 193. Tom Oord is encouraging open theists to consider the view that God *cannot* use force because "God's love always preconditions God's creating and providential activity." Thomas Jay Oord, "Ways to Think about Providence," (May 25th, 2015), http://thomasjayoord.com/index.php/blog/archives/ways-to-think-about-providence#sthash.lTP0C1Wo.dpuf.

(3) The Indwelling Spirit

From the moment the Holy Spirit indwells the believer, several important things become possible related to sanctification, guidance, encouragement, identification with Christ, and communion with God.

The Spirit gently leads in the sanctifying process. Little by little, as we consent, we are led toward the restoration of God's image in us—sanctification. Through the work of the indwelling Spirit, we become more like Jesus.

The Spirit acts as a guide in our synergistic working with God. Through the indwelling Spirit, we hear from God, and get direction in what we should do. The Spirit communicates "yes" or "no" as we contemplate one path or another.

The indwelling Spirit is ὁ παράκλητος—helper, advocate, encourager (John 14:16). That God is *for* us is made real to us through the encouragement of the Spirit.

The Holy Spirit is the Spirit of Christ (Rom. 8:9–10) and creates identification with the risen Jesus. That Christ should indwell the Gentiles means we have hope for—perhaps even proleptic experience of—the glory of union with God.[47]

The indwelling Spirit creates a sense of God's presence. Through the Spirit we have κοινωνία (communion or fellowship) with God (Phil. 2:1).

All whose allegiance is to Jesus share the indwelling Holy Spirit. This shared experience creates κοινωνία among us. To this shared experience, renewalists would add an experience where the Spirit is perceived to come upon a believer, rather than coming from within. We turn now to a discussion of Spirit baptism.

(4) The Baptism of the Spirit

An experience of Spirit baptism is central to being a renewalist.[48] For William Seymour, Spirit baptism involved speaking in tongues, the healing of the sick, casting out demons, and demonstrating the fruit of the Spirit—especially

---

47. Col. 1:27 reads "To them God chose to make known how great among the Gentiles are the riches of the glory of this mystery, which is Christ in you, the hope of glory."

48. The term "renewalist" here is being used in the sense discussed above at p. 41.

V. A CONVERGENCE OF THE TWO TRAJECTORIES

love. In the first volume of *The Apostolic Faith* in a section titled "QUESTIONS ANSWERED—What is the real evidence that a man or woman has received the baptism with the Holy Ghost?" we find this:

> Divine love, which is charity. Charity is the Spirit of Jesus. They will have the fruits of the Spirit. Gal.5:22.... This is the real Bible evidence in their daily walk and conversation; and the outward manifestations; speaking in tongues and the signs following; casting out devils, laying hands on the sick and the sick being healed, and the love of God for souls increasing in their hearts.[49]

Frank Macchia develops this experience of Spirit baptism in a way that takes account of both the Lukan charismatic theology of Spirit baptism but also the Pauline soteriological theology of Spirit baptism.[50] Incorporating both Wesleyan and Pentecostal themes, he says, "Spirit baptism is a baptism into the love of God that sanctifies, renews, and empowers until Spirit baptism turns all of creation into the final dwelling place of God. Along the way, Pentecostals will be justified in calling Christians to a Spirit baptism as a fresh experience of power for witness with charismatic signs following." It's a brilliant description of how the Spirit empowers people to work in the world.

(5) The Spirit at Work in the World

Open theism affirms that the future is open. The future is open to us individually within the constraints of our historical and social contexts. The future is also open to us collectively if we have the imagination to see it. We can follow the dusty path of trying to shape the future by means of economic power and military force or we can try the more difficult path of following the Spirit. It is not just walking with those who walk in the way of peace. People in this group are often characterized by an anger at the way things are. Yes, we should be unsettled by injustice, but living in protest to injustice does not

---

49. Seymour, *The Apostolic Faith*, Vol. 1 No. 11 (January 1908): 2 [(1997): 55; (2013): 311].

50. Roger Stronstad, *The Charismatic Theology of St. Luke: Trajectories from the Old Testament to Luke–Acts*, 2nd ed. (Grand Rapids: Baker Academic, 1984, 2012). Macchia, *Baptized in the Spirit*, 57.

make you a follower of Jesus. Living in a reactionary mode to the injustice we see is not the renewalist option. A renewalist open theist path requires walking in wholeness in obedience to the voice of the Spirit as followers of Jesus. It is being committed to a vision of the kingdom of God lived out. It is a rejection of the cynicism of those who say the teachings of Jesus are not practical. It is a rejection of the alternate visions of a future shaped by national identities and economic self-interest.

The renewalist open theist option doesn't work without the involvement of the Spirit of Jesus. The Spirit provides the power. Compared to the economic power of global economies and the massive military force nations control, relying on a spirit, even the Holy Spirit, might seem inadequate, even pathetic as a force to change the world. But consider that the Spirit has the power to be fully present to me and thousands of miles away to be simultaneously fully present to you. The Spirit is persuading me to follow in a certain way and if you are attentive, influencing you. That is not raw, coercive power, but it is the way divine power usually works in the post-resurrection world. One day, that power could be felt by millions of people simultaneously who reflect God's self-sacrificial love into the world. It is the power to bring about the kingdom of God on earth through followers of Jesus.

This vision is a rejection of the divided loyalties of those who say we owe allegiance to two kingdoms—the kingdom of God, but also the kingdoms of this world.[51] Jesus knew that one kingdom would always give way to the other. Jesus warned about divided loyalties when he talked about money: "No one can serve two masters; for a slave will either hate the one and love the other, or be devoted to the one and despise the other. You cannot serve God and wealth" (Matthew 6:24).

I recently heard Matthew 22:17–22 used to justify loyalty to two kingdoms:[52]

---

51. The two kingdoms doctrine originated with Augustine and Martin Luther (e.g., his "Marburg" sermon) and finds contemporary expression in Chuck Colson, *God & Government: An Insider's View on the Boundaries Between Faith and Politics* (Grand Rapids: Zondervan, 2007), 313.

52. Nomad Extra podcast, "Rick Love—Are Christians Called to Love ISIS?" Uploaded March 6, 2015 (www.peace-catalyst.net). Rick Love said, "As followers of Jesus we have a dual allegiance. Jesus taught that we must render to Caesar the things that are Caesar's and to God the things that are God's."

V. A CONVERGENCE OF THE TWO TRAJECTORIES

Is it lawful to pay taxes to the emperor, or not?" [18] But Jesus, aware of their malice, said, "Why are you putting me to the test, you hypocrites? [19] Show me the coin used for the tax." And they brought him a denarius. [20] Then he said to them, "Whose head is this, and whose title?" [21] They answered, "The emperor's." Then he said to them, "Give therefore to the emperor the things that are the emperor's, and to God the things that are God's." [22] When they heard this, they were amazed; and they left him and went away.

But the passage is not talking about divided loyalties. Jesus is simply saying you fulfill your civic responsibilities. It is not a blanket approval of how governments sometimes act and it not suggesting you give them anything more than their due—certainly not your loyalty which belongs only to God.

I expect that someone might object to this line of thought saying, "But this doesn't sound like either John Wesley or early pentecostalism." The problem here is that this aspect of Wesley has been neglected and, in the case of early pentecostalism, historiographically repressed.[53] Early pentecostalism was deeply pacifist, but those writing the history have sometimes chosen to be revisionist.

Assemblies of God pacifism emerged from its holiness and Quaker heritage. Holiness and Quaker preachers united their quest for perfection with the power of the Holy Spirit to form a Pentecostal peace witness based on prioritizing the life and teachings of Jesus of Nazareth. Their crucifism reflected the Jesus centered and biblically justified Quaker arguments against war and their desire for sanctification. These influences were accompanied by several theological emphases within early Pentecostalism that encour   ˜nviolent ethic.[54]

---

53. Paul Alexander, "The Hidden History of Pentecostal Pacif 2014): 32–35.
54. Paul Alexander, *Peace to War: Shifting Allegiances in th* Series (Telford, Pa.: Cascadia, 2009), 107.

But "its members deleted their pacifist statement in 1967, fifty years after it had been adopted, though perhaps the belief had long since diminished."[55]

John Wesley is similarly committed to a nonviolent ethic. We noted above (p. 113) that for the Christian, "It was impossible for him knowingly and designedly to do harm to any man."[56] While initially sympathetic to the colonists grievances, Wesley was vocal in his opposition to the American war of independence:

> And what is it which drags on these poor victims into the field of blood? It is a great phantom which stalks before them, which they are taught to call, "liberty!" It is this which breathes
> ... into their hearts stern love of war,
> And thirst of vengeance, and contempt of death.[57]

Wesley's commitment to nonviolence comes through in his sermons on Jesus' Sermon on the Mount:

> Meanwhile, let no persecution turn you out of the way of lowliness and meekness, of love and beneficence. "Ye have heard" indeed "that it hath been said, An eye for an eye and a tooth for a tooth." And your miserable teachers have hence allowed you to avenge yourselves, to return evil for evil.
>
> "But I say unto you, that ye resist not evil"—not thus: not by returning it in kind.... So invincible let thy meekness be. And be thy love suitable thereto....
>
> Ye have heard that it hath been said, Thou shalt love thy neighbour, and hate thy enemy.' (God indeed had said only the former part, "Thou shalt love thy neighbour," the children of the devil had added the latter, "and hate they enemy.") "But I say unto you:" (1). "Love your enemies." See that you bear a tender goodwill to

---

55. Ibid., 34.
...mon 4: "Scriptural Christianity" [1744] in Wesley, *Sermons I*, 164–65.
...11: "National Sins and Miseries" [1775] in Wesley, *Sermons III*, 564.

those who are most bitter of spirit against you, who wish you all manner of evil. (2). "Bless them that curse you."... (3). "Do good to them that hate you." Let your actions show that you are as real in love as they in hatred. Return good for evil.... You can never be disabled from doing this; nor can all their malice or violence hinder you.[58]

Wesley emphasizes in this sermon that what is true inwardly in terms of purity of heart be expressed outwardly in our actions. It's interesting that he didn't find a need to dilute Jesus' teaching by saying this nonviolent ethic only applied to some future kingdom. It is for Jesus-followers now.

Jesus taught about the kingdom of God and little else. It is the place where life is lived in wholeness and love in obedience to God. Jesus' Spirit is intent upon seeing Jesus' teachings lived out in reality.

(6) The Spirit and Sanctification

I identified in the previous chapter the fact that part of the core of Wesley's theology is pneumatological.[59] Central to that approach, he clearly distinguishes between justification and sanctification in the soteriological process:

What is 'justification'?... It is evident from what has been already observed that it is not the being made actually just and righteous. This is *sanctification;* which is indeed in some degree the immediate *fruit* of justification, but nevertheless is a distinct gift of God, and of a totally different nature. The one implies what God *does for us* through his Son; the other what he *works in us* by his Spirit.[60]

The lucidity of Wesley's thought here is remarkable. There is no collapsing of sanctification into justification. The logical consequence is an expectation of an experience of sanctification that begins with justification but does not

---

58. Sermon 23: "Upon Our Lord's Sermon on the Mount, III" [1748] in Wesley, *Sermons I*, 528–29.
59. That it is also christological was not argued but is assumed.
60. Sermon 5: "Justification by Faith" [1746] in Wesley, *Sermons I*, 187.

end there. It leaves space for both a subsequent instantaneous crisis experience and gradual transformation and growth. Whether a crisis experience or gradual transformation, the idea of subsequence is implied. That there is something significant to be received from God after justification is essential to renewal theology.

Sanctification was a central theme not only of Wesley but of early pentecostalism. Seymour taught a progression of justification, sanctification, followed by a baptism in the Spirit.[61] Within a couple of decades some major Pentecostal denominations subsumed sanctification under salvation. For example, Aimee Semple McPherson, founder of the International Church of the Foursquare Gospel, in 1922 interpreted Ezekiel's vision in chapter one of the man, lion, ox, and eagle as Jesus as savior, baptizer in the Holy Spirit, healer, and coming king. Viewed against the background of the holiness movement, Jesus as sanctifier is conspicuously absent.[62] With her first husband, Robert Semple, she was a part of William Howard Durham's North Avenue Mission in Chicago for a year and Durham ordained them.[63] The Durham mission for

---

61. Cecil Robeck reports, "Sanctification was the next step in the Christian life, according to mission teaching. As with conversion, holiness leaders had taught that one must engage in an intensive time of prayer in order to receive it." Robeck, *The Azusa Street Mission and Revival*, 173. "Once believers had been sanctified, they were ready to be baptized in the Spirit. Seekers were encouraged to pursue and embrace an intimate encounter with God in which he bestowed upon them this baptism." Ibid., 177. A room on the second floor of the Azusa Street Mission was set aside for this purpose. Ibid., 140.

62. In the description of the vision received in Oakland in July 1922 which defined the "Full Gospel" there is no mention of sanctification (or the teaching of Jesus): "In the clouds of heaven which folded and unfolded in fiery glory, Ezekiel had beheld the Being whose glory no mortal can describe. As he gazed upon the marvelous revelation of the Omnipotent One, he perceived four faces, those of a man, a lion, an ox, and an eagle.

"In the face of the lion, we behold that of the mighty baptizer with the Holy Ghost and fire. The face of the ox typifies the great burden-bearer, who himself took our infirmities and carried our sicknesses, who in his boundless love and divine provision has met our every need. In the face of the eagle, we see reflected soul-enrapturing visions of the coming King, whose pinions soon will cleave the shining heavens, whose voice will vibrate through the universe in thrilling cadences of resurrection power as he comes to catch his waiting bride away. And in the face of the man we behold the Savior, the man of sorrows, acquainted with grief, dying upon the tree for our sins. Here is a perfect gospel, a complete gospel, for body, for soul, for spirit, and for eternity, a gospel facing squarely in every direction." Aimee Semple McPherson, *The Story of My Life: Aimee Semple McPherson* (Waco, Tex.: Word, 1973), 111–12.

63. Edith L. Blumhofer, *Aimee Semple McPherson: Everybody's Sister*, Library of Religious Biography (Grand Rapids: Eerdmans, 1993), 80–85.

V. A CONVERGENCE OF THE TWO TRAJECTORIES

a decade after 1907 was "the de facto worldwide missions and th center for the fast-growing [Pentecostal] movement."[64]

Similarly, the Assemblies of God felt the influence of William Durham who denied a crisis experience of sanctification subsequent to conversion.[65] "Durham called for a new view which assigned sanctification to the moment of conversion based on 'the finished work of Christ on Calvary.' Denying Wesley's concept of a 'residue of sin' in the believer, he taught one was perfectly sanctified at conversion and had no need of a later crisis, or 'second change.'"[66] Wesley had been realistic about residual sin in the believer: "That the corruption of nature does still remain, even in those who are the children of God by faith; that they have in them the seeds of pride and vanity, of anger, lust and evil desire, yea, sin of every kind, is too plain to be denied, being matter of daily experience."[67] Durham's "Finished Work" teaching essentially split pentecostalism into non-Wesleyan Reformed two-stage (salvation followed by the baptism of the Holy Spirit) and Wesleyan three-stage (salvation, sanctification, and baptism of the Holy Spirit) camps.[68] Durham and his followers saw sanctification as a lifelong process. We could argue that this de-emphasis on sanctification is the major factor in producing forms of American pentecostalism and evangelicalism that emphasize conversion—at the expense of discipleship and transformation, both in the individual, and in his or her social context. It is hard to motivate people to be whole-hearted followers of Jesus and his teaching if they have been led to believe that Jesus did everything necessary at Calvary and that is appropriated by a onetime sinner's prayer. Similarly, if it is taught that sanctification is inherent in the past event of justification, motivation for living a life of holiness is undermined and antinomianism is frequently the outcome.

The point of sanctification from Wesley's point-of-view is that following Jesus should produce significant change in the believer and in his or her

---

64. Synan, *The Holiness-Pentecostal Tradition*, 132–33.
65. Edith L. Blumhofer, *Restoring the Faith: The Assemblies of God, Pentecostalism, and American Culture* (Urbana and Chicago: University of Illinois Press, 1993), 124–25.
66. Synan, *The Holiness-Pentecostal Tradition*, 150.
67. Sermon 8: "The First-fruits of the Spirit" [1746] in Wesley, *Sermons I*, 239.
68. See Synan, *The Holiness-Pentecostal Tradition*, 150.

sphere of influence. Growth in sanctification, according to Wesley, should be observable in an increasing capacity to love the neighbor. Jesus' ethic of love of neighbor has been lived out most consistently in Anabaptist communities.[69] John Wesley's engagement with the Moravians from Herrnhut influenced him in this direction.[70] Through Wesley, open theist renewal theology can also incorporate a reading of the New Testament that emphasizes a radical following Jesus, especially in nonviolence. Tom Wright concurs: The kingdom of God "makes its way (as Jesus insists) by nonviolence rather than by violence."[71] When sanctification leads to a renunciation of violence, a pneumatology of love has moved from theology to praxis.

B. TOWARDS AN OPEN THEIST RENEWAL PRAXIS

Wesley writes, "True Christian zeal is no other than *the flame of love*. This is the nature, the inmost essence of it."[72] The last section of this chapter describes the possible praxis of an open theist/renewal community and how the synthesis might be lived out.

1. Following Jesus

In thinking about what living out an open theist renewal theology might be like, it will be helpful to start not with what evangelicalism has looked like in

---

69. Stuart Murray, *The Naked Anabaptist: The Bare Essentials of a Radical Faith* (Scottdale, Pa.: Herald, 2010).

70. Howard A. Snyder, *The Radical Wesley: The Patterns and Practices of a Movement Maker* (Franklin, Tenn.: Seedbed, 1980, 2014).

71. Wright makes the point in discussing how the themes of kingdom and cross intersect in the Gospel of John: "Part of John's meaning of the cross, then, is that it is not only what happens, purely pragmatically, when God's kingdom challenges Caesar's kingdom. It is also *what has to happen* if God's kingdom which makes its way (as Jesus insists) by nonviolence rather than by violence, is to win the day.... This is the 'truth' to which Jesus bears witness—the truth of a kingdom accomplished by the innocent dying in place of the guilty.

"And, in the broader Johannine perspective, we discover that the only word to do justice to this kingdom-and-cross combination is *agape*, 'love.'" N. T. Wright, *How God Became King: The Forgotten Story of the Gospels* (New York: HarperCollins, 2012), 230.

72. Sermon 92: "On Zeal" [1781] in Wesley, *Sermons III*, 312. Pinnock's inspiration for the title of his magnum opus comes not from this passage but St. John of the Cross (b. 1542). Italics are Wesley's. Pinnock, *Flame of Love*, 9.

the recent past, but to ask afresh what it means to be imitators of God and followers of Jesus in the twenty-first century. Openness theology has something powerful to contribute at this point because it emphasizes the condescension of God in surrendering total control of the universe to facilitate free choices in the beings he created. This theme of condescension continues in the incarnation when the Son gives up the prerogatives of heaven to become vulnerable and human. The theme continues in the ministry of Jesus when he serves the needs of humanity in his ministry of teaching, healing, and exorcism as he inaugurates the kingdom of God. And most profoundly the theme of condescension is acted out on the cross as Jesus pours himself out in self-sacrificial love. Being imitators of God means choosing to live lives no longer preoccupied with meeting our own needs but letting ourselves be used up in the loving service of others.[73] But you can't give what you don't have. Wesley knew how to go to the source. "Indeed, supposing we have tasted of the love of God, how can any of us rest till it is our own!"[74]

2. Adventure

Another characteristic of a lived out open theist renewal theology might be inspired by its vision of God as a risk-taker. In the open view, God did not determine everything in advance but took significant risk in giving spiritual beings, including humans, a degree of genuine freedom. God does not always get his way (as evidenced by all the sin and pain in the world) but desires to be a co-worker with willing humans. An open theist renewal theology in praxis takes risks and, as led by the Holy Spirit, takes initiative. It is not content with things as they are, recognizing that if God does not control everything that happens then the status quo may well not represent his will. Realizing that prayerful risk-taking can be godly behavior should have an energizing effect

---

[73]. This issue became the sticking point between Wesley and the Moravians—self-sacrifice versus self-indulgence. Commenting on Sermon 48: "Self-denial" [1760], Albert Outler says of Wesley, "As far back as 1741 he had been shocked by Count von Zinzendorf's scornful dismissal of self-abnegation as a Christian virtue (cf. *JWJ*, September 3, 1741: 'We believers do as we please and nothing more; we laugh at all talk of "mortification"').... But the tendency of the new piety to turn 'Christian liberty' into self-indulgence had persisted; there was evident need for yet another distillation of the ancient Christian wisdom on 'cross-bearing' and self-surrender to the will of God; hence, this present sermon." Wesley, *Sermons II*, 236.

[74]. Sermon 53: "On the Death of George Whitefield" [1770] in ibid., 344.

on a faith community. Learning from Wesley that God is a synergist should lead us to suspect spirituality that sees virtue in leaving everything up to God. Sometimes, he is watching to see what we are going to do. Sometimes, he is waiting for a human partner. John Burnaby (one of John R. W. Stott's teachers at Cambridge) wrote, "The kingdom of God is to be promoted in human history by no other power than the power of love, and ... the power of God's love takes effect in human history in no other way than through the wills and actions of men in whom that love has come to dwell."[75] Wesley could say (with overstatement for effect), "God does nothing but in answer to prayer;...."[76]

An adventurous spirit leads us to pray in a particular way. It is often said that the purpose of prayer is to change us. But from an open theist renewal perspective, there is another entire purpose of prayer and that is to change the world and even to influence God. Vincent Brümmer describes an impretatory form of prayer which results in God doing something *because* we asked.[77] Brümmer suggests modifications to the classical understanding of God's omnipotence, immutability, and omniscience:

> If we are to interpret petitionary prayer as impetratory and not merely as an expression of dependence on God, then we have to presuppose a personal relation between God and ourselves. This entails that God in fact has created an open, non-deterministic universe in which both God and we are personal agents. Since these presuppositions seem to conflict with the doctrines of God's omnipotence, immutability

---

[75]. John Burnaby, "Christian Prayer," in *Soundings: Essays Concerning Christian Understanding*, ed. Alexander Roper Vidler (Cambridge: Cambridge University Press, 1962), 232–33. Cited by Vincent Brümmer, *What Are We Doing When We Pray?: On Prayer and the Nature of Faith*, rev. ed. (Aldershot, England: Ashgate, 2008), 74. Burnaby sent Stott a letter in August 1955 worried that he had become too fundamentalistic. David Bebbington and David Ceri Jones, *Evangelicalism and Fundamentalism in the United Kingdom during the Twentieth Century* (Oxford: Oxford University Press, 2013), 192.

[76]. "Farther Thoughts upon Christian Perfection" in Wesley, *Doctrinal and Controversial Treatises II*, 127. This phrase comes in a series of "Reflections" that Wesley extracted from "Instructions chrestiennes" in Robert Arnauld d'Andilly's *Lettres* (1672) which in turn borrowed from the Abbé de Saint-Cyran, Jean Duvergier de Hauranne's *Lettres Chrétiennes et Spirituelles* (1645). Ibid., 123 n. 112. Cited by Boyd, *Is God to Blame?*, 128.

[77]. Brümmer, *What Are We Doing When We Pray?*, 33, 38–40.

V. A CONVERGENCE OF THE TWO TRAJECTORIES

and omniscience, we are faced by a dilemma which can only be avoided by either denying the impetratory function of prayer or by interpreting the doctrines of divine omnipotence, immutability and omniscience in personal terms so as not to exclude the possibility of personal relations between God and ourselves.[78]

Brümmer's explanation for why impretatory prayer is efficacious is interesting. He suggests it works through a double agency of God and humans. "God realizes his will through the 'actions of human agents, who freely intend to further the purposes of God, seek God's grace to enable them to do so, and do in fact achieve their intended goal.'"[79] This view is a helpful way of understanding how Wesley's synergism works—it's through prayer and double agency.

John Polkinghorne has a similar approach. He uses the analogy of laser light and describes the synergy of divine and human action as "the tuning of divine and human wills to mutual resonance through the collaboration of prayer."[80]

---

78. Ibid., 54–55.

79. Brümmer is quoting Maurice F. Wiles, *God's Action in the World*, Bampton Lectures for 1986 (London: SCM, 1986), 98. Brümmer continues: God "cannot do this by *causing* their choices, since then they would cease to be the agents of these actions. He can however provide the *conditions sine quibus non* for the human agents to realize his will, by (a) making his will known to them in his Son, (b) providentially arranging their factual circumstances as Father and Creator in such as way that they are *enabled* to do what he wills (in the previous section we argued that this is possible without violating the natural order), and (c) inspiring them by his Spirit in order that they may be *motivated* to do his will. In this Trinitarian way, however, God's agency is not coercive but enabling and motivating and therefore does not deny the freedom, responsibility and personal integrity of the human agent through whose action God realizes his will." Brümmer, *What Are We Doing When We Pray?*, 75.

80. Polkinghorne, *Science and Providence*, 82–83. This is the passage where he develops the laser analogy: "The picture that we have been building up in earlier chapters is that of a world of regularity but not of rigidity, within whose evolving history there is room for action initiated both by human will (which we experience directly) and by divine will (which we acknowledge by faith). There must be a delicate balance between structure and flexibility, between the respect for cosmic freedom (which delivers physical process from arbitrary interruption) and the respect for human freedom (which allows us the exercise of choice and responsibility) and the respect for divine freedom (which does not reduce God to the role of an impotent spectator of the history of his creation). It is an immensely difficult task, beyond our powers to accomplish in any detail, to see how this works out, but I claim that the insights of science, and in particular the death of mere mechanism, are consonant with this view. The room for maneuver that exists for the accomplishment of divine and human ends through cosmic process, will surely be enhanced by

God takes the risk that human partners will not do their part in the adventure, but his infinite resourcefulness means he will not ultimately be thwarted in bringing the kingdom of God to earth in its fullness.

3. Compassion

A third characteristic of a lived out open theist renewal theology might be compassion. God is all-in with his love for humanity in the openness vision. One of the most objectionable aspects of Calvinist theology is the callousness it attributes to God if he creates people knowing that they will end up eternally lost. That same hardness is seen if you assign to God control of everything that occurs—it makes him responsible for every bad thing that happens. The open view is radically different. Because the future is partially open, there is plausibility in the assertion that God wills none to be lost. Rather, his heart is *for* us, and he works compassionately in every circumstance to bring the peace and love of the kingdom.[81] Again, as imitators of God, a lived out

---

that collaborative alignment of God's will and ours which lies at the heart of petitionary prayer. People have sometimes spoken in a derogatory way of notions of divine action as 'laser beam' interference. Properly understood, the metaphor is a fruitful one. Laser light is characterized by what the physicists call 'coherence,' that is to say, all the oscillations are in phase, perfectly in step with each other. In that way, effects which otherwise might cancel each other out, can instead afford each other the maximum reinforcement. We can truly use the metaphor of God's laser interaction, not to mean an arbitrarily focused intervention, but as the tuning of divine and human wills to mutual resonance through the collaboration of prayer. The 'laser action' of the virginal conception would result from the complete obedience of Mary's 'Behold, I am the handmaid of the Lord.' Understood in this way it is not inconceivable 'that our asking in faith may make it possible for God to do something that he could not have done without our asking.'" Here Polkinghorne is citing Peter R. Baelz, *Prayer and Providence: A Background Study*, Hulsean Lectures for 1966 (London: SCM, 1968), 118. Polkinghorne continues: "In that way prayer is genuinely instrumental. That instrumentality is located neither solely at the divine end (as if it were a magical demand) but in the personal encounter between God and man by which a new possibility comes into existence. Because of the web of the interrelated process of the world, it is not inconceivable that the new possibility can have consequences for a third person, so that prayer for others, as well as ourselves, seems a coherent possibility. Brümmer points out that another consequence of 'corporate prayer is more effective than individual prayer, not because it brings more pressure to bear on God, but because it enlists more people in the realization of God's will.'" Brümmer, *What Are We Doing When We Pray?*, 54 of the 1984 edition.

81. Wesley pleads for compassion: "One great reason why the rich in general have so little sympathy for the poor is because they so seldom visit them. Hence it is that, according to the common observation, one part of the world does not know what the other suffers. Many of them do not know, because they do not care to know: they keep out of the way of knowing it—and then plead their voluntary ignorance as an excuse for their hardness of heart." Sermon 98: "On Visiting the Sick" [1786] in Wesley, *Sermons III*, 387–88.

V. A CONVERGENCE OF THE TWO TRAJECTORIES

open theist renewal theology would emphasize compassion.[82] Bringing people toward relationship to Christ through the preaching of the gospel is an act of compassion.

Because Jesus' compassion extends to the whole person, our compassion is also holistic. "Life cannot be fully human without a satisfactory physical base beneath it."[83] Wesley and Fletcher's concern for the poor is well-documented.[84] Compassion for the way other people live leads us to make certain lifestyle choices. Clark Pinnock says it well:

> Although we can think globally, we can really act only locally. The watchword has to be downward mobility.... I believe God is calling North American Christians to a life which is simpler—simpler in diet, in housing, in entertainment, and so forth—a life which celebrates God's jubilee, his good news for the poor and a righting of economic wrongs. Let us accept for ourselves the spartan life which we have asked missionaries to live in our stead in the past, and incorporate into our evangelical spirituality dimensions of practical mercy, simplicity, and justice.[85]

This compassion leads us to a liberation from our addiction to consumption.

---

82. Short-term mission trips that allow people from diverse cultural locations to live and work side-by-side can be transformative. For an approach that intentionally engages the poor, see Dale Walker, *Kissing the Face of God: Worship That Changes the World* (Maitland, Fla.: Xulon, 2010). Making room for compassion and enlarged generosity in our lives might mean being less consumerist. Wesley quoting Robert South: "Let our conveniences give way to our neighbour's necessities; and our necessities give way to our neighbour's extremities." Sermon 98: "On Visiting the Sick" [1786] in Wesley, *Sermons III*, 394.

83. Pinnock, "Evangelicals and Liberation," 133.

84. Fletcher died as a result of visiting his poor parishioners during a fever epidemic. Wood, *The Meaning of Pentecost in Early Methodism*, 6. One of Wesley's biographers wrote: "He was humane and charitable; not only administering to the wants of the poor and afflicted, as far as his income would permit, but also using his influence with others to procure them relief." Moore, *Life of the Rev. John Wesley*, 65.

85. Pinnock, "Evangelicals and Liberation," 132–33.

4. Nonviolence

A fourth characteristic of a lived out open theist renewal theology is a consequence of the value God places on human freedom. It recognizes that God's love is mostly non-coercive. God's preferred way of working is to draw people to himself.[86] Issues can be raised related to descriptions of how God works in the Old Testament, but that problem can be set aside for the moment because the open view is Jesus-centric.[87] Jesus taught and modeled a nonviolent and non-coercive love. A commitment to nonviolence would be a natural consequence of an open theist renewal theology as it is lived out.[88]

5. Social Justice

A fifth characteristic of a lived out open theist renewal theology also comes out of Wesley's and open theism's theological emphasis on human freedom. Theology does matter—you become like the God you worship. George

---

86. But what does God do when someone is praying for X which is in line with the kingdom of God and someone else is praying for not-X which will hinder the kingdom? Some relational theologians are of the view that God always works non-coercively, and that may be the case. It may also be the case that as God is influenced by the will of the intercessor, in order to answer a prayer that advances the kingdom, God acts to override human decisions that are headed in the wrong direction.

87. It is Jesus-centric because it sees history, and particularly Old Testament history, as being influenced by God but not determined in every detail. It sees revelation as progressive with its climax in the person of Jesus. It affirms that in Jesus, everything we need to know about God is made known. For example, "For in Christ all the fullness of the Deity lives in bodily form" (Colossians 2:9).

88. Status quo theologies tend to be uncritical of the use and misuse of power and force. Wesley saw clearly how political and military power can undermine following Jesus' teaching. The greatest wound Christianity "ever received, the grand blow which was struck at the very root of that humble, gentle, patient love, which is the fulfilling of the Christian law, the whole essence of true religion, was struck in the fourth century by Constantine the Great, when he called himself a Christian, and poured in a flood of riches, honours, and power upon the Christians, more especially upon the clergy." Sermon 61: "The Mystery of Iniquity" [1783] in Wesley, *Sermons II*, 462. See also Gregory A. Boyd, *The Myth of a Christian Nation: How the Quest for Political Power Is Destroying the Church* (Grand Rapids: Zondervan, 2009). Pinnock wrote, "As for the vocational involvement of believers in the governing process, which is certainly a possibility for them, numerous ethical issues arise. Aside from the day to day dilemmas of compromise all of us face, there is the sword-wielding function of the state, the power of coercion and retribution which is its natural condition since the fall. The state is expected to act in the parameters of the old age, in a manner Christians are commanded to reject for themselves because of the new age. Therefore, it is not self-evident that any and all vocations in the service of government are open to believers, since they are called to live by the standards of the new age, rather than the old." Clark H. Pinnock, "An Evangelical Theology of Human Liberation—Part II," *Sojourners* 5, no. 3 (March 1976): 27.

Whitefield elevated divine sovereignty at the expense of human freedom. He advocated for the legalization of slavery in Georgia and owned slaves after it became legal.[89] John Wesley, in contrast, wrote, "And who cares for thousands, myriads, if not millions of the wretched Africans? Are not whole droves of these poor sheep (human if not rational beings!) continually driven to market, and sold like cattle into the vilest bondage, with no hope of deliverance but by death?"[90] A modern application of Wesley's concern would not only work to eradicate human trafficking but to oppose all forms of oppression—militaristic, socio-political, gender-based, and economic.

Daisy Machado recently mentioned that "Predestination favors the rich."[91] In the Calvinist view, God is in absolute control so the status quo must be as he wants it. In the open theist renewal view, the world is very much not the way God intends it and his sympathies lie with those who are oppressed. Open theist renewalists seek to bring as much as possible of the future kingdom into the present—working to set people free from injustice and suffering.

6. Charismatic Renewal and the Baptism of the Holy Spirit

A sixth characteristic of a lived out open theist renewal theology comes out of the experience of the pentecostal and charismatic movements. A nurturing of renewal is essential. Seeking in prayer an immersion of the Holy Spirit—a baptism of the Holy Spirit—is the precedent of the New Testament and was the fuel for the Azusa Street revival. Wesley, too, encouraged praying to receive charismatic gifts.

The early years of Azusa Street and much of the pentecostal movement have viewed speaking in tongues as a verifiable external evidence of the internal experience of the baptism of the Holy Spirit. There is certainly New Testament precedent for that view, and there is nothing wrong with earnestly

---

89. John Piper, "'I Will Not Be a Velvet-Mouthed Preacher!' The Life and Ministry of George Whitefield: Living and Preaching as Though God Were Real (Because He Is)," (2009), http://www.desiringgod.org/biographies/i-will-not-be-a-velvet-mouthed-preacher [accessed July 23, 2014].

90. Sermon 69: "The Imperfection of Human Knowledge" [1784] in Wesley, *Sermons II*, 579.

91. Daisy L. Machado, "Acres of Diamonds: The American Dream, Latino Immigration, and the Prosperity Gospel" (paper presented at the Society for Pentecostal Studies Annual Meeting, Virginia Beach, Va., March 2, 2012).

praying for it. A positive experience with tongues speaking can lead into the use of gifts that require more faith. Speaking in tongues probably enables more effective prayer. But to insist on it as the only evidence of a baptism of the Holy Spirit seems like an unnecessary codification and the remnant of a modernist approach to faith.[92] It shifts the focus away from the Holy Spirit and the gracious gifting by Jesus. If when somebody is prayed for to receive the baptism of the Holy Spirit and they report an immersive experience of the Spirit but not speaking in tongues, perhaps they should be encouraged to explore what other charismatic gift or gifts they may have been given.[93] It is unfortunate when praying for the baptism in the Holy Spirit degenerates into an exercise in trying to get someone to speak in tongues.[94] It is an immersion in the divine love of the Holy Spirit. If William Seymour is to be believed, what was truly remarkable about the early years of the Azusa Street revival was not just its distinctive teaching about tongues as the evidence of the baptism

---

[92]. While William Seymour taught that speaking in tongues was the evidence of Spirit baptism, he did look for corroborating evidence in the recipient's manner of life: "When we set up tongues to be the Bible evidence of baptism in the Holy Ghost and fire only, we have left the divine word of God and have instituted our own teaching.... While tongues is one of the signs that follows God's Spirit-filled children, they will have to know the truth and do the truth.... How do we take the gift of tongues? We believe that all God's children that have faith in God can pray to God for an outpouring of the Holy Spirit upon the holy sanctified life and receive a great filling of the Holy Spirit and speak in new tongues, as the Spirit gives utterance." Seymour, *Doctrines and Disciplines*, 77. However, Allan Anderson overstates the case when he writes, "Perhaps because of all the hurt Seymour suffered from white Pentecostals, he later repudiated Parham's 'initial evidence' doctrine...." Anderson, *Introduction to Pentecostalism (2nd ed.)*, 42. If we read his language closely, we see that Seymour did not so much renounce tongues as the initial evidence of the baptism of the Holy Spirit as much as was wanting to see it validated by the fruit of love.

[93]. John Fletcher thought that prophecy was the normative gift accompanying the baptism of the Holy Spirit. He was asked about a phrase he had used in a letter: "'That on all who are renewed in love, God bestows the gift of prophecy.' He called for the Bible: then read, and sweetly explained the second chapter of the Acts, observing: To 'prophesy' in the sense he meant, was to magnify God with the new heart of love and the new tongue of praise, as they did, who on the day of pentecost were filled with the Holy Ghost!" Wood, *The Meaning of Pentecost in Early Methodism*, 148.

[94]. Often for Azusa Street recipients of Spirit baptism, it was an experience of divine love. "Though emerging creedal statements and explanations of the Pentecostal distinctive of Spirit baptism identified the purpose of the experience as 'power for witness,' testimonies reveal that participants understood the experience as bringing about an ontological and dispositional change." Kimberly Ervin Alexander and James P. Bowers, "How Godly Love Flourished and Foundered," in *Godly Love: Impediments and Possibilities*, ed. Matthew T. Lee and Amos Yong (Lanham, Md. and Plymouth, UK: Lexington Books, 2012), 132.

of the Holy Spirit but its racial and gender equality, evidence of the radical culture-defying divine love that was manifest, at least initially.[95]

7. Sanctification

A seventh characteristic of a lived out open theist renewal theology would connect with the Wesleyan emphasis on sanctification. The similarity of early Methodist accounts of sanctification to some pentecostal accounts of a person's baptism of the Holy Spirit suggests that an immersive experience of the Holy Spirit can have both a sanctifying and an empowering effect. From a Wesleyan point-of-view, however, it is clearly a mistake to conflate sanctification with justification. From a synergistic renewal point-of-view, it is a mistake to conflate sanctification with the baptism in the Holy Spirit.

It is probably biblical to think of the Holy Spirit as empowering love—empowering for holiness and empowering for service.[96] The New Testament does not seem to model consistently a three-stage sequence but practical wisdom suggests that the emphasis on holiness and the emphasis on charismatic empowerment are each attended to in turn.[97] If somebody has an experience of the baptism of the Holy Spirit, manifests spiritual gifts, but still struggles

---

[95]. Alexander and Bowers write that in the ethos of seeking Christian unity, "Godly love flourished. As defined by their own testimonies, divine love, infused through an infilling of the Spirit, expressed itself in compassion for others, in a desire for unity in the church, and, most notably, in the crossing of culturally imposed or regulated lines of demarcation regarding gender and race. Racial lines were seemingly erased to the horror of those who observed the revival." They reference Robeck, *The Azusa Street Mission and Revival*, 87–128, 129–86. "White ministers, male and female, submitted to the leadership of African-American ones. In addition, there was real, if restricted, elevation of the status of women within the movement." Alexander and Bowers, "How Godly Love Flourished and Foundered," 132–133. However, "it must be acknowledged that the experience of divine love was short-lived." Racism led to the decline of the Azusa Street revival. The larger movement (as exemplified by the Church of God, Cleveland) also saw the fading of the experience of divine love. "The denomination was shaped by a curious mix of the acknowledgement of the important role of spiritual experience and a fundamentalist hermeneutic all poured through the filter of the dominant culture of white male paternalism. In the final analysis, the transformative potential of Pentecostal spiritual experience in the interest of racial and gender equality is largely negated by the adopted hermeneutic and conformity to cultural norms." Ibid., 135.

[96]. At Jesus' baptism, the Father said, "This is my Son, *whom I love*; with him I am well pleased." (Matthew 3:17 NIV).

[97]. Seymour believed that the disciples were already sanctified before they experienced the baptism of the Holy Spirit at Pentecost: "The Disciples were sanctified before the Day of Pentecost. By a careful study of Scripture you will find it is so now. 'Ye are clean through the word which I have spoken unto you' (John 15:3; 13:10); and Jesus had breathed on them the Holy Ghost (John

with overt sin, then in that case prayer for more of the Holy Spirit would be warranted, and even a further crisis experience of sanctification. John the Baptist prophesied Jesus would "baptize you with the Holy Spirit and *fire*" (Luke 3:16). Acts 2:3–4 reads, "Divided tongues, as of *fire*, appeared among them, and a tongue rested on each of them. All were filled with the Holy Spirit and began to speak in other languages, as the Spirit gave them ability." Fire is a frequent biblical metaphor for God's sanctifying presence.[98] The baptism of the Holy Spirit is intended to be experienced in conjunction with God's sanctifying presence.

Wesley did *not* teach that a crisis experience of "Christian perfection" would replace a lifelong growth in holiness. The crisis experience can break the power of sin and enable a believer to choose obedience. That experience is a very important jumping off point. But putting too much emphasis on having attained a *state* of sanctification through one experience could undermine the process of real ongoing transformation into holiness. Wesley was clear that holiness is loving other people, and that it takes time, commitment, and self-sacrifice to learn how to do that.

8. Renewal of Humanity and Renewal of the Earth

An eighth characteristic of a lived out open theist renewal theology comes out of Wesley's view that the goal of salvation is a renewed humanity and a renewed earth.[99] There is in Wesley a theological basis for environmentalism and a resistance to consumerism. This planet is our home for eternity. The biblical image is that heaven will come down.[100] We need to learn to live here in a sustainable way.

20:21, 22)." Seymour, *The Apostolic Faith*, 1, no. 1 (September 1906): 2 [in the section "The Apostolic Faith Movement," (1997): 11; (2013): 11–12].

98. H. Bietenhard, "Fire," in *The New International Dictionary of New Testament Theology*, ed. Colin Brown (Grand Rapids: Zondervan, 1986), 1: 656–57.

99. Theodore Runyon identifies the theme of the new creation as Wesley's *sine qua non*. Runyon, *The New Creation*, 22. "There are three indispensable factors in the new creation: *grace,* the divine initiative to renew the creature and the world; *faith,* the human response to the empowerment that reconstitutes the relational image; and *synergism,* the renewed image working in concert with the Creator to share this renewing power with the world." Ibid., 89. See also Sermon 64: "The New Creation" [1785] in Wesley, *Sermons II*, 500–510.

100. Revelation 21:10.

V. A CONVERGENCE OF THE TWO TRAJECTORIES

However, the renewal of humankind is primary: "Here then we see in the clearest, strongest light, what is real religion: a restoration of man, by him that bruises the serpent's head, to all that the old serpent deprived him of; a restoration not only to the favour, but likewise to the image of God; implying not barely deliverance from sin but the being filled with the fullness of God."[101] For Wesley, the renewal of humanity is its restoration to the full image of God. It entails bruising "the serpent's head," by which he may be alluding to spiritual warfare.

This renewal of the earth involves spiritual warfare because the earth is presently a battleground between those people and spirits aligned with God and those opposed to him and his will.[102] The battle is mostly played out in the thoughts and decisions of people. Wesley was aware of the need for spiritual warfare and devotes a whole sermon to fallen angels where he says, "First, as a general preservative against all the rage, the power, and subtlety of your great adversary, 'put on the panoply,' the whole armour, 'of God,' universal holiness."[103]

It is possible that it is God's intention that Satan and his followers be defeated by humans living out the victory that was won by Jesus on the cross. It is unlikely this will happen until we shake off the pessimism about human action and the dark determinism of Calvinism. Greg Boyd suggests God created humans to help him take back the world from Satan. Satan's power is diminished when people choose to love instead of fear, to forgive instead of retaliate, to share instead of hoard. Perhaps the amillennial view that the conflict between good and evil continues with neither side victorious until Jesus returns is wrong. Wesley's optimistic view is that "the time will come when

---

101. Sermon 62: "The End of Christ's Coming" [1781] in Wesley, *Sermons II*, 482. Theodore Runyon elaborates: "Behind Wesley's understanding of the renewal of the image of God through regeneration lies the Eastern Fathers' notion of 'divinization' (*theosis*), mediated to him indirectly through his Anglican tradition and directly from his reading in the Fathers." Runyon, *The New Creation*, 80.

102. Greg Boyd develops this spiritual warfare theology in two lengthy monographs mentioned earlier, *God at War* (1997) and *Satan and the Problem of Evil* (2001).

103. Sermon 72: "Of Evil Angels" [1783] in Wesley, *Sermons III*, 27.

Christianity will prevail over all, and cover the earth."[104] Maybe we are actually supposed to win this thing.[105]

Azusa Street's theology leaned in a premillennialist direction and so did not emphasize the renewal of the earth, but it was certainly cognizant of spiritual warfare. This passage shows how spiritual warfare was seen to relate to sanctification and Spirit baptism: "A sanctified person is cleansed and filled with divine love, but the one that is baptized with the Holy Ghost has the power of God on his soul and has power with God and men, power over all the kingdoms of Satan and over all his emissaries...."[106] Awareness of the spirit world may have been absorbed from what Walter Hollenweger called the African or black root of pentecostalism.[107] That awareness is still very common in Africa today. It may not be coincidental that the open theist scholar with the most developed theology of spiritual warfare (Greg Boyd) has a pentecostal background. This awareness of spiritual warfare is a significant

---

104. Sermon 4: "Scriptural Christianity" [1744] in Wesley, *Sermons I*, 169.

105. Humans "are charged with carrying on God's creational work of bringing order to chaos...." We are "corulers with God over the earth and cowarriors with God against the forces of chaos for the earth." Boyd, *God at War*, 106–07.

It is hard to win a war if most combatants are unaware it is going on, as is the case in the Western world. Maybe the reason the entertainment industry is problematic is not so much that it promotes immorality as it is with the way it distracts people from the task at hand which is fighting for the restoration of the earth. Perhaps the big issue with professional sports is it diverts billions of dollars and countless hours from the contests that really matter like fighting injustice, poverty, racism, gender inequality, and disease. Events like the Olympic Games and the FIFA World Cup were suspended during the first half of the 1940s because people were aware a war was going on. There is still a spiritual war going on, but most Western people are unaware of it. Local churches, at least, could be more intentional about mobilizing people to fight the war.

Ralph Winter wrote, "Once we are saved I believe we must understand that our mission is to participate all-out in an onslaught against Satan and his works, not lie back and await heaven. Basic to that onslaught are our commendable efforts in calling upon people to accept the Lordship and the Commission of Christ. *But that is merely getting people prepared for war*. The Bible still says, "The Son of God appeared for this purpose, *to destroy the works of the devil.*" 1 Jn. 3:8. The immense tragedy is that the entire Christian world has been significantly duped by Satan, and has only vaguely understood this larger mission." "Growing Up with the Bible: Understanding What It Says, Yielding to What It Means," *International Journal of Frontier Missions* 22, no. 2 (Summer 2005): 73.

106. Seymour, *Azusa Street Papers*, Vol. 2 No. 13 (May 1908): 3 [in the section "THE BAPTISM OF THE HOLY GHOST—The Holy Ghost is Power," (1997): 64; (2013): 365].

107. Hollenweger, *Pentecostalism*, 18–19. The African or black root of pentecostalism was mentioned above at p. 41.

contribution from the pentecostal trajectory towards a Wesleyan theology that sees the eschatological goal as the renewal of the earth.

The hope of salvation is wholeness and restoration—for both people and the planet we will live on, at the renewal of all things. A *renewal* theology leans forward to that reality.

9. Joy in Witness and Living in God's Presence

A ninth characteristic of a lived out open theist renewal theology is that it is hopeful and joyful. One reason it is hopeful is Wesley's understanding that the abundant generosity of God's mercy means many will be saved.[108] Clark Pinnock was also optimistic on this issue.[109] Vaughn Baker has written an excellent open theist rationale for evangelism. He writes, "Could it be argued that what is needed for evangelism to take shape if not to take wings is a more dynamic theology, one more consistent with the biblical witness, the Christian faith and the creeds of the church?"[110] Yes, it could.

An open theist renewal theology is joyful because of its expectation of living in the fullness of the Holy Spirit and growing in the participation in the life of God. Wesley says it comes through living intentionally in the awareness of the presence of God: "Spare no pains to preserve always a deep, a continual, a lively, and a joyful sense of his gracious presence."[111]

Part of living intentionally is identifying and giving up idols: "Many indeed think of being happy with God in heaven; but the being happy in God on earth never entered their thoughts. The less so because from the time they came into the world they are surrounded with idols." Idols "all promise

---

108. Wesley had the expectation of a future global move of the Holy Spirit. "How is it possible to reconcile this [faithful Christians being a small minority in the world] with either the wisdom or goodness of God?... What but the consideration that things will not always be so; that another scene will soon be opened.... 'The earth shall be filled with the knowledge of the Lord, as the waters cover the sea.' The loving knowledge of God, producing uniform, uninterrupted holiness and happiness, shall cover the earth, shall fill every soul of man." Sermon 63: "The General Spread of the Gospel" [1783] in Wesley, *Sermons II*, 488.

109. Clark H. Pinnock, *A Wideness in God's Mercy: The Finality of Jesus Christ in a World of Religions* (Grand Rapids: Zondervan, 1992).

110. Vaughn W. Baker, *Evangelism and the Openness of God: The Implications of Relational Theism for Evangelism and Missions* (Eugene, Ore.: Pickwick, 2013), x.

111. Sermon 118: "On the Omnipresence of God" [1788] in Wesley, *Sermons IV*, 47.

a happiness independent of God."[112] The joy comes from "giving the heart to God."[113]

10. Love of God and Love of Neighbor

A tenth characteristic of a lived out open theist renewal theology would have to be love.[114] Open theists emphasize love as God's defining characteristic.[115] Wesley's exhortation stands: "Here then is the great object of Christian zeal. Let every true believer in Christ apply with all fervency of spirit to the God and Father of our Lord Jesus Christ, that his heart may be more and more *enlarged in love* to God and to all mankind."[116] We express this love in worship to God and compassion to neighbor. Wesley is, of course, getting this from Jesus whose teaching comes down to *love* of God and *love* of neighbor.[117]

---

112. Sermon 120: "The Unity of the Divine Being" [1789] in ibid., 64. He goes into some detail: "These idols, these rivals of God, are innumerable: but they may be nearly reduced to three parts. First, objects of sense, such as gratify one or more of our outward senses. These excite the first kind of 'love of the world,' which St. John terms 'the desire of the flesh.' [1 John 2:16] Secondly, objects of the imagination, things that gratify our fancy, by grandeur, beauty, or novelty. All these make us fair promises of happiness, and thereby prevent our seeking it in God. This the Apostle terms 'the desire of the eyes'; whereby chiefly the imagination is gratified. They are, thirdly, what St. John calls 'the pride of life.' He seems to mean honour, wealth, and whatever directly tends to engender pride." Ibid., 65. "If, by the grace of God, we have avoided or forsaken all these idols, there is still one more dangerous than all the rest, and that is, religion. It will easily be conceived, I mean false religion; that is, any religion which does not imply *the giving the heart to God*. Such is, first, a religion of opinions, or what is commonly called orthodoxy. Into this snare fall thousands of those who profess to hold 'salvation by faith'; indeed all of those who by faith mean only a system of Arminian or Calvinian opinions." Ibid, 66.

113. Sermon 120: "The Unity of the Divine Being" [1789] in ibid., 66.

114. Wesley writes, "It is in consequence of our knowing God loves us that we love him and love our neighbour as ourselves. Gratitude toward our Creator cannot but produce benevolence to our fellow-creatures. The love of Christ constrains us, not only to be harmless, to do no ill to our neighbour, but to be useful, to be 'zealous of good works', 'as we have time to do good unto all men', and be patterns to all of true genuine morality, of justice, mercy, and truth." Sermon 120: "The Unity of the Divine Being" [1789] in ibid., 67.

115. For example, Clark Pinnock writes, "From a Christian perspective, *love* is the first and last word in the biblical portrait of God. According to 1 John 4:8: 'Whoever does not love does not know God, because God is love.' The statement *God is love* is as close as the Bible comes to giving us a definition of the divine reality." Pinnock et al., *The Openness of God*, 18 (italics his). Italics mine.

116. Sermon 92: "On Zeal" [1781] in Wesley, *Sermons III*, 315.

117. For example, "'You shall love the Lord your God with all your heart, and with all your soul, and with all your mind.' This is the greatest and first commandment. And a second is like it: 'You shall love your neighbor as yourself.' On these two commandments hang all the law and the prophets" (Matthew 22:37–40).

V. A CONVERGENCE OF THE TWO TRAJECTORIES

We are to be people "who live entirely for love."[118] We are to love "with the severity and burning flame of the living Christ himself, who seeks to set the whole of world history aflame with the fire of his love."[119] Love is the theme that holds together Wesleyan charismatic-pentecostalism, open theism, and the teaching of Jesus.

---

118. Hans Urs von Balthasar, *Love Alone Is Credible*, 119.
119. Ibid., 120.

Conclusion

This study began with the assertion that John Wesley's theology of love began a trajectory towards open theism just as his emphasis on an experience of holiness and the Holy Spirit began a trajectory towards pentecostalism. Together, these trajectories provide the basis for a constructive open theist renewal theology with the experiential strength of Wesleyan charismatic-pentecostalism and the philosophical advantages of open theism. The first chapter included a review of the literature of open theism. Open theism, as I use the term here, is partly about the nature of the future (it is not predetermined but partially open), and partly about the nature of God (he is open to humanity and love is his defining characteristic). Writers at the intersection of open theism and renewal theology (pentecostal-charismatic and related theology) were noted.

The second chapter looked at problem areas for seeing Wesley as providing an impulse to open theism or pentecostalism. I noted how his understanding of the nature of time progressed over his long ministry from a position that was incompatible with open theism to one that affirms that God is active in time and everlasting rather than timeless. I also saw how Lorenzo Dow McCabe, in the nineteenth century, attempted to bring a mid-course correction to the Wesleyan movement by arguing compellingly on biblical and philosophical grounds that God does not know all future events. This assertion undermines Calvinistic views of free will, predestination, and election but prototypes open theism. The second half of the second chapter documented how Wesley became increasingly open to charismatic manifestations and how he responded to a crisis of misused spiritual gifts provoked by Thomas Maxfield and George Bell.

The third chapter demonstrated how John Wesley and John Fletcher initiated a trajectory towards open theism. Several theological themes pointed in that direction. Wesleyan nondeterministic and synergistic soteriology, with its generous view of God's grace, is congruent with open theism. Wesley emphasized the reality of human freedom, the possibility of working with God for good, and the loving condescension with which God allows his omnipotence to be conditioned by human choices. The late Wesley's deriving of divine omniscience from divine omnipresence moves him significantly toward open theism because open theists affirm God is everywhere. The late Wesley also opens a way for open theism when he rejects the doctrine of divine impassibility and by implication relinquishes divine immutability with respect to God's thinking and feeling (but not his character) and even, it can be argued, is on the threshold of abandoning divine timelessness. Most significantly, for Wesley, love is God's primary characteristic, which is similarly at the core of open theism's theological concern.

The third chapter also explored how Wesley and Fletcher irenically, but with energy, refuted Calvinism's doctrine of predestination and views of election and free will. The parallel with the current open theist debates is striking.

The fourth chapter showed how Wesley's and Fletcher's pneumatological theology and openness to charismatic spirituality set a course to pentecostalism. William Seymour extended an essentially Wesleyan theology while reinterpreting the baptism of the Holy Spirit as an experience after sanctification. The second half of the chapter looked at ways early pentecostalism—seen through issues of *The Apostolic Faith* and Seymour's *Doctrines and Discipline*—exhibited themes important to open theism, particularly divine love.

The fifth chapter described a Wesleyan renewal theology with an open theist identity. Three elements stand out: recovering from Wesley a passion for both personal and social change, absorbing from the pentecostal-charismatic movements a dependence on the power of the Holy Spirit with a willingness be Jesus' hands, feet, and voice, and incorporating the ability of open theism to respond to pressing intellectual issues and to be a catalyst through its emphasis on the openness of the future. An open renewal theology was outlined using categories of God, christology, the church, eschatology, anthropology, and pneumatology. Ten elements of praxis were mentioned: First, Jesus' condescension as he pours himself out in self-sacrificial love shows us how to live. Second, God's risk-taking encourages us to pray and to work synergistically with him to extend his kingdom. Third, we are emulators of God's compassion. Fourth, we imitate Jesus—who taught and modeled a non-violent and non-coercive love. Fifth, we oppose all forms of oppression, modeled on Wesley's opposition to slavery. Sixth, we pray for personal renewal through knowing Jesus and a baptism of the Holy Spirit. Seventh, we invest the time, commitment, and self-sacrifice to grow in sanctification. Eighth, inspired by Wesley's vision of a renewed humanity and a renewed earth, we resist consumerism and materialism and encourage environmentalism and sustainable practices. Ninth, we live joyfully, participating in the life of God, knowing that in his mercy salvation is open to all. Tenth, we live in love—the theme that holds together Wesleyan charismatic-pentecostalism, open theism, and the teaching of Jesus.

So, what does all this suggest for the way forward? Several trips to Africa, particularly to the DR Congo, Rwanda, and Zambia, have reinforced a conviction that theology should be robust enough to work both in the prosperity and privilege of the West but also in the two-thirds world.

Maybe Jesus really meant what he said that the kingdom is among you. It's about seeing the truer reality that lies just beyond perception. The kingdom is meant to be lived into. It's what revival is supposed to lead to. You start with an encounter with Jesus through the Holy Spirit. You are changed, and you begin to change the world around you. That's what open renewal says is possible. The mess we're in isn't inevitable. We can change the world, empowered by the Holy Spirit.

At different points in history, we've seen outbreaks of the Holy Spirit that could have been the catalyst for real change in the world beyond the spiritual benefits to those experiencing it. In my lifetime, I've seen the remarkable power of the charismatic movement usurped for narrowly political and self-serving purposes, instead of becoming the trigger for a world-wide explosion of altruism and expansion of kingdom values. It seems many people have enjoyed the sense of God's proximity without allowing themselves to be deeply transformed into people that truly love their neighbor.

This tendency to see the world in terms of us-versus-them, rather than loving the neighbor, was identified even in the Old Testament. The last verse of Jonah (4:11) is illustrative, where God says, "And should I not be concerned about Nineveh, that great city, in which there are more than a hundred and twenty thousand persons who do not know their right hand from their left, and also many animals?"

Even at Pentecost, maybe we're seeing things go off the rails in Acts 5 with the Ananias and Sapphira incident. Peter deals with them harshly and judgementally and the result is "great fear seized the whole church and ... none of the rest dared to join them" (Acts 5:13). So instead of the community-minded altruism of the Pentecost community expanding in ever broadening circles, it is halted in its tracks.

The pentecostal movement, as large as it is today, could have been the catalyst for world-changing prosperity, equity, and justice had not three factors suppressed it. (1) Clara Lum, editor of *The Apostolic Faith*, became disgruntled, moved to Oregon to work for Florence Crawford (who had become independent from Seymour), and took the mission's mailing list with her.[1] The crowds stopped coming because there was no public communication. (2) Attempts to wrest control from Seymour, e.g., Charles Parham's intervention and setting up a rival congregation. Parham was a racist and troubled by the racial integration at Azusa Street. The establishment of segregated pentecostal denominations is an outgrowth of this attitude. The love expressed through racial integration was essential to the revival. (3) An attempted takeover by William Durham who preached "the finished work of Christ." Durham was from a Calvinist background and resisted the Wesleyan teaching on sanctification. Painting with broad strokes, Reformed theology tends to buttress the status quo (see Daisy Machado;[2] with notable exceptions like Allan Boesak).[3] In my experience, Reformed theology is like green wood. You can make it

---

[1]. Robeck, *The Azusa Street Mission and Revival*, 301.

[2]. Machado, "Acres of Diamonds: The American Dream, Latino Immigration, and the Prosperity Gospel."

[3]. Allan A. Boesak, *Black and Reformed: Apartheid, Liberation, and the Calvinist Tradition* (Maryknoll, N.Y.: Orbis, 1984).

burn but it requires a lot more effort. Wesley's teaching that God is redeeming the whole earth makes working for a better world part of Wesleyan DNA.

> In the last days it will be, God declares,
>> that I will pour out my Spirit upon all flesh,
>>> and your sons and your daughters shall prophesy,
>> and your young men shall see visions,
>>> and your old men shall dream dreams.
>> Even upon my slaves, both men and women,
>>> in those days I will pour out my Spirit;
>> and they shall prophesy (Acts 2:17–18).

The open renewal theology described here affirms that we have a lot to say about what the future will look like. If God has given us this kind of agency, then we need to think in the biggest possible terms about what is possible. Things change when people have a dream or a vision and then speak prophetically. Let's look at some examples in economics.

1. An economic system that emphasizes competing against other people and groups, rather than working for the maximum good, might not be optimal. Capitalism might have to give way to cooperative effort. We can imagine a better way of being productive.

2. The divine right of kings was repudiated in the seventeen and eighteenth centuries. Maybe by analogy it's time for the right of a relatively few to horde wealth needs to be questioned. The labor of others often produced their wealth. The extreme inequities we see in income levels even within western countries is not good for our economies or the thriving of our communities (see economist Robert Reich's film *Inequality for All*,[4] or his book *Saving Capitalism*).[5] In opposition to John Locke, "Wesley did not accept the view of

---
[4]. Jacob Kornbluth and Robert Reich, "Inequality for All," (Documentary film released in 2013)."Inequality for All," (Documentary film released in 2013
[5]. Robert Reich, *Saving Capitalism: For the Many, Not the Few* (New York: Alfred A. Knopf, 2015).

a sacred and inviolable right to property, but rather that the right to property was bound up with its proper use."[6]

Someone might wonder if this is not Marxist class warfare. It is not, for several reasons. Foremost, this change to the social contract must be accomplished without violence or coercion (a little persuasion would be acceptable) or it has nothing to do with Jesus and his ethics. Secondly, it does not propose to set the existing classes against each other but urges a more community-oriented evaluation of what it means to live well. In redistributing their wealth, the super-rich gain a world where their well-being doesn't have to be protected with violence and threats of violence against an increasingly restive underclass. By giving up wealth which they can't possibly spend, they gain a society within which they can live with considerably less fear, and instead enjoy the greater well-being that only shared community can provide. Thirdly, this attitude toward wealth finds its inspiration not in Marx, but in the way the early church handled wealth: "All who believed were together and had all things in common; they would sell their possessions and goods and distribute the proceeds to all, as any had need" (Acts 2:44–45). Wesley dreamed his followers would imitate the early church in this.[7]

3. Nationalism creates substantial inequities between countries (see Jeffrey Sachs, *The Common Wealth*).[8] Our imperialistic past and present must be overcome in favor of a more equitable distribution of wealth and resources. The accident of where you happen to have been born on the planet shouldn't predetermine your future well-being. That a policy is justified if it's in the best interests of *us*, needs to give way to a criterion of what creates the greatest good for everybody (*us* and *them*). Rather, Sachs is right to argue that we need to reinvent global cooperation.[9] Again, the New Testament provides a precedent here in how early believers saw their primary allegiance to Jesus

---

[6]. Thomas W. Madron, "John Wesley on Economics," in *Sanctification and Liberation*, ed. Theodore Runyon (Nashville: Abingdon, 1981), 109.

[7]. Ibid., 108.

[8]. Jeffrey D. Sachs, *The Common Wealth: Economics for a Crowded Planet* (New York: Penguin, 2008).

[9]. Ibid., 295.

rather than a nation-state or empire.[10] They came to see that they were in it together.

These three examples are illustrative of how open renewal theology—with its open-ended view of the future and optimism that God works synergistically—might inspire change. It will be a change toward living out the ethics of the kingdom of God, which Jesus says is already among us. The persuasion of the Holy Spirit can change hearts. Could it be that the next revival will include concern for social and economic justice on a large scale?

In conclusion, an open theist renewal theology can be formed as two trajectories from John Wesley come together. One comes through the pentecostal-charismatic movement. The other comes through a movement which stresses the openness of God. Love is the recurring theme which makes them cohere. It describes God as genuinely humble and, above all, loving. An open theist renewal theology affirms with Hebrews 1:3 that Jesus is the "reflection of God's glory and the exact imprint of God's very being." God's glory is the effulgence of his love.

---

10. Alan Kreider, *The Patient Ferment of the Early Church: The Improbable Rise of Christianity in the Roman Empire* (Grand Rapids: Baker Academic, 2016).

Bibliography

Primary Sources

Fletcher, John. *The Works of the Reverend John Fletcher, Late Vicar of Madeley.* 4 vols. Salem, Ohio: Schmul, rprt. 1974.

———. *Five Checks to Antinomianism.* London: Wesleyan Conference Office, 1872.

Seymour, William J., ed. *The Azusa Street Papers: The Apostolic Faith: The Original 13 Issues.* San Bernardino, Calif.: PentecostalBooks.com, 1906–1908 [reprint 2013]. Thirteen out of the original fifteen issues are also available at pentecostalarchives.org. All fifteen are available as searchable text at http://www.apostolicfaith.org/Library/Index/AzusaPapers.aspx.

———. *The Azusa Street Papers: A Reprint of The Apostolic Faith Mission Publications, Los Angeles, California (1906–1908).* Foley, Ala.: Together in the Harvest, 1906–1908 [reproduction 1997].

———. *The Doctrines and Discipline of the Azusa Street Apostolic Faith Mission of Los Angeles, California.* Edited by Larry Martin. Joplin, Mo.: Christian Life Books, 2000.

Seymour, William J., and others. *Azusa Street Lectures, Letters and Bible Lessons: What the Faithful Believed and Taught at the Pentecostal Revival in Los Angeles.* Edited by Larry Martin. Joplin, Mo.: Christian Life Books, 2008.

Synan, Vinson, and Charles R. Fox, Jr. *William J. Seymour: Pioneer of the Azusa Street Revival.* Alachua, Fla.: Bridge-Logos, 2012. The second half contains a reproduction of the rare 1915 edition of William Seymour's *The Doctrines and Discipline of the Azusa Street Apostolic Faith Mission of Los Angeles, California* and Vinson Synan's introduction.

Wesley, John. *Doctrinal and Controversial Treatises I.* Vol. 12 of The Works of John Wesley. Edited by Randy L. Maddox. Nashville: Abingdon, 2012.

———. *Doctrinal and Controversial Treatises II.* Vol. 13 of The Works of John Wesley. Edited by Paul Wesley Chilcote and Kenneth J. Collins. Nashville: Abingdon, 2013.

———. *Journal and Diaries.* The Works of John Wesley. Edited by W. Reginald Ward and Richard P. Heitzenrater. 7 vols. Nashville: Abingdon, 1990.

———. *The Letters of the Rev. John Wesley, A.M., Sometime Fellow of Lincoln College, Oxford.* Edited by John Telford. 8 vols. London: Epworth, 1931.

———. *Sermons I, 1–33.* Vol. 1 of The Works of John Wesley. Edited by Albert C. Outler. Nashville: Abingdon, 1984. This edition is the standard one relied on here.

———. *Sermons II, 34–70.* Vol. 2 of The Works of John Wesley. Edited by Albert C. Outler. Nashville: Abingdon, 1985.

———. *Sermons III, 71–114.* Vol. 3 of The Works of John Wesley. Edited by Albert C. Outler. Nashville: Abingdon, 1986.

———. *Sermons IV, 115–151.* Vol. 4 of The Works of John Wesley. Edited by Albert C. Outler. Nashville: Abingdon, 1987.

———. *The Sermons of John Wesley: A Collection for the Christian Journey.* Edited by Kenneth J. Collins and Jason Vickers. Nashville: Abingdon, 2013. This edition is particularly valuable, not only for the introductory comments and outlines of the selected sermons, but because it is available in a Kindle edition.

Secondary Sources

Alexander, Kimberly Ervin. "Boundless Love Divine: A Re-evaluation of Early Understandings of the Experience of Spirit Baptism." In *Passover, Pentecost and Parousia: Studies in Celebration of the Life and Ministry of R. Hollis Gause.* Edited by Steven Jack Land, Rickie D. Moore, and John Christopher Thomas. Blandford Forum, Dorset, UK: Deo, 2010.

———. "Standing at the Crossroads: The Battle for the Heart and Soul of Pentecostalism." *Pneuma* 33, no. 3 (2011): 331–49.

Alexander, Kimberly Ervin, and James P. Bowers. "How Godly Love Flourished and Foundered." In *Godly Love: Impediments and Possibilities.* Edited by Matthew T. Lee and Amos Yong. Lanham, Md. and Plymouth, UK: Lexington Books, 2012.

Alexander, Paul. *Peace to War: Shifting Allegiances in the Assemblies of God.* C. Henry Smith Series. Telford, Pa.: Cascadia, 2009.

Althouse, Peter. "Implications of the Kenosis of the Spirit for a Creational Eschatology: A Pentecostal Engagement with Jürgen Moltmann." In *The Spirit Renews the Face of the Earth: Pentecostal Forays in Science and Theology of Creation*. Edited by Amos Yong. Eugene: Wipf & Stock, 2009.

———. *Spirit of the Last Days: Pentecostal Eschatology in Conversation with Jürgen Moltmann*. JPT Supplement Series 25. London: T & T Clark, 2003.

Anderson, Allan. *An Introduction to Pentecostalism: Global Charismatic Christianity*. Cambridge: Cambridge University Press, 2004.

———. *An Introduction to Pentecostalism: Global Charismatic Christianity*. 2nd ed. Cambridge: Cambridge University Press, 2014.

Archer, Kenneth J. *The Gospel Revisited: Towards a Pentecostal Theology of Worship and Witness*. Eugene, Ore.: Pickwick/Wipf & Stock, 2011.

———. "Open Theism View: Prayer Changes Things." *The Pneuma Review* 5, no. 2 (Spring 2002): 32–53.

———. *A Pentecostal Hermeneutic for the Twenty-First Century: Spirit, Scripture and Community*. London and New York: T&T Clark, 2004.

Armerding, Carl E., ed., Harvie M. Conn, Kenneth Hamilton, Stephen C. Knapp, and Clark H. Pinnock. *Evangelicals and Liberation*. Nutley, N.J.: Presbyterian and Reformed, 1977.

Arminius, Jacobus. *The Writings of James Arminius Translated from the Latin in Three Volumes*. Translated by James Nichols (vols. 1 & 2), and W. R. Bagnell (vol. 3). Grand Rapids: Baker, 1956.

Asamoah-Gyadu, J. Kwabena. *African Charismatics*. Leiden and Boston: Brill, 2005.

Audi, Robert, ed. *The Cambridge Dictionary of Philosophy*. Cambridge: Cambridge University Press, 1999.

Augustine of Hippo. *Concerning the City of God, against the Pagans*. Translated by Henry Bettenson. Harmondsworth, Middlesex, England and Baltimore, Md.: Penguin, 1467, 1972.

Aulén, Gustaf. *Christus Victor: An Historical Study of the Three Main Types of the Idea of Atonement*. Translated by A. G. Hebert. New York: Macmillan, 1969.

Baelz, Peter R. *Prayer and Providence: A Background Study*. Hulsean Lectures for 1966. London: SCM, 1968.

Baker, Frank. "Thomas Maxfield's First Sermon." *Proceedings of the Wesley Historical Society* 27, no. 1 (March 1949): 7–15.

Baker, Vaughn W. *Evangelism and the Openness of God: The Implications of Relational Theism for Evangelism and Missions*. Eugene, Ore.: Pickwick, 2013.

Barbour, Ian G. *Issues in Science and Religion*. London: SCM, 1966.

Barth, Karl. *Church Dogmatics*. Translated by Geoffrey W. Bromiley, Vol. III, Part 3. Edinburgh: T&T Clark, 1960.

Basinger, David. "Practical Implications." In *The Openness of God: A Biblical Challenge to the Traditional Understanding of God*. Downers Grove: InterVarsity Press, 1994.

Basinger, David, and Randall Basinger. *Predestination and Free Will: Four Views of Divine Sovereignty and Human Freedom*. Downers Grove: InterVarsity, 1986.

Bebbington, David, and David Ceri Jones. *Evangelicalism and Fundamentalism in the United Kingdom during the Twentieth Century*. Oxford: Oxford University Press, 2013.

Bebbington, David. *Evangelicalism in Modern Britain: A History from the 1730s to the 1980s*. Grand Rapids: Baker, 1989.

Beilby, James K., Paul R. Eddy, Gregory A. Boyd, William Lane Craig, Paul Helm, and David Hunt. *Divine Foreknowledge: Four Views*. Downers Grove: InterVarsity, 2001.

Beilby, James K., Paul R. Eddy, Steven E. Eenderlein, Michael F. Bird, James D. G. Dunn, Michael S. Horton, Veli-Matti Kärkkäinen, Gerald O'Collins, S.J., and Oliver Rafferty, S.J. *Justification: Five Views*. Downers Grove: InterVarsity, 2011.

Bell, Rob. *Love Wins: A Book About Heaven, Hell, and the Fate of Every Person Who Ever Lived*. New York: HarperCollins, 2011.

Bellusci, David C., and Christoph Ehland. *Amor Dei in the Sixteenth and Seventeenth Centuries*. Value Inquiry Book Series. Amsterdam: Editions Rodopi, 2013.

Benson, Joseph, John Wesley, and Joshua Gilpin (Vicar of Wrockwardine). *The Life of the Rev. John W. de la Fléchère: Compiled from the Narrative of Rev. Mr. Wesley; the Biographical Notes of Rev. Mr. Gilpin; From His Own Letters, And Other Authentic Documents, Many of Which Were Never Before Published*. London: T. Mason and G. Lane, 1840.

Berridge, John. *The Christian World Unmasked*. 2nd ed. London: Edward and Charles Dilly, 1773.

Beverley, James A. *Holy Laughter and the Toronto Blessing: An Investigative Report*. Grand Rapids: Zondervan, 1995.

Bietenhard, H. "Fire." In *The New International Dictionary of New Testament Theology*. Edited by Colin Brown, 656–57. Grand Rapids: Zondervan, 1986.

Birx, H. James, ed. *Encyclopedia of Time: Science, Philosophy, Theology & Culture*. 3 vols. Los Angeles: Sage, 2009.

Blumhofer, Edith L. *Aimee Semple McPherson: Everybody's Sister*. Library of Religious Biography. Grand Rapids: Eerdmans, 1993.

———. *Restoring the Faith: The Assemblies of God, Pentecostalism, and American Culture*. Urbana and Chicago: University of Illinois Press, 1993.
Boesak, Allan A. *Black and Reformed: Apartheid, Liberation, and the Calvinist Tradition*. Maryknoll, N.Y.: Orbis, 1984.
Boyd, Gregory A. *God at War: The Bible and Spiritual Conflict*. Downers Grove: InterVarsity, 1997.
———. *God of the Possible: A Biblical Introduction to the Open View of God*. Grand Rapids: Baker, 2000.
———. *Is God to Blame?: Moving Beyond Pat Answers to the Problem of Evil*. Downers Grove: InterVarsity, 2003.
———. *Oneness Pentecostals and the Trinity: A World-wide Movement Assessed by a Former Oneness Pentecostal*. Grand Rapids: Baker, 1992.
———. *Present Perfect: Finding God in the Now*. Grand Rapids: Zondervan, 2010.
———. *Repenting of Religion: Turning from Judgment to the Love of God*. Grand Rapids: Baker, 2004.
———. *Satan and the Problem of Evil: Constructing a Trinitarian Warfare Theodicy*. Downers Grove: InterVarsity, 2001.
———. *The Myth of a Christian Nation: How the Quest for Political Power Is Destroying the Church*. Grand Rapids: Zondervan, 2009.
———. *The Myth of a Christian Religion: Losing Your Religion for the Beauty of a Revolution*. Grand Rapids: Zondervan, 2009.
———. *Trinity and Process: A Critical Evaluation and Reconstruction of Hartshorne's Di-Polar Theism Towards a Trinitarian Metaphysics*. New York, San Francisco, and Bern: Peter Lang, 1992.
Boyd, Gregory A., and Paul R. Eddy. *Across the Spectrum: Understanding Issues in Evangelical Theology*. 2nd ed. Grand Rapids: Baker Academic, 2009.
Bradbury, Thomas. *Grove Chapel Pulpit: Twenty-four Sermons*, Vol. 4. London: Robert Banks, 1880.
Bray, Gerald Lewis. *The Personal God*. Carlisle, U.K.: Paternoster Press, 1998.
Brümmer, Vincent. *What Are We Doing When We Pray?: On Prayer and the Nature of Faith*. Rev. ed. Aldershot, England: Ashgate, 2008.
Bundy, David D. *Keswick: A Bibliographic Introduction to the Higher Life Movements*. Wilmore, Ky.: B. L. Fisher Library, Asbury Theological Seminary, 1975.
Burgess, Stanley M., and Eduard M. van der Maas, eds. *The New International Dictionary of Pentecostal and Charismatic Movements*. Grand Rapids: Zondervan, 2003.
Burnaby, John. "Christian Prayer." In *Soundings: Essays Concerning Christian Understanding*. Edited by Alexander Roper Vidler. Cambridge: Cambridge University Press, 1962.

Callen, Barry L. *Clark H. Pinnock: Journey Toward Renewal: An Intellectual Biography*. Nappanee, Ind.: Evangel, 2000.

———. *God as Loving Grace: The Biblically Revealed Nature and Work of God*. Nappanee, Ind.: Evangel, 1996.

———. "John Wesley and Relational Theology." In *Relational Theology: A Contemporary Introduction*. Edited by Brint Montgomery, Thomas Jay Oord, and Karen Winslow. Eugene, Ore.: Point Loma Press/Wipf & Stock, 2012.

Calvin, John. *Institutes of the Christian Religion*. Translated by Ford Lewis Battles. The Library of Christian Classics, Vol. XX. Edited by John T. McNeill. Philadelphia: Westminster, 1960.

Castelo, Daniel, ed. *Holiness as a Liberal Art*. Eugene, Ore.: Pickwick/Wipf & Stock, 2012.

Charnock, Stephen. *Discourses upon the Existence and Attributes of God*. 2 vols. Grand Rapids: Baker, 1853 [Robert Carter & Brothers], rprt. 1996.

Clarke, Clifton R. "Ogbu Kalu and Africa's Christianity: A Tribute." *Pneuma* 32 (2010): 107–20.

Clayton, Allen L. "The Significance of William H. Durham for Pentecostal Historigraphy." *Pneuma* 1, no. 1 (1979): 27–42.

Cobb, John B., and David Ray Griffin. *Process Theology: An Introductory Exposition*. Philadelphia: Westminster Press, 1976.

Cobb, John B., and Clark H. Pinnock. *Searching for an Adequate God: A Dialogue Between Process and Free Will Theists*. Grand Rapids: Eerdmans, 2000.

Collins, Kenneth J. "A Hermeneutical Model for the Wesleyan *Ordo Salutis*." *Wesleyan Theological Journal* 19, no. 2 (Fall 1984): 23–37.

———. *A Real Christian: The Life of John Wesley*. Nashville: Abingdon, 1999.

———. "Recent Trends in Wesley Studies and Wesleyan/Holiness Scholarship." *Wesleyan Theological Journal* 35, no. 1 (Spring 2000): 67–86.

———. *The Theology of John Wesley: Holy Love and the Shape of Grace*. Nashville: Abingdon, 2007.

Coppedge, Allan. *Shaping the Wesleyan Message: John Wesley in Theological Debate*. Nappanee, Ind.: Francis Asbury Press, 1987, 2003.

Coveney, Peter, and Roger Highfield. *The Arrow of Time: A Voyage Through Science to Solve Time's Greatest Mystery*. New York: Fawcett Columbine, 1990.

Craig, William Lane. *Divine Foreknowledge and Human Freedom: The Coherence of Theism: Omniscience*. Brill's Studies in Intellectual History 19. New York: Leiden, 1990.

———. *The Only Wise God: The Compatibility of Divine Foreknowledge and Human Freedom*. Grand Rapids: Baker, 1987.

Crockett, W. V., J. Walvoord, Z. J. Hayes, and Clark H. Pinnock. *Four Views on Hell*. Grand Rapids: Zondervan, 1997.

Cross, F. L., and E. A. Livingstone, eds. *Dictionary of the Christian Church*. 3rd ed. Oxford: Oxford University Press, 1997.

Cullmann, Oscar. *Christ and Time: The Primitive Christian Conception of Time and History*. Translated by Floyd V. Filson. Philadelphia: Westminster, 1950.

Culp, John. "A Dialog with the Process Theology of John B. Cobb, Jr." *Wesleyan Theological Journal* 15, no. 2 (Spring 1980): 33–58.

Dart, John. "College to Close Out 'Open Theism' Scholar." *Christian Century* 121, no. 26 (Dec 28, 2004): 12.

Dayton, Donald W. "Methodism and Pentecostalism." In *The Oxford Handbook of Methodist Studies*. Edited by William J. Abraham, and James E. Kirby, 171–87. Oxford and New York: Oxford University Press, 2008.

———. "Some Doubts about the Usefulness of the Category 'Evangelical'." In *The Variety of American Evangelicalism*. Edited by Donald W. Dayton and Robert K. Johnston, 245–51. Downers Grove: InterVarsity, 1991.

———. *Theological Roots of Pentecostalism*. Peabody, Mass.: Hendrickson, 1987.

Del Colle, Ralph. *Christ and the Spirit: Spirit-Christology in Trinitarian Perspective*. New York: Oxford University Press, 1994.

Dewey, Orville. *The Works of the Rev. Orville Dewey, D. D., Pastor of The Church of the Messiah, New York*. London: Simms and McIntyre, 1844.

Dorner, Isaak August. *A System of Christian Doctrine*. Translated by Alfred Cave. Edinburgh: T&T Clark, 1880.

Elliott, George. "Orthodoxy of Bowne." *Methodist Review* 105, no. 3 (May 1922): 399–413.

Elliott, Matthew A. *Faithful Feelings: Re-thinking Emotion in the New Testament*. Grand Rapids: Kregel, 2006.

English, John C. "John Wesley's Scientific Education." *Methodist History* 30, no. 1 (October 1991): 42–51.

Erickson, Millard J. *Christian Theology*. 2nd ed. Grand Rapids: Baker, 1998.

Fletcher, John. *An Equal Check to Pharisaism and Antinomianism*. 4 vols. The Works of the Reverend John Fletcher, Late Vicar of Madeley I. Salem, Ohio: Schmul, 1774 [reprint 1974].

Flew, Antony. *A Dictionary of Philosophy*. 2nd ed. New York: St. Martin's, 1984.

Foote, William C., and William Wilberforce Rand. *Bible Student's Companion: Containing Bible Text-Book, Concordance, Table of Proper Names, Twelve Maps, Indexes, Etc*. New York: American Tract Society, 1876.

Fox, Charles R., Jr., and Vinson Synan. *William J. Seymour: Pioneer of the Azusa Street Revival*. Alachua, Fla.: Bridge-Logos, 2012.

Frame, John M. *No Other God: A Response to Open Theism*. Phillipsburg, N.J.: P&R, 2001.
Fretheim, Terence E. *The Suffering of God: An Old Testament Perspective*. Philadelphia: Fortress, 1984.
Ganssle, Gregory E., ed. *God and Time: Four Views*. Downers Grove: InterVarsity, 2001.
Gasaway, Brantley W. *Progressive Evangelicals and the Pursuit of Social Justice*. Chapel Hill: University of North Carolina Press, 2014.
Gill, John, ed. *Christ Alone Exalted, in the Perfection and Encouragement of the Saints, Notwithstanding Sins and Trials: Being the Complete Works of Tobias Crisp... Containing Fifty-two Sermons, on Several Select Texts of Scripture*. 7th ed. London: John Bennett, 1832.
Gingerich, Ray, and Ted Grimsrud, eds. *Transforming the Powers: Peace, Justice, and the Domination System*. Minneapolis, Minn.: Fortress, 2006.
Girard, René. *I See Satan Fall Like Lightning*. Maryknoll, N.Y.: Orbis, 2001.
Grant, Miles. *Foreknowledge: Is God's Prescience Eternal and Universal? The Eternal Principles that Control Conditional and Positive Prophecy—A Golden Mean between Arminianism and Calvinism*. Boston, Mass.: Miles Grant, 1896.
Griffin, David Ray. *Evil Revisited: Responses and Reconsiderations*. Albany: State University of New York Press, 1991.
———. *God, Power, and Evil: A Process Theodicy*. Louisville: Westminster John Knox, 2004.
Grudem, Wayne. *Systematic Theology: An Introduction to Biblical Doctrine*. Leicester, England: InterVarsity and Grand Rapids: Zondervan, 1994, 2000.
Gunter, W. Stephen. *The Limits of 'Love Divine': John Wesley's Response to Antinomianism and Enthusiasm*. Nashville: Kingswood, 1989.
Guthrie, Stan. "Open or Closed Case?: Controversial Theologian John Sanders on Way Out at Huntington." *Christianity Today* 48, no. 12 (Dec 2004). http://www.christianitytoday.com/ct/2004/decemberweb-only/12-20-32.0.html.
Hall, Christopher A., and John Sanders. *Does God Have a Future?: A Debate on Divine Providence*. Grand Rapids: Baker Academic, 2003.
Harmon, Nolan B., ed. *The Encyclopedia of World Methodism*. 2 vols. Nashville, Tenn.: United Methodist Publishing House, 1974.
Hartshorne, Charles. *Omnipotence and Other Theological Mistakes*. Albany: State University of New York Press, 1984.
Hasker, William. "Foreknowledge and Necessity." *Faith and Philosophy* 2 (April 1985): 121–57.

―――. *God, Time, and Knowledge*. Cornell Studies in the Philosophy of Religion. Ithaca, N.Y.: Cornell University Press, 1989.
―――. *Metaphysics and the Tri-Personal God*. Oxford Studies in Analytic Theology. Oxford: Oxford University Press, 2013.
―――. "A Philosophical Perspective." In *The Openness of God: A Biblical Challenge to the Traditional Understanding of God*. Downers Grove: InterVarsity Press, 1994.
―――. *Providence, Evil and the Openness of God*. London: Routledge, 2004.
―――. "The Social Analogy in Modern Trinitarian Thought." Ph.D. thesis, University of Edinburgh, 1961.
Hasker, William, Thomas Jay Oord, and Dean Zimmerman. *God in an Open Universe: Science, Metaphysics, and Open Theism*. Eugene, Ore.: Wipf & Stock, 2011.
Haught, John F. *God After Darwin: A Theology of Evolution*. 2nd ed. Boulder, Colo.: Westview, 2008.
―――. *God and the New Atheism: A Critical Response to Dawkins, Harris, and Hitchens*. Louisville: Westminster, 2008.
Hayes, Joel S. *The Foreknowledge of God or, The Omniscience of God Consistent with His Own Holiness and Man's Free Agency*. Nashville: Publishing House of the M. E. Church, 1890.
Heitzenrater, Richard P. *Wesley and the People Called Methodists*. Nashville: Abingdon, 1995.
Helm, Paul. "Divine Timeless Eternity." In *God and Time: Four Views*. Edited by Gregory E. Ganssle. Downers Grove: InterVarsity, 2001.
―――. *The Providence of God*. Downers Grove: InterVarsity, 1994.
Heschel, Abraham. *The Prophets*. 2 vols. New York: Harper & Row, 1962.
Hollenweger, Walter J. *Pentecostalism: Origins and Developments Worldwide*. Peabody, Mass.: Hendrickson, 1997.
Janiak, Andrew. "Kant's Views on Space and Time." In *The Stanford Encyclopedia of Philosophy*. Edited by Edward N. Zalta, 2009. http://plato.stanford.edu/archives/win2012/entries/kant-spacetime/.
Jennings, Daniel R. *The Supernatural Occurrences of John Wesley*. Oklahoma City, Okla.: Sean Multimedia, 2005, 2012.
Johnson, B. C. "God and the Problem of Evil." In *Philosophy and Contemporary Issues*. Edited by John Burr, and Milton Goldinger, 158–63. New York: Macmillan, 1992.
Johnson, Todd, and Kenneth R. Ross, eds. *The Atlas of Global Christianity*. Edinburgh: Edinburgh University Press, 2009.
Johnston, Robert K. "Clark H. Pinnock." In *Handbook of Evangelical Theologians*. Edited by Walter Elwell. Grand Rapids: Baker, 1993.

Kalu, Ogbu. *African Pentecostalism: An Introduction*. Oxford: Oxford University Press, 2008.
Kärkkäinen, Veli-Matti. "'Truth on Fire': Pentecostal Theology of Mission and the Challenges of a New Millennium." *Asian Journal of Pentecostal Studies* 3, no. 1 (2000): 33–60.
Kenny, Anthony John Patrick. *The God of the Philosophers*. Oxford: Clarendon Press, 1979.
King, William McGuire. "God's Nescience of Future Contingents: A Nineteenth-Century Wesleyan Theory." *Process Studies* 9 (Fall 1979): 105–15.
Kitamori, Kazoh. *Theology of the Pain of God*. 5th ed. Eugene, Ore.: Wipf & Stock, 1958.
Knight III, Henry H., ed. *From Aldersgate to Azusa Street: Wesleyan, Holiness, and Pentecostal Visions of the New Creation*. Eugene, Ore.: Pickwick, 2010.
König, Adriö. *Here Am I!: A Christian Reflection on God*. Grand Rapids: Eerdmans, 1982.
Kornbluth, Jacob and Robert Reich. "Inequality for All." Documentary film released in 2013.
Kreider, Alan. *The Patient Ferment of the Early Church: The Improbable Rise of Christianity in the Roman Empire*. Grand Rapids: Baker Academic, 2016.
Kushner, Harold. *When Bad Things Happen to Good People*. New York: Schocken, 1981.
Land, Steven Jack. *Pentecostal Spirituality: A Passion for the Kingdom*. Cleveland, Tenn.: CPT, 2010.
Land, Steven Jack, Rickie D. Moore, and John Christopher Thomas. *Passover, Pentecost and Parousia: Studies in Celebration of the Life and Ministry of R. Hollis Gause*. Journal of Pentecostal Theology Supplement Series. Blandford Forum, Dorset, UK: Deo, 2010.
Larson, David. "The Spectrum Blog." (12 Nov 2007). http://spectrummagazine.org/blog/2007/11/12/ richard-rice-discusses-open-theism.
Le Poidevin, Robin, and Murray MacBeath. *The Philosophy of Time*. Oxford Readings in Philosophy. Oxford: Oxford University Press, 1993.
Lederle, Henry I. *Theology with Spirit: The Future of the Pentecostal & Charismatic Movements in the Twenty-first Century*. Tulsa, Okla.: Word and Spirit, 2010.
Lee, Matthew T., and Amos Yong. *Godly Love: Impediments and Possibilities*. Lanham, Md. and Plymouth, UK: Lexington Books, 2012.
Leftow, Brian. "Immutability." In *The Stanford Encyclopedia of Philosophy*. Edited by Edward N. Zalta, 2011. http://plato.stanford.edu/archives/win2012/entries/immutability/.

Lucas, John R. *Freedom and Grace*. London: SPCK, 1976.
Lugo, Luis. "Spirit and Power: A Ten-Country Survey of Pentecostals." *The Pew Forum on Religion and Public Life*. Washington, D.C.: The Pew Research Center, October 2006.
Lukashow, Tom. "Historical Research." *The Open View* (2014). http://theopenview.org/historical-research/. [Accessed 12 May 2014].
Macchia, Frank D. *Baptized in the Spirit: A Global Pentecostal Theology*. Grand Rapids: Zondervan, 2006.
Machado, Daisy L. "Acres of Diamonds: The American Dream, Latino Immigration, and the Prosperity Gospel." Society for Pentecostal Studies Annual Meeting. Virginia Beach, Va., March 2, 2012.
Maddox, Randy L. "From Everlasting to Everlasting: John Wesley on Eternity and Time." *Methodist History* 31, no. 3 (April 1993): 185–187.
———. "John Wesley and Eastern Orthodoxy: Influences, Convergences and Differences." *Asbury Theological Journal* 45, no. 2 (Fall 1990): 29–53.
———. "John Wesley's Reading: Evidence in the Book Collection at Wesley's House, London." *Methodist History* 41, no. 3 (April 2003): 118–133.
———. "John Wesley's Reading: Evidence in the Kingswood School Archives." *Methodist History* 41, no. 2 (January 2003): 49–67.
———. "Kingswood School Library Holdings (ca. 1775)." *Methodist History* 41, no. 1 (October 2002): 342–370.
———. "Remnants of John Wesley's Personal Library." *Methodist History* 42, no. 2 (2004): 122–28.
———. *Responsible Grace: John Wesley's Practical Theology*. Nashville: Kingswood, 1994.
———. "Seeking a Response-able God: The Wesleyan Tradition and Process Theology." In *Thy Nature and Thy Name Is Love: Wesleyan and Process Theologies in Dialogue*. Edited by Bryan P. Stone and Thomas Jay Oord, 111–42. Nashville: Kingswood, 2001.
———. "Wesley and the Question of Truth or Salvation through Other Religions." *Wesleyan Theological Journal* (Spring/Fall 1992): 7–29.
Madron, Thomas W. "John Wesley on Economics." In *Sanctification and Liberation*. Edited by Theodore Runyon, 102–15. Nashville: Abingdon, 1981.
Mander, W. J. *The Philosophy of John Norris*. Oxford: Oxford University Press, 2008.
Mandryk, Jason, and Patrick Johnstone. *Operation World*. 7th ed. Colorado Springs, Colo.: Biblica, 2010.
Marshall, I. Howard. *New Testament Theology: Many Witnesses, One Gospel*. Downers Grove: IVP Academic and Nottingham, England: Apollos, 2004.

McCabe, Lorenzo D. *Divine Nescience of Future Contingencies a Necessity: Being an Introduction to "The Foreknowledge of God, and Cognate Themes."* New York: Phillips & Hunt, 1882.

———. *The Foreknowledge of God, and Cognate Themes in Theology and Philosophy*. Cincinnati: Walden & Stowe, 1882.

McClure, John, and Don Williams. *Theological and Philosophical Statements*. Stafford, Tex.: Vineyard USA, 2004.

McConnell, Francis John. *The Christlike God: A Survey of the Divine Attributes from the Christian Point of View*. New York: Abingdon, 1927.

McDaniel, Jay B., and Donna Bowman. *Handbook of Process Theology*. St. Louis, Mo.: Chalice Press, 2006.

McGiffert, Arthur Cushman. *A History of Christian Thought: Volume II, The West from Tertullian to Erasmus*. New York and London: Charles Scribner's Sons, 1933, 1954.

McLaughlin, Bruce. "From Whence Evil?" *Perspectives on Science and the Christian Faith: Journal of the American Scientific Affiliation* 56, no. 3 (September 2004): 237–38.

McMurphy, Kathleen B. "John Wesley and the End of the World." *Ministry: International Journal for Pastors* 33 (April 1960): 32–33.

McPherson, Aimee Semple. *The Story of My Life: Aimee Semple McPherson*. Waco, Tex.: Word, 1973.

McTaggart, J. M. E. *The Nature of Existence*, Vol. 2. Cambridge: Cambridge University Press, 1927.

———. "The Unreality of Time." In *The Philosophy of Time*. Edited by Robin Le Poidevin and Murray MacBeath. Oxford: Oxford University Press, 1993.

Medina, Néstor. *Mestizaje: (Re)mapping Race, Culture, and Faith in Latina/o Catholicism*. Maryknoll, N.Y.: Orbis, 2009.

Menzel, Christopher. "Alethic Modalities." In *The Cambridge Dictionary of Philosophy*. Edited by Robert Audi. Cambridge: Cambridge University Press, 1999.

Menzies, William W. "The Reformed Roots of Pentecostalism." *PentecoStudies* 6, no. 2 (2007).

Molina, Luis de. *On Divine Foreknowledge*. Translated by Alfred J. Freddoso. Part IV of the *Concordia*. Ithaca and London: Cornell University Press, 1588, 1988.

Moltmann, Jürgen. *The Crucified God: The Cross of Christ as the Foundation and Criticism of Christian Theology (Der gekreuzigte Gott)*. Translated by R. A. Wilson and John Bowden. 2nd ed. New York: HarperCollins, 1974, 1991.

———. *Science and Wisdom*. Translated by Margaret Kohl. Minneapolis, Minn.: Fortress, 2003.

―――. "Sighs, Signs, and Significance: Natural Science and a Hermeneutics of Nature." In *Divine Grace and Emerging Creation: Wesleyan Forays in Science and Theology of Creation*. Edited by Thomas Jay Oord, 106–21. Eugene: Wipf & Stock, 2009.

―――. *Trinity and the Kingdom: The Doctrine of God*. Translated by Margaret Kohl. Minneapolis, Minn.: Fortress, 1993.

Montgomery, Brint, Thomas Jay Oord, and Karen Winslow, eds. *Relational Theology: A Contemporary Introduction*. Eugene, Ore.: Point Loma Press/Wipf & Stock, 2012.

Moore, Henry. *The Life of the Rev. John Wesley, A.M., Fellow of Lincoln College, Oxford; in Which Are Included, the Life of His Brother, the Rev. Charles Wesley, A.M., Student of Christ Church, and Memoirs of Their Family: Comprehending an Account of the Great Revival of Religion, in Which They Were the First and Chief Instruments*. London: J. Kershaw, 1824.

Murphy, Nancey, George F. R. Ellis, and Timothy O'Connor, eds. *Downward Causation and the Neurobiology of Free Will*. New York: Springer, 2009.

Myers, Bryant L. *Walking with the Poor: Principles and Practices of Transformational Development*. Maryknoll, N.Y.: Orbis, 1999.

Murray, Stuart. *The Naked Anabaptist: The Bare Essentials of a Radical Faith*. Scottdale, Pa.: Herald, 2010.

Naglee, David Ingersoll. *From Everlasting to Everlasting: John Wesley on Eternity and Time*. American University Studies, Series 7, Theology and Religion, Book 65. New York: Peter Lang, 1991.

Neff, David. "Dispatch from Atlanta: What Fireworks? Anxieties and Attack Turn to Grace as the Evangelical Theological Society Votes on Open Theism Proponents' Membership." *Christianity Today* 47, no. 11 (Nov 2003). http://www.christianitytoday.com/ct/2003/novemberweb-only/11-17-41.0.html.

Newport, Kenneth G. C. "George Bell, Prophet and Enthusiast." *Methodist History* 35, no. 2 (January 1997): 95–105.

Newton, John Thomas. "Neoplatonism and Augustine's Doctrine of the Person and Work of Christ: A Study of the Philosophical Structure Underlying Augustine's Christology." Ph.D. dissertation, Emory University, 1969.

New York Times. "Two Acquittals for Prof. Borden P. Bowne: Exoneration of Original Charges Followed by a Second Set. East Conference Applauds: Rev. Dr. Buckley Declares the Professor's Accuser Liable to Prosecution in Courts." April 9, 1904.

Norgate, Gerald le Grys. "Maxfield, Thomas (d.1784)." In *Dictionary of National Biography*. Vol. 37. London: Smith, Elder & Co., 1885–1900.

Norris, John. *A Collection of Miscellanies: Consisting of Poems, Essays, Discourses, and Letters, Occasionally Written.* Oxford: John Crosley Bookseller, 1687; reprint 1978, New York and London: Garland.

Olsen, Ted. "ETS Leadership Issues Recommendations on Kicking Out Open Theists: Evangelical Theological Society's Executive Committee Unanimously Recommends Clark Pinnock Stay; Majority Says John Sanders Should Go." *Christianity Today* 47, no. 10 (October 2003). http://www.christianitytoday.com/ct/2003/octoberweb-only/10-27-41.0.html.

Olson, Roger, Timothy George, Douglas F. Kelly, and Alister E. McGrath. "Has God Been Held Hostage by Philosophy? A Forum on Free-will Theism, a New Paradigm for Understanding God." *Christianity Today* 39, no. 1 (January 1995): 30–34.

Oord, Thomas Jay. *Creation Made Free: Open Theology Engaging Science.* Eugene, Ore.: Wipf & Stock, 2010.

———. *Defining Love: A Philosophical, Scientific, and Theological Engagement.* Grand Rapids: Baker/Brazos Press, 2010.

———, ed. *Divine Grace and Emerging Creation: Wesleyan Forays in Science and Theology of Creation.* Eugene: Wipf & Stock, 2009.

———, ed. *The Many Facets of Love: Philosophical Explorations.* Newcastle, UK: Cambridge Scholars Publishing, 2007.

———. *The Nature of Love: A Theology.* St. Louis, Mo.: Chalice Press, 2010.

———. *Science of Love: The Wisdom of Well-Being.* Philadelphia and London: Templeton Foundation Press, 2004.

———. *The Uncontrolling Love of God: An Open and Relational Account of Providence.* Downers Grove: IVP Academic, 2015 (forthcoming).

———. "Ways to Think about Providence." (May 25th, 2015). http://thomasjayoord.com/index.php/blog/archives/ways-to-think-about-providence#sthash.lTP0C1Wo.dpuf.

———. "What Is Relational Theology?" In *Relational Theology: A Contemporary Introduction.* Edited by Brint Montgomery, Thomas Jay Oord, and Karen Winslow, 1–6. Eugene, Ore.: Point Loma Press/Wipf & Stock, 2012.

Orobator, Agbonkhianmeghe E. *Theology Brewed in an African Pot.* Maryknoll, N.Y.: Orbis, 2008.

Padget, Alan. "Eternity as Relative Timelessness." In *God and Time: Four Views.* Edited by Gregory E. Ganssle. Downers Grove: InterVarsity, 2001.

Pannenberg, Wolfhart. *Systematic Theology: Volume I.* Translated by Geoffrey W. Bromiley. Grand Rapids: Eerdmans, 1991.

Park, Tae Soo. *A Biblical Response to Open Theism: Christology in the Four Gospels.* Saarbrücken, Germany: VDM Verlag Dr. Müller, 2010.

Peacocke, Arthur R. *Creation and the World of Science: The Re-shaping of Belief*. Oxford: Oxford University Press, 1979, 2004.

Peterson, Douglas. *Not by Might Nor by Power*. Oxford: Regnum Books International, 1996.

Pinnock, Clark H. "Acts 4:12—No Other Name Under Heaven." In *Through No Fault of Their Own?: The Fate of Those Who Have Never Heard*. Edited by William V. Crockett, and James G. Sigountos. Grand Rapids: Baker, 1991.

———. "Afterword." In *Clark H. Pinnock: Journey Toward Renewal: An Intellectual Biography*. Edited by Barry L. Callen, 269–72. Nappanee, Ind.: Evangel, 2000.

———. "The Beauty of God: John Wesley's Reform and Its Aftermath." *Wesleyan Theological Journal* 38, no. 2 (2003): 57–68.

———. "Biblical Authority in Christian Witness and Nurture." *Theological Conference of the International Federation of Free Evangelical Churches*, August 29–September 4, 1971, 1–5.

———. *Biblical Revelation: The Foundation of Christian Theology*. Chicago: Moody, 1971.

———. "Book Review: *Catch the Fire:* No Small Feat." *Spread the Fire* 1, no. 1 (1995): 16, 27.

———. "A Bridge and Some Points of Growth: A Reply To Cross and Macchia." *Journal of Pentecostal Theology* 6, no. 13 (1998): 49.

———. "A Call for the Liberation of North American Christians." In *Evangelicals and Liberation*. Edited by Carl E. Armerding. Nutley, N.J.: Presbyterian and Reformed, 1977.

———. "Can't Tell God How and Where to Work." *The Canadian Baptist* (March 1995): 3–4.

———. "Church in the Power of the Holy Spirit: The Promise of Pentecostal Ecclesiology." *Journal of Pentecostal Theology* 14, no. 2 (2006): 147.

———. "Confessions of a Post-Conservative Evangelical Theologian." *Dialog: A Journal of Theology* 45, no. 4 (2006): 382–88.

———. *A Defense of Biblical Infallibility*. International Library of Philosophy and Theology: Biblical and Theological Studies. Philadelphia: Presbyterian and Reformed, 1967.

———. "Divine Relationality: A Pentecostal Contribution to the Doctrine of God." *Journal of Pentecostal Theology* 8, no. 16 (2000): 3.

———. "Evangelical Theologians Facing the Future: An Ancient and a Future Paradigm." *Wesleyan Theological Journal* 33, no. 2 (1998).

———. "An Evangelical Theology: Conservative and Contemporary." *Christianity Today* 23, no. 7 (Jan 5, 1979): 23–29.

———. "An Evangelical Theology of Human Liberation—Part I." *Sojourners* 5, no. 2 (February 1976): 30–33.

———. "An Evangelical Theology of Human Liberation—Part II." *Sojourners* 5, no. 3 (March 1976): 26–29.

———. *Flame of Love: A Theology of the Holy Spirit*. Downers Grove: InterVarsity Press, 1996.

———. "From Augustine to Arminius: A Pilgrimage in Theology." In *The Grace of God, the Will of Man*, 15–30. Grand Rapids: Zondervan, 1989.

———. "God Limits His Knowledge." In *Predestination and Free Will: Four Views of Divine Sovereignty and Human Freedom*. Edited by David Basinger and Randall Basinger, 141–62. Downers Grove: InterVarsity, 1986.

———, ed. *The Grace of God, the Will of Man: A Case for Arminianism*. Grand Rapids: Zondervan, 1989.

———. *Grace Unlimited*. Minneapolis, Minn.: Bethany House, 1975.

———. "The Harrowing of Heaven." *Christianity Today* 14, no. 19 (June 19, 1970): 7–8.

———. "How I Use the Bible in Doing Theology." In *Use of the Bible in Theology: Evangelical Options*. Edited by Robert K. Johnston, 18–34. Atlanta: John Knox, 1984.

———. "How My Mind Has Changed." In *Clark H. Pinnock: Journey Toward Renewal: An Intellectual Biography*. Edited by Barry L. Callen, 219–67. Nappanee, Ind.: Evangel, 2000.

———. "Inclusivism." In *Four Views on Salvation in a Pluralistic World*. Edited by Dennis L. Okholm, and Timothy R. Phillips. Grand Rapids: Zondervan, 1996.

———. "An Interview with Clark Pinnock." *Modern Reformation* 37 (1998).

———. "Liberation Theology: An Evangelical View from the Third World." *Journal of the American Academy of Religion* 49, no. 4 (1981): 734.

———. *Most Moved Mover: A Theology of God's Openness*. Carlisle, U.K.: Paternoster, 2001.

———. "The New Pentecostalism: Reflections by a Well-Wisher." *Christianity Today* 17, no. 24 (Sept 14, 1973): 6–10.

———. "The Ongoing Struggle Over Biblical Inerrancy." *Journal of the American Scientific Affiliation* 31, no. 2 (June 1979): 69–74.

———. "Open Theism: An Answer to My Critics." *Dialog: A Journal of Theology* 44, no. 3 (2005): 237–45.

———. "Open Theism: 'What Is This? A New Teaching?—and with Authority!'" *Ashland Theological Journal* 34 (2002): 39–54.

———. "Opening the Church to the Charismatic Dimension." *Christianity Today* 25, no. 11 (June 12, 1981): 16.

———. "A Pilgrim on the Way." *Christianity Today* 42, no. 2 (Feb 9, 1998): 43.

———. "Prospects for Systematic Theology." In *Toward a Theology for the Future*. Edited by David F. Wells, and Clark H. Pinnock, 93–124. Carol Stream, Ill.: Creation House, 1971.

———. *Reason Enough: A Case for the Christian Faith*. Downers Grove: InterVarsity, 1980.

———. "Reconstructing Evangelical Theology: Is the Open View of God a Good Idea?" *Andrews University Seminary Studies* 41, no. 2 (2003): 215–27.

———. "The Recovery of the Holy Spirit in Evangelical Theology." *Journal of Pentecostal Theology* 13, no. 1 (2004): 3.

———. "Response #2." In *From the Margins: A Celebration of the Theological Work of Donald W. Dayton*. Edited by Christian T. Collins Winn, 285–87. Eugene, Ore.: Pickwick/Wipf & Stock, 2007.

———. "Response to Daniel Strange and Amos Yong." *The Evangelical Quarterly* 71, no. 4 (1999): 349–57.

———. "Review of Frank D. Macchia's *Baptized in the Spirit: A Global Pentecostal Theology*." *Journal of Pentecostal Theology* 16, no. 2 (2008): 1–4.

———. "The Role of the Spirit in Interpretation." *Journal of the Evangelical Theological Society* 36, no. 4 (1993): 491–97.

———. "The Role of the Spirit in Redemption." *Asbury Theological Journal* 52 (1997): 55–62.

———. *The Scripture Principle*. San Francisco: Harper & Row, 1984.

———. *Set Forth Your Case: Studies in Christian Apologetics*. Chicago: Moody, 1971.

———. "Should Baptists Catch the Fire?" *Canadian Baptist* (March 1995).

———. *Three Keys to Spiritual Renewal*. Minneapolis, Minn.: Bethany House, 1985.

———. "Toward an Evangelical Theology of Religions." *Journal of the Evangelical Theological Society* (Sept 1990): 359–68.

———. *Tracking the Maze: Finding Our Way Through Modern Theology from an Evangelical Perspective*. San Francisco: Harper & Row, 1990.

———. *Truth on Fire: The Message of Galatians*. Grand Rapids: Baker, 1972.

———. *Unbounded Love: A Good News Theology for the 21st Century*. Downers Grove: InterVarsity, 1994.

———. *A Wideness in God's Mercy: The Finality of Jesus Christ in a World of Religions*. Grand Rapids: Zondervan, 1992.

———. "The Work of the Holy Spirit in Hermeneutics." *Journal of Pentecostal Theology* 1, no. 2 (1993): 3.

Pinnock, Clark H., and D. Brown. *Theological Crossfire: An Evangelical/Liberal Dialogue*. Grand Rapids: Zondervan, 1990.

Pinnock, Clark H., and Barry L. Callen. *The Scripture Principle: Reclaiming the Full Authority of the Bible*. 2nd ed. Grand Rapids: Baker Academic, 2002.

Pinnock, Clark H., and Grant R. Osborne. "A Truce Proposal for the Tongues Controversy." *Christianity Today* 16, no. 1 (Oct 8, 1971): 6–9.

Pinnock, Clark H., Richard Rice, John Sanders, William Hasker, and David Basinger. *The Openness of God: A Biblical Challenge to the Traditional Understanding of God*. Downers Grove: InterVarsity Press, 1994.

Piper, John. "'I Will Not Be a Velvet-Mouthed Preacher!' The Life and Ministry of George Whitefield: Living and Preaching as Though God Were Real (Because He Is)." (2009). http://www.desiringgod.org/biographies/i-will-not-be-a-velvet-mouthed-preacher. [Accessed July 23, 2014].

Piper, John, Justin Taylor, and Paul Kjoss Helseth. *Beyond the Bounds: Open Theism and the Undermining of Biblical Christianity*. Wheaton, Ill.: Crossway, 2003.

Polkinghorne, John C. *Belief in God in an Age of Science*. New Haven, Conn.: Yale University Press, 1998.

———. *Science and Creation: The Search for Understanding*. Philadelphia: Templeton Foundation, 1988, 2006.

———. *Science and Providence: God's Interaction with the World*. Philadelphia: Templeton Press, 2005.

———, ed. *The Work of Love: Creation as Kenosis*. Grand Rapids: Eerdmans, 2001.

Pomerville, Paul. *The Third Force in Missions: A Pentecostal Contribution to Mission Theology*. Peabody, Mass.: Hendrickson, 1985.

Porter, George M. "Things That May Be Only? Lorenzo Dow McCabe and Some Neglected Nineteenth Century Roots of Open Theism in North America." *Forum of The Oxford Society of Scholars Meeting in Rewley House/Kellogg College* (January 12–14, 2004). http://opentheism.info/information/things-may/. [Accessed 14 May 2014].

Rahner, Karl, and Herbert Vorgrimler. *Theological Dictionary*. New York: Herder and Herder, 1965.

———. *The Trinity*. Translated by Joseph Donceel. New York: Herder and Herder, 1970.

Randall, Rory. "The Nature of Love: A Theology—By Thomas Jay Oord." *Religious Studies Review* 37 (2011): 36.

Rhoda, Alan R. "The Fivefold Openness of the Future." In *God in an Open Universe: Science, Metaphysics, and Open Theism*. Edited by William Hasker, Thomas Jay Oord, and Dean Zimmerman, 69–93. Eugene, Ore.: Wipf & Stock, 2011.

Rhoda, Alan R., Gregory A. Boyd, and Thomas G. Belt. "Open Theism, Omniscience, and the Nature of the Future." *Faith and Philosophy* 23, no. 24 (2006): 432–59.

Rice, Richard. "Biblical Support for a New Perspective." In *The Openness of God: A Biblical Challenge to the Traditional Understanding of God.* Edited by Clark H. Pinnock. Downers Grove: InterVarsity Press, 1994.

———. *God's Foreknowledge and Man's Free Will.* Minneapolis, Minn.: Bethany House, 1985.

———. *The Openness of God: The Relationship of Divine Foreknowledge and Human Free Will.* Nashville, Tenn.: Review and Herald, 1980.

———. "Process Theism and the Open View of God: The Crucial Difference." In *Searching for an Adequate God: A Dialogue Between Process and Free Will Theists.* Edited by John B. Cobb, and Clark H. Pinnock. Grand Rapids: Eerdmans, 2000.

———. *The Reign of God.* 2nd ed. Berrien Springs, Mich.: Andrews University Press, 1997.

Rifkin, Jeremy. *The Emerging Order: God in the Age of Scarcity.* New York: G. P. Putnam's Sons/Ballantine, 1979, rprt. 1983.

Robinson, Michael D. *The Storms of Providence: Navigating the Waters of Calvinism, Arminianism, and Open Theism.* Lanham, Md.: University Press of America, 2003.

Robeck, Cecil M., Jr. "William J. Seymour and the 'Bible Evidence'." In *Initial Evidence: Historical and Biblical Perspectives on the Pentecostal Doctrine of Spirit Baptism.* Edited by Gary B. McGee. Peabody, Mass.: Hendrickson, 1991.

———. *The Azusa Street Mission and Revival: The Birth of the Global Pentecostal Movement.* Nashville: Thomas Nelson, 2006.

Roennfeldt, Ray C. W. *Clark H. Pinnock on Biblical Authority: An Evolving Position.* Berrien Springs, Mich.: Andrews Univ. Press, 1993.

Rogers, Hester Ann. *Life and Correspondence of Mrs. Hester Ann Rogers: With Corrections and Additions, Comprising an Introduction by Thomas O. Summers.* Nashville: Publishing House of the M. E. Church, South, 1855, rprt. 1870.

Roy, Steven C. *How Much Does God Foreknow?: A Comprehensive Biblical Study.* Downers Grove: IVP Academic, 2006.

Runyon, Theodore. *The New Creation: John Wesley's Theology Today.* Nashville, Tenn.: Abingdon, 1998.

Russell, Robert John. *Time in Eternity: Pannenberg, Physics, and Eschatology in Creative Mutual Interaction.* Notre Dame, Ind.: University of Notre Dame Press, 2012.

Ryan, Maxwell. "A Conversation with Clark Pinnock." *Christian Week* 14, no. 5 (2000). http://www.christianweek.org/stories/vol14/no05/story4.htm.

Sachs, Jeffrey D. *The Common Wealth: Economics for a Crowded Planet*. New York: Penguin, 2008.

———. *The End of Poverty: Economic Possibilities for Our Time*. New York: Penguin, 2005.

Saia, Michael R. *Does God Know the Future?: A Biblical Investigation of Foreknowledge and Free Will*. Fairfax, Va.: Xulon, 2002.

Sanders, John. *The God Who Risks: A Theology of Providence*. Downers Grove: InterVarsity Press, 1998.

———. "Historical Considerations." In *The Openness of God: A Biblical Challenge to the Traditional Understanding of God*. Edited by Clark H. Pinnock. Downers Grove: InterVarsity Press, 1994.

———. "Open Theism: A Radical Revision or Miniscule Modification of Arminianism?" *Wesleyan Theological Journal* 38, no. 2 (2003): 69–102.

———. *What About Those Who Have Never Heard?: Three Views on the Destiny of the Unevangelized*. Downers Grove: InterVarsity Press, 1995.

Scaer, David P. "The Rise and Fall of Clark H. Pinnock." *Concordia Theological Quarterly* 46, no. 1 (Jan 1982): 40–42.

Schlossberg, Herbert, Pierre Berthoud, Clark H. Pinnock, and Marvin Olasky, ed. *Freedom, Justice, and Hope: Toward a Strategy for the Poor and Oppressed*. Westchester, Ill.: Crossway, 1988.

Schreiner, Thomas R., and Bruce A. Ware, eds. *The Grace of God, The Bondage of the Will*. 2 vols. Grand Rapids: Baker, 1995.

Sia, Santiago. *God in Process Thought: A Study in Charles Hartshorne's Concept of God*. Dordrecht, Boston, and Lancaster: Martinus Nijhoff, 1985.

Snyder, Howard A. "The Church as Holy and Charismatic." *Wesleyan Theological Journal* 15, no. 2 (Spring 1980): 7–32.

———. *The Radical Wesley: The Patterns and Practices of a Movement Maker*. Franklin, Tenn.: Seedbed, 1980, 2014.

Snodderly, Beth. "The Warfare Missiology of Ralph D. Winter." William Carey International University, www.wciu.edu/docs/resources/34_warfare_missiology.pdf.

Southey, Robert. *The Life of Wesley; And the Rise and Progress of Methodism*. Rev. ed. London and New York: Frederick Warne and Co., 1889.

Spittler, Russell P. "Glossolalia." In *The New International Dictionary of Pentecostal and Charismatic Movements*. Edited by Stanley M. Burgess and Eduard M. van der Maas, 670–76. Grand Rapids: Zondervan, 2003.

Stone, Bryan P., and Thomas Jay Oord, eds. *Thy Nature and Thy Name Is Love: Wesleyan and Process Theologies in Dialogue*. Nashville: Kingswood, 2001.

BIBLIOGRAPHY

Strange, Daniel. "Clark H. Pinnock: The Evolution of an Evangelical Maverick." *The Evangelical Quarterly* 71, no. 4 (1999): 311–26.

Stronstad, Roger. *The Charismatic Theology of St. Luke: Trajectories from the Old Testament to Luke–Acts*. 2nd ed. Grand Rapids.: Baker Academic, 1984, 2012.

———. *The Prophethood of All Believers: A Study in Luke's Charismatic Theology*. Cleveland, Tenn.: CPT, 2010.

Sutton, Matthew Avery. *Aimee Semple McPherson and the Resurrection of Christian America*. Cambridge, Mass. and London: Harvard University Press, 2007.

Synan, Vinson. "A Healer In the House? A Historical Perspective on Healing in the Pentecostal/Charismatic Tradition." *Asian Journal of Pentecostal Studies* 3, no. 2 (2000): 189–201.

———. *The Holiness-Pentecostal Tradition: Charismatic Movements in the Twentieth Century*. 2nd ed. Grand Rapids: Eerdmans, 1997.

———, ed. *Spirit-Empowered Christianity in the Twenty-First Century*. Lake Mary, Fla.: Charisma House, 2011.

Tiessen, David Alstad. "The Openness Model of God: An Evangelical Paradigm in Light of Its Nineteenth-Century Wesleyan Precedent." *Didaskalia* (Spring 2000): 77–101.

Tillich, Paul. "God as Being and as Living (1951)." In *Paul Tillich: Theologian of the Boundaries*. Edited by Mark Kline Taylor. The Making of Modern Theology. London: Collins, 1987.

Tomkins, Stephen. *John Wesley: A Biography*. Grand Rapids, Mich. and Cambridge, U.K.: Eerdmans, 2003.

Toplady, A. B., Vicar of Broad-Hembury, Augustus. *The Doctrine of Absolute Predestination Stated and Asserted: Translated in Great Measure from the Latin of Jerom Zanchius, with Some Account of His Life Prefixed, And An Appendix Concerning the Fate of the Ancients; Also A Caveat Against Unsound Doctrine, to Which Is Added, A Letter to the Rev. John Wesley*. New York: George Lindsay, 1811 [rprt. from 1772 original].

Tucker, Susan I. *Enthusiasm, A Study in Semantic Change*. Cambridge: Cambridge University Press, 1972.

Tyerman, Luke. *The Life and Times of the Rev. John Wesley M.A.* 3 vols. London: Hodder and Stoughton, 1870–1871.

Volf, Miroslav. *Exclusion and Embrace: A Theological Exploration of Identity, Otherness, and Reconciliation*. Nashville: Abingdon, 1996.

———. "Response to DeVan's Review Essay of *Allah: A Christian Perspective*." *Christian Scholar's Review* XLI, no. 2 (Winter 2012): 187–92.

von Balthasar, Hans Urs. *Love Alone Is Credible*. Translated by D. C. Schindler. San Francisco: Ignatius, 1963, 2004.

Vondey, Wolfgang. "Renew Your Mind ... And the Rest Will Follow." *Renewal Dynamics* (February 24, 2010). http://renewaldynamics.com/2010/02/24/renew-your-mind-and-the-rest-will-follow/. [Accessed 11/1/2012].

Wacker, Grant. *Heaven Below: Early Pentecostals and American Culture*. Cambridge, Mass. and London: Harvard University Press, 2003.

Waldvogel, Edith L. "The "Overcoming" Life: A Study in the Reformed Evangelical Contribution to Pentecostalism." *Pneuma* 1, no. 1 (1979): 7–19.

Walker, Dale. *Kissing the Face of God: Worship That Changes the World*. Maitland, Fla.: Xulon, 2010.

Ware, Bruce A. *God's Lesser Glory: The Diminished God of Open Theism*. Wheaton, Ill.: Crossway Books, 2000.

Warfield, Benjamin B. "The Cessation of the Charismata." In *Counterfeit Miracles*. New York: Scribner, 1918.

Warrington, Keith. *Pentecostal Theology: A Theology of Encounter*. New York and London: T&T Clark, 2008.

Watson, JoAnn Ford. "Contemporary Views on the Problem of Evil." *Ashland Theological Journal* 24 (1992): 27–33.

Wilkinson, David. *When I Pray, What Does God Do?* Oxford: Monarch/Lion Hudson, 2015.

Williams, J. Rodman. *Renewal Theology: Systematic Theology from a Charismatic Perspective*. Grand Rapids: Zondervan, 1996.

Wiles, Maurice F. *God's Action in the World*. Bampton Lectures for 1986. London: SCM, 1986.

Wink, Walter. *Engaging the Powers: Discernment and Resistance in a World of Domination*. The Powers, Volume Three. Minneapolis, Minn.: Fortress, 1992.

———. *Naming the Powers: The Language of Power in the New Testament*. The Powers, Volume One. Philadelphia: Fortress, 1984.

———. *The Powers That Be: Theology for a New Millennium*. New York and London: Doubleday, 1998.

———. *Unmasking the Powers: The Invisible Forces That Determine Human Existence*. The Powers, Volume Two. Philadelphia: Fortress, 1986.

Winter, Ralph D. "Growing Up with the Bible: Understanding What It Says, Yielding to What It Means." *International Journal of Frontier Missions* 22, no. 2 (Summer 2005): 69–74.

———. "The Kingdom Strikes Back." In *Perspectives on the World Christian Movement Reader*. Edited by Ralph D. Winter and Steven C. Hawthorne, 209–27. Pasadena, Calif.: William Carey Library, 1999.

———. "The Most Precarious Mission Frontier." *International Journal of Frontier Missions* 21, no. 4 (Winter 2004): 167–72.

Wolchover, Natalie. "Time's Arrow Traced to Quantum Source." *Quanta Magazine* (April 16, 2014): Simons Foundation. https://www.quantamagazine.org/20140416-times-arrow-traced-to-quantum-source/.

Wolterstorff, Nicholas. "God Everlasting." In *God and the Good: Essays in Honor of Henry Stob*. Edited by Clifton Orlebeke and Lewis Smedes, 181–203. Grand Rapids: Eerdmans, 1975.

Wood, Laurence W. "Historiographical Criticisms of Randy Maddox's Response." *Pietist and Wesleyan Studies* 34, no. 2 (Fall 1999): 111–135.

———. "John Fletcher and the Rediscovery of Pentecost in Methodism." *The Asbury Theological Journal* 53, no. 1 (Spring 1998): 7–34.

———. *The Meaning of Pentecost in Early Methodism: Rediscovering John Fletcher as John Wesley's Vindicator and Designated Successor*. Pietist and Wesleyan Studies. Lanham, Md.: Scarecrow, 2002.

———. "Pentecostal Sanctification in Wesley and Early Methodism." *Wesleyan Theological Journal* 34, no. 1 (Spring 1999): 24–63.

Wright, N. T. *How God Became King: The Forgotten Story of the Gospels*. New York: HarperCollins, 2012.

———. *Justification: God's Plan & Paul's Vision*. Downers Grove: InterVarsity, 2009.

———. *Paul and the Faithfulness of God*. 2 vols. Minneapolis, Minn.: Fortress, 2013.

Wynkoop, Mildred Bangs. *A Theology of Love: The Dynamic of Wesleyanism*. Kansas City, Mo.: Beacon Hill, 1972.

———. *Foundations of Wesleyan-Arminian Theology*. Kansas City, Mo.: Beacon Hill, 1967.

Yong, Amos. "Divine Omniscience and Future Contingents: Weighing the Presuppositional Issues in the Contemporary Debate." *Evangelical Review of Theology* 26, no. 3 (2002): 240–64.

———. "Possibility and Actuality: The Doctrine of Creation and Its Implications for Divine Omniscience." *Wesleyan Philosophical Society Online Journal* 1, no. 1 (2007).

———. "Poured Out on All Flesh: The Spirit, World Pentecostalism, and the Renewal of Theology and Praxis in the 21st Century." *PentecoStudies* 6, no. 1 (2007): 16–46.

———. "Relational Theology and the Holy Spirit." In *Relational Theology: A Contemporary Introduction*. Edited by Brint Montgomery, Thomas Jay Oord, and Karen Winslow, 18–20. Eugene, Ore.: Point Loma Press/Wipf & Stock, 2012.

———. *The Spirit Poured Out on All Flesh: Pentecostalism and the Possibility of Global Theology*. Grand Rapids: Baker Academic, 2005.

———, ed. *The Spirit Renews the Face of the Earth: Pentecostal Forays in Science and Theology of Creation*. Eugene: Wipf & Stock, 2009.

———. "Whither Theological Inclusivism? The Development and Critique of an Evangelical Theology of Religions." *The Evangelical Quarterly* 71, no. 4 (1999): 327–48.

Zahnd, Brian. *Beauty Will Save the World*. Lake Mary, Fla.: Charisma House, 2012.

———. *A Farewell to Mars: An Evangelical Pastor's Journey Toward the Biblical Gospel of Peace*. Colorado Springs, Colo.: David C. Cook, 2014.

Zahnd, Brian, and Miroslav Volf. *Unconditional?* Lake Mary, Fla.: Charisma House, 2010.

Indexes

SCRIPTURE INDEX

Genesis 1:29–30, *142*
Genesis 20:3, *65*
Exodus 12:31, *138 n 20*
Exodus 14:4, 8, 17, *138 n 20*
Exodus 4:21, 7:3, 8:15, 8:32, 9:12, 9:34, 10:1, 20, 27, 11:10, *137 n 20*
Exodus 6:3, *129 n 59*
Ezekiel 34:21, *140*
Numbers 23:19, *21*
1 Samuel 15:29, *21*
Psalm 139:7–10, *129 n 59*
Psalm 34:15, *98*
Psalm 83:18, *98*
Psalm 90:2, *11*
Isaiah 38:1, *65*
Jonah 3:4, 9–10, *65*
Jonah 4:11, *174*
Malachi 3:6, *21*
Matthew 10:29–30, *72*
Matthew 22:17–22, *148*
Matthew 22:37–40, *168 n 117*
Matthew 24:24, *123*
Matthew 3:17, *163 n 96*
Mark 15:34, *144 n 42*
Mark 2:17, *136 n 13*
Mark 3:29, *136 n 12*
Mark 8:34, *127*, *139*
Luke 3:16, *164*
Luke 5:20, *136 n 12*
Luke 7:28, *136 n 12*
John 13:10, *163 n 97*
John 13:13–17, *126*
John 13:34, *13 n 21*
John 14:16, *146*
John 15:3, *163 n 97*
John 20:21–22, *163 n 97*
Acts 15:18, *112*
Acts 2:17–18, *175*
Acts 2:3–4, *164*
Acts 2:44–45, *176*
Acts 4:31, *74*
Acts 5:13, *174*
Romans 1:20, *142 n 34*
Romans 2:13, 16, *109*
Romans 8:28, *61 n 34*
Romans 8:29–30, *110*
Romans 8:9–10, *146*
1 Corinthians 13:4–5, *13 n 23*
1 Corinthians 2:2, *125*
Galatians 5:22, *147*
Philippians 2:1, *146*
Colossians 1:15–19, *133*
Colossians 1:27, *146 n 47*
Colossians 2:9, *160 n 87*
2 Timothy 2:19, *106 n 48*
Hebrews 1:3, *177*
Hebrews 10:26, *20*
Hebrews 13:8, *128*
Hebrews 2:14, *142 n 34*

Hebrews 3:12, *20*
Hebrews 6:17, *99 n 29*
James 1:17, *21*
James 2:24, *109*
2 Peter 1:3–4, *121 n 30*
1 John 2:16, *168 n 112*
1 John 3:8, *166 n 105*
1 John 4:8, *168 n 115*
Revelation 19:6, *129 n 60*
Revelation 21:10, *164 n 100*

NAME AND SUBJECT INDEX

Alexander, Estrelda, iv
Alexander, Kimberly Ervin, iv, 41, 120–21
allegiance, 50, 71, 137, 146, 148–49, 176
amillennialism, 165
Anderson, Allan, 113–14, 120, 162
anthropology, 132, 135, 138, 140, 172
antinomianism, 85, 107–09, 153
Apostolic Faith Mission, 3, 114–15, 119, 122, 129
Apostolic Faith newspaper, 2, 121–25, 129, 136, 147, 163, 172
Archer, Kenneth J., iv, 38, 40–41, 45–46, 48, 131
Arminian theology, 4, 15, 19, 36, 42, 46, 66, 137, 168
A-theory of time, 56, 58, 61, 67–68
Augustine of Hippo, iii, 8, 23, 52–56, 58, 62, 68, 75, 98, 104–05, 111, 148
Aulén, Gustaf, 136
Azusa Street revival, 2, 39–40, 43, 113–16, 119–24, 126, 129, 152, 161–63, 166, 174

Barth, Karl, 54, 119
Basinger, David, 17–18, 20, 26
Boyd, Gregory A., 19, 24, 28–29, 32, 36, 45–48, 62, 97, 131, 136, 141–43, 156, 160, 165–66

Brown, Colin, iii, 164
Brümmer, Vincent, 59, 156–58
B-theory of time, 56–57, 61, 67–68
Bundy, David D., 127
Burgess, Stanley M., iii, 39, 116
Burnaby, John, 156

Callen, Barry L., 43
Calvin, John, 4, 8, 23, 63, 65, 108, 110
Calvinism, iii, 9, 19, 28, 42, 46, 49–50, 62, 66, 70, 91, 98, 104–10, 112, 123, 138, 158, 161, 165, 172, 174
change, 10, 14, 21–22, 26, 28, 32, 34, 36–37, 40, 53, 62–65, 68–70, 74–75, 81, 98–100, 111, 128, 131, 137, 148, 153, 156, 162, 172–73, 175–77
charismatic gifts, 4, 74, 91, 118, 161
charismatic manifestations, 74, 76, 87, 89, 147, 171
charismatic theology, 1, 2, 4–5, 39–40, 46, 48, 74, 77, 82, 87, 91, 113, 118–19, 131, 133–34, 147, 161–63, 169, 171–73, 177
Charnock, Stephen, 8, 9, 24
christology, 13–14, 21, 26, 29, 31, 35, 40–41, 64–66, 69, 71–72, 75, 83, 103, 109, 118, 123–24, 131, 133–34, 136–37, 139, 141–42, 144–55, 159–68, 172–73, 176–77
Christus Victor interpretation of the atonement, 136
church, *see* ecclesiology
Classical theism, 3, 8, 11–14, 20–21, 25–27, 30–31, 35–38, 45, 54, 94
Cobb Jr., John B., 17, 30
Collins, Kenneth J., 23, 79, 83, 101
community, 34–36, 41, 132, 134, 154, 156, 176
compassion, 10, 58, 98, 100, 122, 129, 137, 158–59, 163, 168, 173
consumerism, 140, 164, 173
Coveney, Peter, 34–35, 57–58

creation, 11, 21, 23, 27, 38, 46–47, 54, 59, 66–67, 73, 90, 100, 105–06, 141–44, 147, 157, 164
Cullmann, Oscar, 57

Dayton, Donald W., 4, 5, 8, 44, 77, 119
determinism, 14, 31, 64–65, 70, 90, 98, 100, 129, 132, 137, 156, 165
divine image, 65
divine love, *see* love, God's love
divine right of kings, 175
divine will, 47
Durham, William Howard, 152–53, 174

ecclesiology, iii, 2, 7, 9, 12, 22, 35, 46, 59, 67, 74–75, 78, 110, 113–15, 125, 134–35, 163, 167, 172, 176
economics, 68, 71, 139–40, 147–48, 159, 161, 175, 177
election, 12, 50, 62, 66, 91, 98, 106, 123, 171, 172
empire, 177
enthusiasm, iii, 78–80, 84, 87, 89
environmentalism, 52, 164, 173
see also Wesley, John, and renewed earth
eschatology, 12, 135, 144, 167, 172
eternity, 9, 10–11, 25, 45, 53, 55, 57, 59, 65, 95–96, 100, 152, 164
evangelical, 2, 7–8, 35, 46, 49, 51, 117, 131, 133, 137, 156, 159
everlasting, 11, 55, 57, 59, 63, 66, 73, 76, 79, 100, 106, 171
evil, 14, 25, 32–33, 47, 54, 60–61, 72, 105, 138, 142, 150–51, 153, 165
exorcism, 11, 32, 76, 146, 155
experience, 1, 3, 5, 10, 21, 25–27, 33, 39, 44, 48, 50, 53, 56, 58, 67, 76–77, 80, 83, 88, 94, 99, 100–02, 114–17, 120–21, 123, 141, 144–47, 151, 157, 161–64, 171–72, 174

faithfulness, 9, 22, 87, 91, 99
Fletcher, John, 1–5, 43–44, 48–51, 89, 107–13, 116–21, 131, 159, 162, 172
following Jesus, 153, 160
foreknowledge, 9, 17–20, 22, 29–31, 37, 59, 62, 66, 69–70, 89, 100
Foundry, the, 77, 78, 81
free will, 14, 31–32, 59–60, 62, 89, 94, 107, 129, 135–38, 142, 171–72
freedom, 4, 10, 13, 16, 27, 30–32, 35–37, 45, 47, 60, 64–65, 69–73, 82, 90, 93–94, 97, 100, 117, 127, 129, 132, 135, 137, 140, 150, 155, 157, 160, 172
future, 2, 9, 14, 18, 21–22, 25–38, 42, 45–46, 52–53, 55–70, 73, 89, 96–100, 125, 129, 132–137, 140, 144, 147, 151, 158, 161, 167, 171–72, 175–77
future exhaustively known by God, 9, 27, 29–31, 38, 63, 64, 68, 70, 73, 89, 94, 97–100

Gasque, W. Ward, iii
George Bell, 77–81, 171
grace of God, 4, 10, 12, 27, 38, 48, 66, 79, 80, 83, 85, 87, 90–91, 101, 106, 109, 111, 117, 119–21, 127, 131, 138, 141, 145, 157, 164, 172
Greek philosophy, 8, 22
Neoplatonism, iii, 11, 22, 26, 52–54, 59, 98
Grudem, Wayne, 9–12, 29, 35
guidance, 26, 47

Hasker, William, 15, 18, 20, 25–26, 29, 32, 37, 60, 142
healing, 41, 47, 75, 80–81, 114, 146–47, 155
Hebrew prophets, 140
Heschel, Abraham, iii, 36

history, iii, 14, 22–27, 33, 37–40, 47,
  57, 59, 63, 68, 97, 110, 114, 120,
  123, 125, 135, 143, 149, 156–57,
  160, 169, 173
holiness, iii, 1, 2, 5, 9–10, 29, 43–44,
  52, 75, 80, 83, 85, 95–96, 99,
  107–10, 114–21, 126, 141, 149,
  152–53, 163–65, 167, 171
Hollenweger, Walter J., 41, 115–17, 166
Holy Spirit, iii, 1, 3, 8–12, 27, 35,
  39–48, 51, 59, 65, 67, 70, 73–76,
  80, 83–84, 87–88, 91, 98, 102, 110,
  113–21, 127, 129, 131, 134–37,
  140–55, 157, 161–64, 166–67,
  171–73, 175, 177
Hubbard, David Allan, iii
humility, 54, 58, 82–84, 101, 126, 129,
  132, 155, 160, 172–73, 177

immutability, 8–10, 14, 20, 22, 25–26,
  31, 36–37, 54, 56, 98–100, 129,
  156, 172
impassibility, 3, 8–10, 13–14, 22, 25–
  27, 31, 36, 56, 98–100, 130, 172
influence, iii, iv, 8, 9, 14, 23, 25, 29,
  36, 38, 45, 49, 52, 54, 73–74, 77,
  98, 121, 123, 138, 140, 142, 149,
  154, 156, 159–60
injustice, 60, 147, 161–66
inner witness of the Spirit, 84

Jesus, *see* christology
justice, iv, 10, 12, 101, 139–40, 154,
  159, 168, 177
justification, 12, 27, 36, 46, 61, 83,
  88, 91, 106–09, 119, 130, 145,
  151–53, 163

Kalu, Ogbu, 113
kenosis, 94, 143–44
  see also self-limitation
kingdom of God, 39, 42, 71, 133–35,
  137, 148, 151, 154–56, 158,
  160, 177

König, Adriö, 21, 22
Kreider, Alan, 177

Lady Huntingdon, 77, 81–82, 99, 107
love, 1, 4, 13, 31, 33, 35, 51, 68, 74,
  75, 80, 82, 85, 91, 101–04, 106,
  117, 119–24, 127, 129, 132–33,
  137, 141, 144–45, 147–48, 150–52,
  154, 160, 162–63, 168, 171
  definition, 13
  God's love, 3, 4, 8, 10–13, 21–22,
    24, 27, 30, 43, 45–46, 49,
    58, 61–66, 68–69, 71, 79, 83,
    90–91, 95–96, 99–103, 106,
    110, 118, 121–23, 129–32,
    135, 140, 144, 147, 152, 155,
    157–58, 160, 162–64, 166, 168,
    172, 177
  for God, 25, 103, 105
  of neighbor, 13–14, 42, 71, 75, 85,
    103, 112, 116, 154, 156, 165,
    168, 173

Machado, Daisy L., 161, 174
Maddox, Randy L., 1–2, 52, 54,
  70, 112
materialism, 140, 173
Maxfield, Thomas, 4, 77–78, 80–82,
  84, 87–89, 99, 171
Maxfield–Bell crisis, 4, 77, 82
McCabe, Lorenzo D., 4, 17, 61–70, 89,
  95, 171
McPherson, Aimee Semple, 152
Methodists and Methodism, 4, 44,
  50–51, 62, 71, 77–81, 84, 88, 99,
  109, 114, 118–20, 122, 159, 162
Moltmann, Jürgen, 8, 36–37, 143–44
monergism, 27, 46, 90, 105

Naglee, David Ingersoll, 53–54, 93, 100
nescience, *see* foreknowledge
Newton, Sir Isaac, 34, 57–58, 67
non-coercive, 13, 71, 138, 140,
  160, 173

nonviolence, 103, 133, 138, 149–50, 154, 160

omnicontrolling, 31, 129
omnipotence, 4, 8, 9–10, 18, 20, 23, 27, 93, 95, 129, 135, 144, 156, 172
see also Wesley, John, and God's power
omnipresence, 4, 9–11, 59, 73, 95–96, 129, 144, 172
omniscience, 4, 8–9, 18, 21, 23, 38, 59, 95–96, 129, 144, 156, 157, 172
open theism, 3, 12, 15, 17, 19, 28–29, 46, 61–62, 89–90, 97, 112–13, 122
Oord, Thomas Jay, iv, 13, 15, 37, 43, 45, 70, 104, 124, 138, 145
Openness theology, 17, 27, 142, 155
see also open theism
Outler, Albert C., 1–2, 33, 52, 55, 59, 61, 80, 83, 91, 106, 117, 138, 140, 145

pacifism, *see* nonviolence
Pannenberg, Wolfhart, 23
Parham, Charles Fox, 39, 114–16, 120, 162
pathos, 36
pentecostalism, 1–2, 4, 40–41, 49, 74, 75, 77, 113–19, 122, 129, 149, 152–53, 166, 169, 171–73
perfection, 10, 26, 80, 82, 101-02, 106–07, 111, 117, 119, 149, 164
persuasion, 30, 63, 138, 140, 145, 176, 177
Pinnock, Clark H., iii, 4, 7, 17–21, 23–25, 30, 45, 46, 48, 90–91, 94, 97, 99, 104–05, 112, 121–23, 131, 139–40, 142, 154, 159, 160, 167–68
Piper, John, 29, 31, 161
pneumatology, 42, 48, 90, 117, 131–32, 141, 151, 154, 172–73
Polkinghorne, John, 32, 137–38, 142–44, 157–58

Porter, George M., 17, 59, 62
poverty, 139, 166
power, 2, 9, 10, 12, 23, 25, 27, 30, 32–33, 42–43, 66, 71–72, 75–77, 79–80, 87, 93, 95, 98, 100, 105, 111, 119, 121, 123, 131–32, 134–36, 141–43, 145, 147–149, 152, 155–56, 160, 162, 164–66, 172–73
praxis, 132, 154–55, 173
prayer, 11, 26, 29, 33, 38–39, 42, 44, 46–47, 59, 66, 75–77, 80, 82–83, 86, 115, 119, 126, 152, 156–62, 164
impretatory, 156–57
premillennialism, 166
prescience, *see* foreknowledge
prevenient grace, 83, 91, 117, 138, 141, 145
process theology, 23, 43
property, 176
prophecy, 22, 29, 40, 76, 81–82, 84, 87, 91, 118, 134, 162
proto-pentecostal, 51, 89, 118
providence, 4, 11, 66, 71, 73, 89, 112, 145

racial and social barriers, 116, 163
Relational theology, 12–13, 31, 33, 43, 45, 95, 124, 129, 135–136, 160, 164
Renewal theology, 1, 3, 5, 7, 9, 39–49, 51, 74, 80, 113, 122, 131–37, 140–41, 145, 152–68, 171, 172–75, 177
restoration, 43, 83, 90, 132, 135, 146, 165–67
Rhoda, Alan R., 15–16, 62
Rice, Richard, 17, 19, 20–22, 24, 30, 43, 61
righteousness, 10, 12, 74, 79, 91, 107, 108
risk, 67, 85, 105, 132, 155, 158, 173
Robeck, Cecil M., Jr., 2, 114–16, 120, 124, 126, 152, 163, 174

Runyon, Theodore, 83, 164–65, 176

Sachs, Jeffrey D., 176
sanctification, 12, 36, 50–51, 74, 80–89, 91, 102, 107, 117, 119, 120–21, 127, 130, 145–47, 149, 151–53, 162–64, 166, 172–74
Sanders, John, iv, 3, 7–8, 18–20, 22–24, 27, 31, 38, 66, 97, 138, 145
Satan, 11, 19, 32, 36, 47–48, 97, 123, 136, 141–42, 165–66
self-limitation, 105, 143
self-sacrificial love, 14, 134, 148, 155, 173
Seymour, William J., iv, 2, 39, 114–16, 119–26, 128, 129, 131, 136, 146–47, 152, 162, 163, 166, 172
slavery, 43, 114, 161, 173, 175
soteriology, 1–2, 4, 12, 90–91, 99, 106, 117, 141, 147, 151, 172
sovereignty, 9–10, 12, 27, 43, 100, 123, 161
speaking in tongues, 39, 75, 80, 115–16, 146–47, 161–62
Spirit, *see* Holy Spirit
Spirit baptism, 119, 130, 146, 161
spiritual disciplines, 83
spiritual warfare, 32, 47, 75, 141–43, 165–66
spirituality, 3, 9, 41, 46, 116–18, 120, 143, 156, 159, 172
Stronstad, Roger, 134, 147
suffering, 4, 9, 25–26, 32–33, 36–37, 47, 60–61, 66, 129, 139, 161
sustainability, 164, 173
Synan, Vinson, iii, 41, 80, 113, 115, 153
synergism, 2, 5, 27, 45–46, 91, 138, 146, 157, 163–164, 172

theodicy, 32–33, 35, 45, 48, 54, 59–60, 66, 70, 142
time, iii, iv, 1–2, 4, 10–11, 18, 25, 27–29, 33–38, 45, 48, 50, 52–59, 61, 63–64, 67–71, 73, 76–79, 82, 86, 89, 96, 100, 110–11, 115, 118, 120, 123, 126, 129, 132, 136, 140, 152, 164–65, 167–68, 171, 173
time's arrow, 34, 35
timeless, God as, 11, 22, 25–26, 29, 57–59, 67, 100, 123, 171
timelessness, 10–11, 70, 100, 172
Toplady, A. B., 99, 105, 107
Trinity, 11, 18, 20, 24, 38, 46, 68, 95, 105, 124, 132, 144

violence, 78, 96, 142, 151, 154, 176
Volf, Miroslav, 133
von Balthasar, Hans Urs, 13, 169

Wesley, Charles, 44, 50, 77–78, 84
Wesley, John
 and A-theory of time, 58
 and awareness of the presence of God, 167
 and B-theory of time, 56, 61, 171
 and charismatic gifts, 74–75, 79, 161
 and class, band, and society meetings, 134
 and concern for the poor, 43, 159
 and controversy with Calvinists, 42, 49, 104–12, 172
 and critique of the doctrine of God's impassibility, 98–100
 and Eastern spirituality, 117
 and future global move of the Holy Spirit, 167
 and God's foreknowledge, 55, 58, 62–63, 95
 and God's power, 93–95, 105
 and God's prevenient grace, 91, 145
 and human freedom, 72, 94
 and impassibility, 10
 and John Fletcher, 48–51, 118
 and nature of time, 52–55, 59
 and nonviolence, 103, 149–51

and open theism, 1, 3, 45, 64, 70–71, 89–90, 96–97, 99, 112–13, 131, 171–72
and opposition to slavery, 43
and pentecostal-holiness movement, iii, 5, 43–44, 121
and personal and social change, 131, 172
and politico-economic power, 71
and predestination, 63, 105–06, 110
and proto-pentecostalism, 74, 77, 87, 117–19, 122, 172
and renewal of humankind, 165
and renewed earth, 135, 164–65, 175
and salvation, 138, 167
and sanctification, 80, 102, 120, 151–53, 164
and Satan, 136
and social justice, 71, 160, 175, 176
and spiritual warfare, 165
and synergism, 156, 157
and the American war of independence, 71, 150
and the Apostolic Faith Mission, 123
and the experience of God's love, 90, 102–03, 168
and the Maxfield-Bell controversy, 77, 81, 84, 87
and the way of love, 91, 100, 103, 116, 122, 154–55, 168, 177
and theodicy, 60–61
and unusual manifestations of the Holy Spirit, 76, 80
ideas, 57, 110
influence on William J. Seymour, 114
life, 49
opposition to Augustine, 75
pneumatological theology of, 117, 141
preaching in prison, 76
sermons, 2, 90
theology of love, 1, 90
view of providence, 71, 73
Wesley, Susanna, 77, 105
Whitefield, George, 42, 50, 75–78, 81, 99, 105–06, 118, 155, 161
Williams, J. Rodman, 24, 40
Wink, Walter, 47
Winter, Ralph D., 47, 142, 166
wisdom, iv, 9, 46, 55, 63, 72–73, 79, 84, 95–96, 129, 155, 163, 167
Wood, Laurence W., 51, 81, 109, 118–20, 122, 159, 162
Wright, N. T., 91, 133, 154

Yong, Amos, iv, 13, 41–42, 44–46, 48, 131, 144–45, 162

Zahnd, Brian, 133

**ALSO FROM
SacraSage Press...**

GOD CAN'T
How to Believe in God and Love after Tragedy, Abuse, and Other Evils

THOMAS JAY OORD

OPEN AND RELATIONAL THEOLOGY
An Introduction to Life-Changing Ideas

THOMAS JAY OORD

DIVINE SELF-INVESTMENT
An Open and Relational Constructive Christology

Studies in Open and Relational Theology

TRIPP FULLER

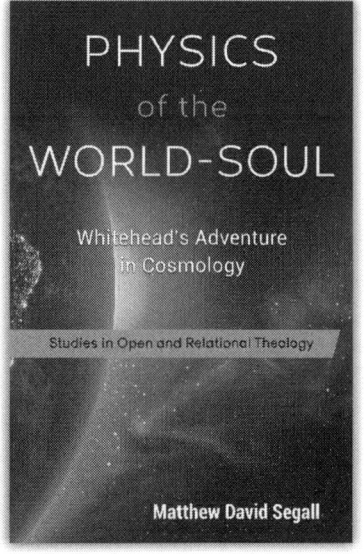

PHYSICS of the WORLD-SOUL
Whitehead's Adventure in Cosmology

Studies in Open and Relational Theology

Matthew David Segall

SACRASAGEPRESS.COM

ALSO FROM
SacraSage Press...

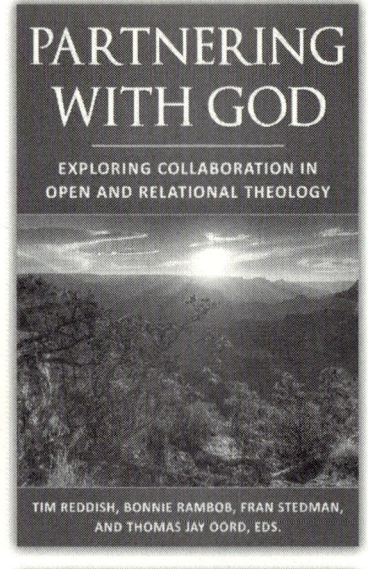

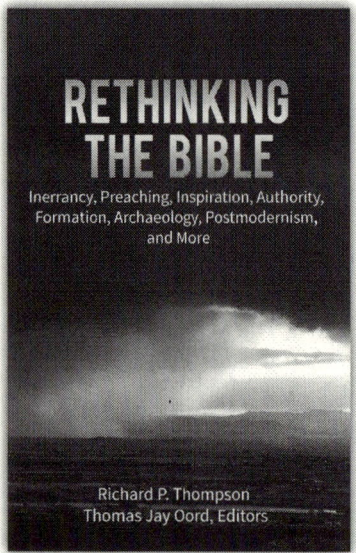

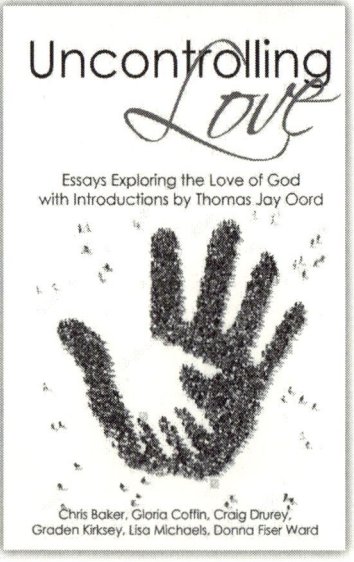

OPEN AND RELATIONAL LEADERSHIP
Leading with Love
Roland Hearn, Sheri D. Kling, & Thomas Jay Oord, EDITORS

PARTNERING WITH GOD
EXPLORING COLLABORATION IN OPEN AND RELATIONAL THEOLOGY
TIM REDDISH, BONNIE RAMBOB, FRAN STEDMAN, AND THOMAS JAY OORD, EDS.

RETHINKING THE BIBLE
Inerrancy, Preaching, Inspiration, Authority, Formation, Archaeology, Postmodernism, and More
Richard P. Thompson, Thomas Jay Oord, Editors

Uncontrolling Love
Essays Exploring the Love of God with Introductions by Thomas Jay Oord
Chris Baker, Gloria Coffin, Craig Drurey, Graden Kirksey, Lisa Michaels, Donna Fiser Ward

SACRASAGEPRESS.COM

Made in the USA
Middletown, DE
29 September 2021